Balderdash & Piffle

Alex Games

BOOKS

takeaway media

This book is published to accompany the television series
entitled *Balderdash & Piffle*, which was first broadcast
in 2006 on BBC2. The series was produced by Takeaway
Media for BBC Television.
Executive producer: Neil Cameron
Series editor: Archie Baron

Published by BBC Books,
BBC Worldwide Limited, Woodlands
80 Wood Lane, London W12 0TT

First published 2006

ISBN 0 563 49336 4

Commissioning editor: Stuart Cooper
Project editor: Cameron Fitch
Copy-editor: Trish Burgess
Designed and typeset by: Smith & Gilmour, London
Illustrator: David Smithson
Production controller: David Brimble
Set in Caslon and Akzidenz Grotesk
Printed and bound in Great Britain by CPI Bath

For more information about this and other BBC books,
please visit our website on www.bbcshop.com
or telephone 08700 777 001.

Contents

Note: Words and phrases discussed and/or defined in the text appear in **bold** type and are all listed in the index on pages 295–304. Foreign words appear in *italic* type. Unless stated otherwise, all definitions of words and phrases cited in the text are taken from *The Oxford English Dictionary* (*OED*).

Foreword

When I was a child, I made a list of my favourite words. Ferret. Tinsel. Quagmire. They were my top three.

I made the more traditional lists too: boys I liked, Barbie outfits, revenges to be exacted on horrible schoolteachers.

But, while teachers and Barbies dominate our lives for a limited period of time, and boys become far less enigmatic with exposure, words remain mysteriously fascinating for ever.

I still think I picked a good three. Ferret, tinsel, quagmire, all of them strange and perfect in their various ways. 'Ferret' squirms slightly as you say it: a mischievous, wriggly little word. 'Tinsel' is sharp and silvery against the teeth. You can get bogged down in 'quagmire', with its juicy start and claggy centre.

This is why there is no such thing as a perfect translation. The precise relationship between a word or phrase and its meaning is peculiar to every language.

You might say to a friend, 'I'll see you at teatime', meaning only an approximation of four o'clock. But tucked away inside the word 'teatime', to a British ear, is a chill winter afternoon: darkness outside, a little orange glow around the streetlamps, and a pile of hot buttered crumpets on a table by the hearth. (And tucked away inside the word 'crumpets' is a little parade of Victorian prostitutes, from the time when the word came to mean an attractive woman, for reasons which I can't possibly spell out here.)

Your plan, when you meet this friend at teatime, may involve neither chill winds nor tea, and I certainly hope it doesn't involve prostitutes. But every time you use an English word, it whispers a little story. Words are like the best sort of grandparents: still engaged and busy in the modern world, but full of colourful tales about the place they were born, the years of their youth, and the job they used to do. The question is, are we always listening?

The reason I wanted to work on the series *Balderdash & Piffle*, when I usually consider myself far too fat and croaky to appear on television, is the opportunity it offered to investigate some of our more curious words and phrases at first hand. TV producers usually ring up and ask whether I might like to be a guest on their hilarious new panel game, pressing a buzzer and competing with stand-up comics to shout one-liners at a slightly frightened audience.

But this one said: 'Let's hire a Mini and travel to the birthplace of "codswallop" and "ploughman's lunch".' It was an irresistible adventure. Off we could go to… ferret out the truth.

World-class Scrabble players, I have read, are familiar with literally thousands of words without knowing their meaning. The letters are simply point-scoring symbols, and definitions don't matter. This is one of approximately fourteen reasons why I will never be a world-class Scrabble player. I can't imagine hearing a new word without wanting to know its meaning, and knowing its history is even better. We can understand our own history, as a nation, through these little tales.

When you know your etymology, the words 'ferret out' should summon you immediately back to 1580, when gamekeepers sent half-tame ferrets down rabbit holes to flush out their tasty occupants. The word 'ferret' itself, coming from the Old French *fuiret* and previously the Latin *fur, furis* (a thief), speaks to you of people moving across Europe in ancient times, bringing their languages with them and noticing, even then, that there is something suspicious and untrustworthy about ferrets. 'Look at zem,' some Old French wordsmith must have muttered, 'Like leetle thieves.' Except he probably thought it in French. It must surely be worth knowing as much of this stuff as possible. Unlocking the history of words gives so much more weight, colour and poetry to every conversation we have. Why not let images of sixteenth-century gamekeepers dance in the mind, and sixteenth-century wives cooking delicious rabbit pies, rather than letting 'ferret out' become a flat one-dimensional phrase with no further meaning than its figurative one? Why not keep those stories alive?

I admit, I only know about ferreting because I just looked it up. I don't know half as much as I would like to about the origins of words; despite my fascination, I was awfully lazy about detective work for the first thirty years of my life. But I'm on the case now. My best excuse is that I never had a Mini before.

Victoria Coren

THE POWER OF WORDS

This book is about **WORDS** and where they come from. It is <u>NOT</u> a <u>DICTIONARY</u>, an **ENCYCLOPAEDIA**, a manual or a TEXTBOOK. It is, rather, a bit like a **CHAT SHOW.**

The Power of Words

Human beings have their limits. We can't soar gracefully through the air like an eagle, nor can we swim unaided to the ocean floor like a sea-lion and stay there for hours without surfacing. Our night vision is hopeless compared to that of an owl. Most of us can't run as fast as an over-excited spaniel, let alone a cheetah, and we can't change colour according to our environment. Our skin blisters in the sun, we get frostbite if we're too high up a mountain, and our young are helpless if left to fend for themselves during their first ten years or so.

So far, then, the prospects for the human race are not bright, so what exactly are we good at? Well, we can talk. And we can write and read. We may not be able to talk to the animals, but we can talk about them, and we can talk each other; and our capacity for self-awareness, for encoding and decoding complex messages, our love of playing games and debunking each other marks us out as distinctive. Of course, some of us are better than others at speaking our own language, but not being a fluent speaker is no obstacle to holding high office (just ask the current occupant of the White House). So it isn't purely the quality of our speech that counts. In different ways we all have the capacity for writing, and it is that capacity that separates us from the other species with which we share the planet.

There is, inevitably, a bit of a battle to be named the world's earliest writing centre. We know that the Sumerians of Uruk in southern Mesopotamia – modern-day Iraq – were keeping records of goods and services as long ago as 3400–3300 BC. In Abydos, 400km (250 miles) south of Cairo, ancient Egyptian hieroglyphics at the tomb of King Scorpion recording linen and oil deliveries have been dated to between 3300 and 3200 BC. Then, in May 1999, it was disclosed that archaeologists at a site called Harappa in Pakistan had found deliberately-incised marks on pottery which could date back to 3500 BC. The first forms of writing, at any rate, emerged over 5000 years ago. It wasn't pure literature, then, and it took some time before language evolved to achieve the subtlety of Homer's *Iliad* (and then 2750 years later, *Nuts* magazine) but it all proves that our ancestors were adept at communicating with their fellow beings.

The hunger for language is rooted in our culture. The inarticulate speech of small children is known as **babble**, a word that, if not purely imitative of the way babies speak, may be related to the biblical tower of Babel. In that famous story from Genesis, the peoples of the world came together to build a tower so that we could have a squint inside God's living-room, and God – in a striking blow for the right to privacy, which nearly all subsequent celebrities would gladly endorse – knocked the whole project on the head, not with the soon-to-be conventional weaponry of thunder, lightning, disease or slaughter, but with a much wilier ruse. He cast them down with language: one morning, they all woke up unable to understand what each other was saying. End of tower.

The Babel story is one way the ancient world explained the incredible variety of tongues, but these days, our towers reach not up to the sky, but horizontally, across different communities. As long as we're not trying to puncture the heavens, language can be a formidable means of generating consent. Consequently, words themselves have taken on a variety of different meanings over the years.

Meaningful noises

Words are our most valuable currency, and over the years they have taken on a host of different meanings. Anyone skilled with words is known as a **wordsmith**, a sense borrowed from the days of blacksmiths, forges and anvils, as they hammer new words out of flexible letters. We give our **word of honour**, or we say that someone is **as good as their word**. In the City of London, the Stock Exchange has operated since its founding in 1801 on the principle of **My word is my bond**, a motto which – Latinized into *Dictum Meum Pactum* – was incorporated into its coat of arms in 1923. Two simple words, 'I do', can commit two people to each other for life when uttered as part of a marriage service. But words can also fail us, and we can be lost for them. They can be honeyed or twisted. They can send us to war, or move us to tears.

Words have power. Prayers are recited every day for the living and the dead, for the rulers and the weak. As religion evolved, some faiths created names for their God so sacrosanct that they cannot even be spoken: so now the fear is not of a physical tower ascending to heaven, but of a simple word on the lips of a mortal scraping the heavenly underbelly by its mere utterance. Words have political significance. To talk of Madras or Calcutta these days is to betray that you are locked in a Raj-like time warp: in modern India you must talk of Chennai and Kolkata. Salisbury used to be the capital of Rhodesia; now Harare is the capital of Zimbabwe. You can say **cant** and **wink** on the radio or TV in Britain at any time of the day, but if you change one letter in either of those words, the broadcaster's switchboard will light up with complaints and hundreds of angry letter-writers will reach for their pens or keyboards. Being **stuck for words** is a dilemma. **Verbal diarrhoea**, on the other hand, is a condition that the hearer is usually able to diagnose a lot faster than the speaker. But, then, isn't the **gift of the gab** said to be a blessing? The power of words is indisputable. In the beginning, after all, was the word. And it will probably be there at the end, too.

Starting at the beginning

This book is about words and where they come from. It's not a dictionary, an encyclopaedia, a manual or a textbook. Nor is it about grammar, punctuation or style, though all those elements come into the story at various points. It is an unashamedly personal selection of words which have undergone interesting and unexpected journeys on the way from what they originally meant to what they mean today. It is not intended as an academic study, and it steers well clear of scholarly dialect or specialist language, though we have taken pains to ensure that our definitions and etymological[1] explanations are correct. It is, rather, a bit like a chat show in which the guests are not people with products to plug – that really would be shameless – but words with interesting stories to tell. The only make-up we have resorted to is an element of **bold type** so that it's easy for you, the reader, to identify the notable word or phrase. And the only time we shall allow ourselves to pause for a glass of water is at the end of the book when, out of sheer goodwill, we shall add a list of further suggestions, to help you to take your investigation of the subject a stage further.

But don't feel you have to. After all, any fluent English speaker has thousands of words at their fingertips – or, rather, on their tongue. Among friends, colleagues or family, most of us are capable of astonishing fluency. We can talk – frequently for hours – without having to consult a dictionary, thesaurus, vocabulary book or grammar primer. William Shakespeare is said to have had a working vocabulary of between 17,000 and 20,000 words. The linguistics

---

1 Etymology – the study of the original meaning of words. *Etumos* – true (Greek). For 'Ology' – see Chapter 8, page 206.

expert David Crystal estimates that most modern professional people have a vocabulary of around 50,000 words. So we're all experts, and we are all authorities, though few of us will write plays as good as Shakespeare's. Some of us might make the odd boob on paper, or when typing, but essentially we have an entire dictionary in our heads.

For most British people, English is their mother tongue. But even further afield, English is an amazingly successful language. It is spoken and taught the world over, frequently by people who have never even been to Britain. English is the most popular second language in the world, which goes some way towards explaining why most British people have such an appalling record when it comes to speaking other people's languages. Across the world, English is the language that most people want to learn. There are more Chinese speakers than the approximately 375 million people who use English as their mother tongue, but most of them are in China. English is the most widely spoken language in the world today, used regularly by over 700 million people in over 100 countries. A recent survey found that more than four-fifths of all international organizations use English as either their main, or one of their main, operating languages, and that more than 80 per cent of all internet home pages are written in English.

Unpacking the language

The power of words derives from their extraordinary economy. Here is a three-word sentence, just about the simplest unit of sense that you can get: 'Petrol prices soar'. A mere three words, yet each word comes pre-bundled with an entire world of implied meanings. The words conjure up an image of a fully operational world behind those sixteen letters: we may think of petrol stations and long queues, or oil tankers on the oceans. It doesn't matter what we think of: words draw pictures in our heads. And we can do our own predictive texting too. If we had to choose a word to come after 'petrol', many of us (based on our past experience) would probably choose 'prices'. And, to complete the sentence, many of us would be more likely to choose **soar** than 'plummet'. Words relate very directly to the associations that we have already made with them in the past. We also have a sense of familiarity with certain word groups, which is why more of us – at least in Britain – would choose 'soar' than, say, **escalate**. We all have a mental thesaurus, and we are combing through it all the time, making choices in search of the best word to communicate meaning.

Learning such associations is a natural process for children, but acquiring them in a new language at a later age can be difficult. Nonetheless, more people are studying English than ever before. The British Council estimates that English has official or special status in at least seventy-five countries, with a total population of over two billion. The appetite for English is growing fast because it is still the language of business, technology, finance, medicine, travel, scholarship and, to a lesser extent, the media. There are various reasons for this, and they don't all relate to Britain's imperial past or to America's cultural and economic dominance. English is a hard language to master, but an easy language to pick up in some basic sense. Grammatically, it doesn't have complicated final forms or rules about agreement based on declensions and conjugations. Learning English is a national obsession in some countries, such as Japan. Across Europe, most schools teach English as a compulsory subject, but the evidence suggests that most pupils need little encouragement to learn the language of J-Lo, Eminem, Craig David and Brad Pitt.

Fashion aside, the English language is a fascinating subject even for native speakers, and relevant to us all in our daily lives. Take the word **run**, for example. *The Oxford English Dictionary* (*OED*) entries for both noun and verb forms stretch to over 55,000 words, or sixty-one pages – the length of a short novel. Hardly surprising, though, when you think of the number of possible meanings. A sprinter **runs**, and so does a wet nose. An escaped prisoner is **on the run**, but a **play can run to** three and a half hours. A cricketer **makes runs**, but can be **run out**. An invalid looks **run down**, perhaps from an attack of **the runs**, while a new car needs **running in**. Commodity speculators might trigger a **run on** oil, which leads to us **running up** quite a bill at the petrol station. Are you being evasive? You're giving someone the **run-around**. Didn't hear what was said? **Run it by me** one more time.

Precision matters

Choosing the right word can make all the difference between making sense and causing offence – or worse. There is a marked difference between **bumping into** an old friend, and **bumping off** an old friend (or enemy), and it is one that just about all native speakers of English appreciate. Learners, no matter how adept, have to acquire this skill, and it can take time. A German friend recalls asking a well-known British actor what he thought of the charitable event that they were both attending. Unfortunately, though, instead of asking him, 'What do you **make of** events like these?' she asked, 'What do you **make out of** events like these?' and was surprised when he gave her a very moody stare.

We all know the advice given to a journalist that 'Dog Bites Man' is no story. 'Man Bites Dog' is news. In English, word order is vital to making sense. Imagine if you saw a newspaper headline that read: 'Pet Shops Run Out of Hamsters.' It wouldn't raise many eyebrows. We might pause to wonder what caused this sudden dearth of pouched rodents. Possibly a flurry of school projects or an unguarded comment by a teen idol who happens to like them. It's not a major event, at any rate. But change the word order, and the story becomes much more dramatic: 'Hamsters Run Out of Pet Shops.' Now that's news!

You can have great fun looking up words in a big dictionary. English has hundreds of colourfully disparaging terms, so let's look at those in the title of this book: **balderdash** and **piffle**. Neither is particularly common these days, and in essence they mean the same thing: 'twaddle'. But what history lurks behind these words?

First we'll look at the *OED* entries for them, which show in miniature the skill of the lexicographer,[2] the technical term for someone who writes or compiles dictionaries.

> **balderdash**, *n*.
> †1. ? Froth or frothy liquid. *Obs.*
>   1596: NASHE *Saffron Walden* To Rdr. II Two blunderkins, hauing their braines stuft with nought but balder-dash.
>   1599: *–Lent. Stuffe* 8 They would no more…have their heads washed with his bubbly spume or barbers balderdash.

The entry tells us first that the word 'balderdash' is a noun. The † means that the definition is obsolete (no longer used in that sense). This is reinforced by the question mark, indicating that the editors were not sure of the meaning from the available evidence, and the abbreviation 'Obs'. The earliest definition, therefore, however uncertain, is of a 'Froth or frothy liquid'.

---

2 Dr Johnson, in his *Dictionary* of 1755, clearly relished defining the word as 'a writer of dictionaries; a harmless drudge, that busies himself in tracing the original, and detailing the signification of words'.

Next comes the evidence from the printed page. The earliest quotation found to back up the definition is from 1596. The author is named as NASHE, and in the *OED*'s online version, an on-screen hyperlink takes us to the *OED*'s Bibliography, which tells us the author's full name, Thomas Nashe, and gives a short list of his works – 15 in all – including the one cited above, *Have with you to Saffron-walden*. 'To Rdr'. means 'to reader', so this quotation can be found in the part of the book entitled 'To The Reader.'

Thomas Nashe was born in 1567 and died in 1601. Clearly the word had not yet taken on its modern meaning. The second quotation is from the same author (indicated by the long dash): *Nashes Lenten Stuffe* from 1599. He obviously liked the word 'balderdash' a good deal: we are left wondering what barbers did with it. Was it drinkable, or somewhat like a shampoo or rub?

Those who are, by now, intrigued by Thomas Nashe and can get to their local library might be interested to see more of his contribution to the English language. Using the online *OED*'s Simple Search button, we can draw down a list of the English words for which Nashe is named as the 'first cited author'. It comes to a very impressive 705. Although not much known these days, Nashe was obviously a master of offensive words: **dish-wash** was used first by him, in its literal sense and as a term of abuse. Other Nashe words include **conundrum, helter-skelter, grandiloquent, harlequin, impecunious, silver-tongued** and – you saw it here first – **dildo.**

To be a first quoted author in the *OED* is a considerable feather in any writer's cap, and Nashe's score puts him in elevated company. Geoffrey Chaucer has 2018 entries to his name, William Shakespeare has over 1700, Jane Austen has exactly sixty and Charles Dickens has 262.

The second definition of 'balderdash' looks like this:

†2. A jumbled mixture of liquors, e.g. of milk and beer, beer and wine, brandy and mineral waters. *Obs.*

1611: CHAPMAN *May-day* III. Dram. Wks. 1873: II. 374 S'fut winesucker, what have you fild vs heere? baldre~dash? 1629: B. JONSON *New Inn* I. ii, Beer or butter-milk, mingled together … It is against my free-hold … To drink such balder-dash. 1637: J. TAYLOR (Water P.) *Drink & Welc.* (Worc.), Beer, by a mixture of wine hath lost both name and nature, and is called balderdash. 1693: W. ROBERTSON *Phraseol. Gen.* 198 Balderdash; of drink; Mixta Potio.

b. *attrib.* 1641: HEYWOOD *Reader, here you'll*, etc. 6 Where sope hath fayl'd without, Balderdash wines within will worke no doubt. 1680: *Revenge* v. 68 Ballderdash Wine.

Here we meet such writers as George Chapman, Ben Jonson, Jeremy Taylor and William Robertson. We see the variety of ways in which the word was spelt, as well as archaic spellings of other words, such as 'filled', 'us' and 'here'. And we can also see that the word now applies to something drinkable, probably cheap grog, the sixteenth-century equivalent of Tennents Extra or McEwans.

In the next two definitions, the word has set out on what we will soon recognize as a familiar journey from a physical object to something more abstract or figurative.

3. *transf.* A senseless jumble of words; nonsense, trash, spoken or written.

1674: MARVELL *Reh. Transp.* II. 243 Did ever Divine rattle out such prophane Balderdash! 1721: AMHERST *Terræ Fil.* 257 Trap's second-brew'd balderdash runs thus: Pyrrhus tells you, etc. 1812: *Edin. Rev.* XX. 419 The balderdash which men must talk at popular meetings. 1849: MACAULAY *Hist. Eng.* I. 351, I am almost ashamed to quote such nauseous balderdash. 1854: THACKERAY *Newcomes* I. 10 To defile the ears of young boys with this wicked balderdash. 1865: CARLYLE *Fredk.* Gt. II. VII. v. 287 No end of florid inflated tautologic ornamental balderdash.

There, within that short paragraph, are some of our finest writers: Andrew Marvell, Thomas Babington Macaulay, William Thackeray and Thomas Carlyle, as well as the lesser-known Nicholas Amherst, all brought together for a purpose that they could never have anticipated: to attest to the same sense of 'balderdash' as the one in which the *Edinburgh Review* uses it.

And in its final definition, 'balderdash' comes to mean:

4. *dial.* Filthy, obscene language or writing.

Without any further examples, the *OED* follows this with a longish discussion of the etymological origins (historical formation and development) of 'balderdash'. It suggests that although the first two definitions mean 'frothy talk' or 'a senseless farrago' or 'jumble of words', the majority of etymologists have taken the third meaning as the original. From this point, they have sought to locate its roots in languages beyond these shores. They find the English dialect word 'balde', meaning 'to use coarse language', but they want more, so continental Europe is scoured for a time when the language mulch was in a more formative state. The linguists peer into our muddy shared linguistic past. They see the Dutch word *balderen*, meaning 'to roar, thunder'. Cousin or coincidence? Next they see the Norwegian *baldra* and Icelandic *baldrast* or *ballrast*, which mean 'to make a clatter'. Possibly. Back to the UK, perhaps, where they note the Welsh word *baldordd*, meaning 'idle noisy talk, chatter'. That explains the 'dash' part of the word too, though another linguist conjectured a reference to 'the froth and foam made by barbers in dashing their balls backward and forward in hot water'. Quite what the barbers were trying to achieve by doing this with their balls, or indeed which balls they were doing it with, remains a mystery.

Whatever it was, though, the practice has, mercifully, fallen out of favour amongst contemporary barbers.

Meanwhile, here is the great American writer H.L. Mencken (1880–1956) scornfully dismissing the prose style of US president Warren G. Harding (in office 1921–3):

> He writes the worst English that I have ever encountered. It reminds me of a string of wet sponges; it reminds me of tattered washing on the line; it reminds me of stale bean soup, of college yells, of dogs barking idiotically through endless nights. It is so bad that a sort of grandeur creeps into it. It drags itself out of the dark abysm of **pish**, and crawls insanely up the topmost pinnacle of **posh**. It is **rumble and bumble**. It is **flap and doodle**. It is **balder and dash**.

How about the other word from our title? The *OED* entry for 'piffle' takes us straight to the verb form, as follows:

> **piffle**, *v. dial.* and *slang*
> *intr.* To talk or act in a feeble, trifling, or ineffective way.
> 1847–78: HALLIWELL, *Pifle*, to be squeamish or delicate. 1896: KIPLING *Seven Seas, Mary Gloster* (1897) 146 They piddled and piffled with iron; I'd given my orders for steel! 1897: *Sunday Times* 2 Jan. 6/7 Their defence is sound, and their attack altogether good, save a tendency to 'piffle' in front of goal at times.

That's more straightforward. Dialect, slang, an intransitive verb (one having no object, such as 'to stand', as opposed to a transitive verb, such as 'to push', which needs to push something). We note with interest some lines from Rudyard Kipling. It's also relevant that the popular press, here in the shape of the Sunday Times, has a crucial role to play in the citing of sources. Who, though, is Halliwell? James Orchard Halliwell (1820–89) was a much-admired

Shakespearean scholar, who went up to Trinity College, Cambridge, aged seventeen. Widely regarded as a genius, his fame so preceded him that he was granted access to Trinity's unique collection of priceless manuscripts. Some months after his admission, the college discovered that over a dozen of them had gone missing. The culprit was Halliwell, and his punishment earned him a spell not in Dartmoor High Security Prison but – possibly worse – Jesus College, Cambridge, where he remained a great scholar and married the daughter of the eccentric book hoarder Sir Thomas Phillipps. Here, then, within the skein of a simple word, a thumbnail sketch of an entire family history emerges. Phillipps described his own appetite for manuscripts (written on vellum[3]) as that of 'a perfect vello-maniac', so the two men were obviously well matched, even if Sir Thomas may have had to check his son-in-law's pockets before he let him leave.

The entry continues:

> Hence **piffle** *n.*, foolish or formal nonsense; twaddle; trash; also used as a derisive retort; **piffler**, a trifler, a twaddler; **piffling** *vbl. n.* and *ppl. a.*
>
> 1890: *Sat. Rev.* 1 Feb. 152/2 If there is … a certain amount of the 'piffle' (to use a University phrase) thought to be incumbent on earnest young princes in our century, there is a complete absence of insincerity. 1900: O. ONIONS *Compl. Bachelor* ii. 18 He'd talk a lot of piffle, wouldn't

> he? 1914: 'HIGH JINKS, JR.' *Choice Slang* 16 *Oh piffle*, an exclamation denoting inconsequence of the subject in question. 1920: 'B.L. STANDISH' *Man on First* xviii. 127 'The Hawks have the lead on us, still.' 'Piffle!' said Cady. 'We'll even things up to-morrow.' 1959: ELIZABETHAN Apr. 10/1 I gave you a bar of chocolate on the train from London. So piffle! 1892: *Star* 14 July 1 The nervousness of the other juvenile and titled piffler. 1896: *Westm. Gaz.* 4 Dec. 2/1 Lord; but this chap is dull… Dull! He's a perfect piffler. 1864: MRS. E. LYNN LINTON *Lake Country* 309 Pyklin an' pyflin,

---

3 Calfskin that has been soaked, limed, shaved, stretched and dried – a type of parchment.

thoo gits nowt doon. 1894: *Westm. Gaz.* 21 May 2/3 He seems … to have
convinced himself that he is an old man, and settled down to a piffling
eld. 1916: 'BOYD CABLE' *Action Front* 17 You don't think a pifflin' little
Pip-Squeak shell could go through *his* head? 1927: *Daily Express* 26 July
3/4 The Bench consider that this is a piffling offence, and … that a
warning would have been sufficient. 1927: *Observer* 13 Nov. 10/4 The
mechanical parts of the moving-pictures are superb, but the
imaginative and intellectual parts are piffling. 1963: *Times* 12 June 8/7
The sum involved was piffling compared with the firm's £25m. a year
turnover. 1973: J. WAINWRIGHT *Pride of Pigs* 56 The lesser hooks being
pulled in for the piffling crimes, while the big boys work the blinders.

Here is a veritable treasure trove of quotations, all shrouded in the
mysterious and sometimes exotic wrapping paper of history. We find
university usages, exclamations, the word standing on its own or
joined to others. We see a dialect spelling, sporting journals, financial
news, war titles, obscure diaries, political journals and film reviews:
a body of evidence spanning a period of 83 years.

About this book

The appeal of words is that most of them have been around for a
great many years, and like any sprightly senior citizen, have travelled
a bit, seen a lot and have some good stories to tell. As soon as you
start looking at words, you find that they have a tendency to veer
off in the most curious directions. In fact, this book could equally
have been called *Make & Do* or *Tea & Biscuits* or *Rhubarb & Custard*.
They all bring their own histories with them, and all are worth the
chase. This book is about our fascination with language, especially
with the English language. It aims to show how English has
consistently refashioned itself, or been refashioned, throughout its

long history. At every stage of its development, though, the questions we really want to ask are how does English reflect the period in which it was used, and which words from that time do we still use?

The chapters of this book are arranged by themes. Chapter 1, for example, deals with the origins of the English language. Every time you look out of a **window,** you are looking straight through a word with Viking roots, and one that represents a victory over two other contenders for the same title. Originally, or at least from 890 (the time of King Alfred, and we have the documents to prove it) to about 1225, we used to look through **eyethurls.**[4] This word was comprehensively trounced by the Middle English **fenester** (not a million miles from the French *fenêtre*, which shows how close the two languages once were), which made its pitch between at least 1290 and 1548. In 1225, the same year of the eyethurl's last recorded appearance, the word 'window' made its first appearance: as perfect an act of baton-passing as a 4 × 100-metre relay team. It originated from the Old Norse *vindauga*, which in turn came from *vindr* (wind) and *auga* (eye), which was clearly what you would have experienced had you stuck your head out of a window before supplies of glass were readily available in the thirteenth century.

Within the linguistic churn that this book covers – from Anglo-Saxon to Estuary English – we look at the epic poem *Beowulf*, which is still scaring the faint-hearted over a thousand years after it was written. We find out a little about Celtic place names, and how important it was to have the right ending, such as *–dunum*, and Saxon endings such as *–ham* and *–stead*. And we also meet some Norman barons who brought French across the Channel, and the scholars who reintroduced Latin to Britain.

Chapter 2 looks at some of the early attempts to standardize the English language, such as Dr Johnson's *Dictionary*. When Johnson

---

4 'Thurl' or 'thirl' is the Old English for 'hole, bore, perforation or aperture.'

turned his London garret into the production office for a book that would 'fix the English language', he little knew that it would take him and his small team eight years. But the work they eventually produced – late, over budget, packed with idiosyncrasies and as lively and provocative as the man himself – was one of the greatest cultural works of the eighteenth century. Following on from this, Chapter 3 looks at the extraordinary labour that went into the compilation of The *OED*, a project begun just over a hundred years after Johnson's publication and that took seventy years to complete. We look at the pioneering work of Frederick Furnivall and Sir James Murray on the *OED* in the mid-nineteenth century and at the present-day *OED Online*, available since 2000.

In Chapter 4 we look at the Bible – the book that Christians and atheists alike constantly quote, although they may not know they're doing so. No matter how staunchly secular, many people pepper their speech with biblical expressions, such as **out of the mouths of babes,** which comes from the book of Psalms. If they talk of sticking to **the straight and narrow** or see something as a **sign of the times**, they are quoting the book of Matthew. If they try to be **all things to all men** or **suffer fools gladly,** they are quoting Corinthians, and if they **fight the good fight** or scorn **filthy lucre**, they are borrowing from the book of Timothy.

Similarly, the words of Shakespeare live on in daily speech, from **what the dickens** (*The Merry Wives of Windsor*) to a **foregone conclusion** (*Othello*). The expression **all Greek to me** is borrowed from *Julius Caesar*, and **playing fast and loose** comes from *Antony and Cleopatra*. And so it goes on: **cold comfort** is from *King John*, **making a virtue of necessity** is from *Pericles*, and the first recorded use of the word **obscene** is in *Richard III*. Without Shakespeare, would we be using words such as **accommodation, assassination,**

barefaced, **countless**, **courtship**, **dwindle**, **eventful**, **fancy-free**, **lack-lustre**, **laughable**, **premeditated** and **submerge**? Perhaps not, as Shakespeare popularized them, if not invented them.

Words can mean the same or something quite different, depending on where your feet are planted on these islands. In Chapter 5 we chart the journey that English took within the British Isles, and the endless varieties of English within Britain. In the past, varieties of dialect speech may have been exploited for comic purpose, and it may even have been thought that standard English would one day supplant the huge wealth of accents and dialects that have given English its colour and character. Fortunately, we have moved away from such ideas, and every variation in speech is now welcomed as part of the family. Whether we wear **trousers** and **trainers**, or **kecks** and **pumps**, whether you say 'Do you **know**?' or 'D'ye **ken**?', we now recognize that the heart of a language is nourished by its extremities.

All communities feed the body, in the broadest sense of the word. Words that were coined by the black community form a discrete language, but many of its distinctive words – from **irie** to **massive**, from **skanking** to **spliff** – were coined behind a wall of racial separation, leaked out and entered the mainstream. Black English, with its roots in creolized forms of English from the days of slavery, has always had a two-way relationship with the mainstream English language. So whereas a word such as *mambo* comes from Cuban Spanish and then Haitian Creole, words from other gated communities – be they children, women, gays – are entering the English language at an unprecedented rate. Such communities are gated because access to them is not guaranteed, but the gate can be opened at will, and that's when words – whether invented or with a meaning specific to that community – slip out.

When British explorers travelled the world, they brought back far more than commodities and strange animals. As Chapter 6 reveals, new terms came too, including the Arabic words **cotton**, **marzipan** and **sherbet**. From Calcutta in India came **calico**, while **gauze** came from Gaza, **ombudsman** from Sweden, **molasses** from Portugal, **tycoon** from Japan and **hoard** from Turkey. These words and many others have given English its fascinating profile.

Just as secular people use the Bible, so non-sportsmen and women use the language of sport (Chapter 7). Some sports are ancient, but their language remains young. For example, if you've ever been **hoodwinked**, you may not have known that you are using a falconry term that is at least 200 years old. It derives from the practice of covering a falcon's face with a hood so as to remove the prey from its talons. Similarly, the word **boozing** is related to the Middle English word 'bowse', the term used to describe the drinking action of a bird of prey.

We use sporting language all the time, even when we're sitting down. If you've ever **crossed a line, hit the ground running, hit a bullseye** or **fallen short of your mark,** you are employing a phrase that was created in a very different context. If you've ever been the **butt** of someone's joke, that's an archery term. The old sports have the deepest roots. Don't confuse today's **quarrel** with the one from 1350, which meant 'a short, heavy, square-headed arrow or bolt, formerly used in shooting with the cross-bow or arbalest'. And if you've ever been told to **brace** yourself, 'bracing' is what used to be done to a bow to make it strong enough to take the arrow.

Popular entertainment is responsible for producing a long list of words in common currency. The **64-dollar question** was originally a catchphrase from American television. A boxing manager called Joe Jacobs was the first to utter the immortal words '**We was robbed**' when his boxer Max Schmeling lost on points to Jack Sharkey in 1932. If you say **pass** when you don't know the answer to something, you are using a word which came into prominence on the British quiz show *Mastermind*.

Of course, if it hadn't been for science and technology (Chapter 8), we wouldn't have a telly in the first place. We have drawn thousands of words from science, and many are still in daily use. Anyone who says they 'went **ballistic**' is using an eighteenth-century term that reflects that age's fascination with projectile science. When something **passes the litmus test**, or reaches a **critical mass**, even when we get to **boiling point**, we are drawing on scientific vocabulary. And if you **park your tanks** on someone's lawn, or **bring up the rear**, or feel **outflanked** or **ambushed**, you're conscripting military language for non-military purposes. As we shall see, this happens more than we might have expected.

As we scan the wilder shores of language, we must look at the furthest coast of all: taboo[5] words, swear words, obscene and profane language, and words that are designed to hurt. Chapter 9 examines language with its trousers down and its underwear around its ankles. Words uttered in anger or passion: the mysterious origins of the word **fuck** and its ruder medieval equivalent of **swive**. Why, when Mrs Patrick Campbell said the word **bloody** during the first night of George Bernard Shaw's *Pygmalion* on 11 April 1914, the event was marked with sensational newspaper headlines. The history of swearing and of **blue[6] language** occupies a distinguished place in word history.

---

5 A word brought home in the accounts of Captain James Cook, following his travels in the Pacific (1777): 'Not one of them would sit down, or eat a bit of any thing ... On expressing my surprize at this, they were all *taboo*, as they said; which word has a very comprehensive meaning; but, in general, signifies that a thing is forbidden. Why they were laid under such restraints, at present, was not explained.'

6 Blue had the meaning of 'smutty' throughout the nineteenth century. The first 'blue movie' was noted by *Punch* magazine in 1965.

A more shameful place is rightly given to racist and derogatory language, and this chapter also turns its eye to this. Some of these pejorative terms have now been appropriated by the intended targets. **Queer, dyke** and **nigger** are obvious examples; **damn kids** has not undergone the same transition.

Whizz, bang! Ouch! Er… In Chapter 10 we regress to the most basic language of all – words that are almost non-words, but that are nonetheless a vital part of our vocabulary. When we say things go **pop** and **splash**, we are using **onomatopoeia**, an elaborate word for describing the most basic of sounds – the sounds of the world around us. From the external to the internal, we come to the sounds we make. We all know how it feels to stub a toe, but when did that inchoate shriek of pain crystallize around the four-letter word 'ouch'? And then there are other words, all sharply expressive in their way but with more coherent and complex meanings.

The French philosopher Voltaire (1694–1778) said that 'if God did not exist, it would be necessary to invent him.' That may also be true of nonsense words, and once they have been created, they are so evocative that it's hard to imagine a world without them, as Oscar Wilde demonstrated when he borrowed Lord Bunbury's name and turned it into an excuse for not doing things.[7] From the pages of the *Beano* to the *Lord of the Rings*, we take a look at made-up language that with time and use has become 'real'.

Chapter 11 is all about 'now' words, 'it' words, words of the month, the week, the day, the year. **Jargon, lingo, slang** – the word on the street, in the club, on the net. Some have stuck with us, others we have shrugged off as trends move on. Looking at each decade from

---

7 As Algernon says in Act One of *The Importance of Being Earnest* (1895): 'I have Bunburyed all over Shropshire on two separate occasions.' … 'I have invented an invaluable permanent invalid called Bunbury, in order that I may be able to go down into the country whenever I choose.'

the early twentieth century to the present, it may come as a surprise to learn just how old some slang words are. We may not often say something we like is the **bee's knees** these days, but **wicked** is common currency. Yet both entered the language in the 1920s. You may wish to know the words that were judged our favourites in 1980, and how the rather harsher realities of life in modern Britain caught up with a similar survey twenty years later. This is the history of the way we speak – pins on the map for future linguists to follow.

And that leads us, finally, to those historical black holes of the dictionary: those mysterious words marked 'origin unknown' or 'etymology obscure'. Chapter 12 is the great paper-chase, both of this book and of the BBC TV series that it accompanies. The public is invited to get digging, and to share its findings with the editors of the *OED* in a search for the earliest verifiable usage of fifty of the most talked-about words in the English language.

This book is for anyone who is interested in talking, reading, writing or hearing English. It is not a textbook or a scientific book – it is for the general reader. And it aims to be part of a broader debate, in which it forms part of the BBC series from which it is drawn. Readers are encouraged to take up the challenge, to join in the public craze for language that is sweeping the nation, just as garden or home makeovers or unblinking studies of self-publicists stuck in a jungle have fascinated the public until now. Websites about words are attracting new viewers all the time. In today's *zeitgeist* – one of those foreign words that has bedded down nicely in modern English – words are cool, and books, websites, newspapers and magazines all feed on and profit from the British love affair with its language.

From the soaraway success of Lynne Truss's *Eats, Shoots and Leaves* to Michael Quinion's invaluable *POSH* and Susie Dent's fascinating *Larpers and Shroomers*, an abiding interest in the spoken and written word characterizes our fascination with the crucial and the trivial, and is as popular with **bloggers** and **rappers** as it is in the columns of the *Spectator*. Word-searching is a dangerous and rather delicious addiction, but one that is open to everyone. The English language is currently the scene of the nation's favourite quarry. 'Digging a hole' can sometimes be a synonym for getting yourself into deeper and deeper trouble, but not on this occasion. If you need any further encouragement, just grab a spade and start digging.

THE TRUE PRONUNCIATION of the country's name is ENG-A-LAND, recalled most accurately in its <u>NATIONAL</u> football CHANT.

Our Mongrel Tongue

The English language is a great borrower of words. But once it's borrowed them, it likes to hang on to them, and there they stay, like migrant workers, working productively under new economic conditions. English is basically a Germanic tongue, but it has cross-pollinated ceaselessly for centuries, and is correspondingly multi-faceted. Sir James Murray, the first and arguably still the most renowned editor of the *OED*, began classifying the English language in 1884. Having noticed that English frequently contains a whole series of words to describe the same thing, he began to compile lists of English words in terms of their 'register' or tone. The four registers he devised are illustrated in the following example. A priest might describe a bride as looking **euphoric** or **elated** on this joyous occasion (literary), while she tells him she is **happy** (common). She might then tell her friends that she is **chuffed** (colloquial), unless she is in Liverpool, where she might be **made up** (slang). Each synonym has its proper time and place in a sentence, and a native English speaker will automatically know when to use which particular word.

Each word is equally 'correct' of course, and, as a lexicographer, Murray was naturally most interested in describing the richness of the English language and the vast range and diversity of the synonyms themselves. But one way of deciphering meaning or register is to study the numerous linguistic sources from which the synonyms derive. A word's history may not give its current meaning, but it can help to understand the nuances with which each word in English is now imbued. 'Euphoric' is classical Greek in origin and therefore likely to have entered the language via religious scholars during the Renaissance. 'Elated' is Latin, which came into English with William the Conqueror, whose coronation in 1066 was conducted in both Latin and French – the source for 'joyous'. The word 'happy' derives from the Old Icelandic word 'happy', one of a group of languages including Old Norse which was spoken in Scandinavia by the Vikings, and particularly the Norwegians, until about AD 1000 and which is still closely connected to modern Icelandic. No one really knows the origins of 'chuffed', while 'made up' is Shakespearean, but didn't come to mean 'chuffed' until as late as 1956. The scholar Geoffrey Hughes gave an example of the nature of our mongrel tongue in the following diagram:

Anglo-Saxon:	a	to the		of the English
Norman French:	guide			language
Latin and Greek:		lexical history		

Adapted from: Geoffrey Hughes, *A History of English Words*, Blackwell, 2000

This multi-layered representation goes some way to revealing why our language, with all its versatility and subtlety, is such a linguistic soup. Every word becomes a time capsule, containing its own past within itself. To understand the nature of the mongrel, we need to travel back to the dawn of Englishness.

The Celts

'Britain, formerly known as Albion, is an island in the ocean, facing between north and west, and lying at a considerable distance from the coasts of Germany, Gaul and Spain, which together form the greater part of Europe,' wrote the Venerable Bede (c.673–735) in his *History of the English Church and People*, completed in 731. He entered the monastery of St Paul in Jarrow, Northumberland, at the age of seven, and went on to become a renowned scholar, composing over thirty books in Latin, which was still the primary language of monastic scholarship. In Bede's day the British Isles were an ethnic melting pot and the people divided into five main groups: 'At the present time there are in Britain, in harmony with the five books of the divine law, five languages and four nations – English, British, Scots and Picts.' Bede points out that Latin, 'by the study of the Scriptures', is the fifth grouping since it is 'common to (whom we would now call Celts) who gave their name to the land'.

But despite writing in Latin, Bede firmly believed that it was important to translate important religious texts into the new, fully merged language of the people. The first translation of his book into this language – Old English – is said to have been made by or under the influence of King Alfred the Great almost 150 years later as an inspiration for his English subjects and an acknowledgment of the quality of the Venerable Bede's writing. (It is, incidentally, the linguistically gifted King Alfred who is credited with one of the first recorded appearances of the word **Englisc** in his late-ninth-century translation of another Latin work – Pope Gregory's *Pastoral Care*. Who was the last British monarch who could have undertaken either of these tasks?) Judging by the number of other texts that Bede would have had to consult, it strongly suggests that the island's speakers were at least bilingual at the time, and that this was considered the norm, or even a bare minimum.

There are those who, for political reasons, now use the word Anglo-Saxon as if that were the beginning of British culture. In fact, the Anglo-Saxons were an invading race, who displaced the original natives of this land, along with their language and culture. The first-known inhabitants of these islands were the Celts, who also travelled to Scotland. They were followed, in about the fourth century AD, by a tribe called the Picts, who had arrived from Ireland, since the Irish inhabitants (who spoke Gaelic) would not allow the Picts to live there. The Picts used an alphabet called Ogham, which consisted of a series of scrapes into stone. It was hard work and it doesn't truly survive in any other form except runic artefacts. The *OED* now contains no words directly derived from Ogham, though some are listed as 'recorded in an Ogham inscription'. One is **neve**, which turned into 'nephew'. Another is the **O'** prefix in Irish names.

Julius Caesar attempted to invade the islands and tame the Celts in 55BC, but he was unsuccessful. Almost a hundred years later the Emperor Claudius tried again. The Celts dispersed and retreated north and westwards, but maintained links with the Romans, coexisting relatively peacefully and speaking their respective languages, with the Celts presumably speaking Latin too for trade purposes. Almost 400 years later, however, the Roman Empire began to collapse and a power vacuum was created at the heart of it. The troops hastily withdrew to Rome in the early fifth century and the Celts began to be attacked from the north by the Scots and the Picts (who finally merged in 850 and thenceforth spoke a unified Scottish tongue).

In 494 the Celtic king Vortigern turned to the Anglo-Saxons (modern Danes and Germans) for military assistance. These tribes spoke a wide range of different Germanic dialects, and whole new linguistic threads were now added to the native British tongue. One of these Germanic tribes in particular had been referred to by the Romans as the '*Angli*', and within 150 years of their arrival, the whole area of their invasion became known as **Englaland** (land of the Angles). As Bede was to recount some 300 years after the event, the Angles and Saxons, led by the 'brother-commanders' Hengist and Horsa, arrived in three long ships in 449. The tribal groupings were, in fact, relatively straightforward geographically, with the Angles from Denmark arriving along the northern half of the east coast, while the Saxons from northern Europe came aground along the Thames and the south coast. It may not be surprising that the invaders took some time learning to communicate with the locals, but it is possible that the invaders could not even understand each other. They had a common oral heritage, but wildly varying pronunciation and vocabulary. There were dozens of different localized dialects, and their influence spread rapidly through central, southern and northeastern England, generally along major rivers. The Celts remained in Cornwall, Wales and Cumbria, while the Angles occupied most of eastern Britain (modern-day East Anglia) and the east Midlands. The Jutes, who came from Jutland in modern-day Denmark, occupied the land east of the River Medway, southern Hampshire and the Isle of Wight. The Germanic Saxons settled in southern England west of the Medway, particularly along the south coast, the Thames valley, and the western Midlands around the River Avon in Warwickshire. Of the invading Germanic tongues, Frisian (from an area around the modern Netherlands) was probably the tongue closest to modern English. The Frisian for a **broomstick**, for example, is *bromstich*.

Very few Celtic words survived to be passed on in normal speech. An enormous number of place names have Celtic prefixes or suffixes, and these, logically, steadily increase from the east to the west of England and into Wales and Cornwall, since these were the places to which the Celts fled. The Celtic family of languages today includes Breton, Welsh, Manx, Scottish Gaelic, Irish Gaelic and Cornish, but all surviving Celtic words in modern English are related to geography and landscape – the hills they walked upon, the streams they crossed and the paths where they led their herds. Celtic words really are the roots of Britishness, from **cwm** (valley) to **tor** (hill). There are a few words of dubious Celtic origin, such as **bin** (receptacle), which may actually derive from the early Latin word *benna*, while **ass** probably comes from the Celtic word *assen*, but equally may be from the Latin word *asinus*.

The reasons for the almost total disappearance of Celtic remain, frankly, mysterious. It is just about possible that the rural Celtic way of life had so little in common with the Anglo-Saxons that they simply didn't need their vocabulary, or that life was so similar that the Anglo-Saxons already had a word for everything they needed. Or that, just like the subsequent Normans, the Anglo-Saxons considered the Celts too 'common' to use their vocabulary, or, conversely, so closely integrated into the now disgraced Roman Empire that they wanted nothing to do with their language. It is also true that since almost all the Celts who resisted the invasion were evicted across the Welsh border, the Anglo-Saxons may simply not have come into much contact with their vocabulary.

Aside from geography, the only other major area of influence of Celtic on Old English was, rather surprisingly, in first names. The Anglo-Saxon nobility adopted Celtic first names with great relish. Caedwalla was the king of Wessex in 685, while Caedmon was a seventh-century stable boy who became England's first Christian poet. It may simply be that the Anglo-Saxons liked the sound of the new names (all of which began with 'C'), but still, noble Celtic names must have been socially acceptable. It remains even more of a mystery, therefore, why so little else from the culture survived.

The vocabulary left by the retreating Roman soldiers, however, made somewhat more of a mark. Where the Celts had inhabited hills and valleys, the Romans had constructed long-lasting buildings (and roads), and the names for these remained common currency. *Strata*, for example, meant a 'paved street' – more durable than the humble 'road' – so Britain's Roman roads had names such as Icknield Street, Ermine Street and Watling Street, the last extending 180 miles between London and Chester. Chester itself came from the Latin word *castra*, meaning a 'camp', which resurfaces in Chichester, Cirencester, Lancaster and Worcester.

Latin also gave us important words, such as **wine** (from *vinum*), which led to Britain's proud tradition of wine-making, or at least wine-drinking. In that first visit of the Romans to Britain, not a great many words changed hands before the invaders limped back to mop up the remnants of the Roman Empire, which had imploded owing to a combination of factors, including lead poisoning and incest. We moulded *cucina* into **kitchen** and took on many Latin loan words in that department, such as *caseus* (**cheese**), *pisum* (**pea**) and *prunus* (**prune**). The much-debated **cheap**, originally a noun rather than an adjective, meaning a 'bargain', is generally recognized to have derived from the Latin *caupo* (a petty trader), a few of whom can still be found trading at Cheapside in London. As well as commercial terms, we also borrowed Latin units of measurement. The Latin *uncia*, meaning 'one-twelfth', became the Anglo-Saxon 'unce/ince', and the Modern English 'ounce/inch'. But the Romans did metric too: *millia* meant a thousand paces, which we transformed into the (non-metric) 'mile'.

As these examples show, the first generation of Latin words were one or two-syllabled, and related very specifically to the Britons' basic needs. More complicated constructions, and the more complex thought processes that they conveyed, would come later. This process, however, was effectively restricted to the southern part of these islands when Emperor Hadrian, during the course of his AD 122 imperial tour, glanced north and decided that a wall was needed to protect the soft southerners from the hairy hordes. The wall took six years to build and stretched 117km (73 miles) from Wallsend on the Tyne to Bowness-on-Solway in the West. South of this line, Latin words are more common in the English tongue.

The Angles

According to the Venerable Bede's history (which may not be strictly accurate since it was written 300 years after the events it describes), the Anglo-Saxon invasion actually refers to three distinct groups of people: Angles, Saxons and Jutes. The Anglians headed north, from where the Northumbrian and Mercian dialects derive. The Saxons, including the West-Saxons in what became known as Wessex, went south. The Jutes headed for Kent, where the Kentish dialect became a particularly hybrid linguistic soup, since the Romans had made their biggest mark there, too. Numerically, there were more Saxons than Angles, but the Angles, in true German style, must have got up especially early as they were first in line when it came to naming the country 'Englaland' in Old English, since shortened to 'England'. The true pronunciation of the country's name is 'Eng-a-Land', recalled most accurately in our national football chant. The most common theory of how England got its name is that early Latin writers used the term *Angli Saxones* as an easy way of distinguishing them from the 'Old Saxons' on the Continent and that, as in many double-barrelled names, only the first half stuck.

Under the Anglo-Saxons a further wave of place-naming occurred, with the ending –**ing** denoting a Saxon founder. Buckingham, for example, breaks down as 'the home of the sons of Bucca', where the

Old English 'hám' means 'home'. It also appears at the front of such place names as Hampstead or Hampton. Nottingham, meanwhile, was first settled in pre-Roman times and was originally called *Tigguo Cobauc*, which means 'a place of cavy dwellings'. Nottingham's modern name, however, derives from later settlements that were built by Anglo-Saxon invaders after AD 600. These settlements were named after their chieftain – Snot – who brought his people together in an area of the city where the historic Lace Market can now be found. This place became known as Snotingaham – 'the home of Snot's people'. While most of the '–ing' towns were in the southeast of England, the words **Sussex** (a contraction of South Saxon), **Essex** (East Saxon) and **Middlesex** are also Saxon words. The word **Saxon** itself comes from the word *seax* (sword). There is a district called Angel in the province of Schleswig in Germany, and this may be where the original Angles came from.

The Anglo-Saxon language soon became known as **English** (Bede refers to a monastery 'namned on Englisc' – named in English – and King Alfred, who coined the term, used it in a treaty between the English and the Danish). We now refer to this early Anglo-Saxon language as Old English, and by this time its vocabulary included such words as **dog**. The *OED* really has no idea where this sprang from, although it was originally written 'docga'. At the time, the generic name for a dog, as in many other Teutonic (generally German) languages, was *hund* (later 'hound'). The *OED* says that the 'English dog' was used to mean a powerful breed or race of dogs. But the word was clearly a winner since, by about the late sixteenth century, in the days before quarantine, the animal had spread all across Europe. The Danes, Dutch and Germans were referring to *dogge*, the Swedes to *dogg*, the Italians, Spanish and Portuguese to *dogo*, and even the French to *dogue*. When we compare certain basic Anglo-Saxon and Latin words, we see that even though they come from the same roots, they have mutated along different lines as English developed. Latin began its existence in England as the language of political power, and this would have made it the language of choice for the educated and the aspirational. Even the Celts had taken some of the early learning on board, since the Welsh *eglwys* (church) came from the originally Greek *ecclesia*, and *ysgol* (school) from *schola*. This trend also touched Old English – it is even possible that aristocratic Britons continued to use Latin as their chosen tongue long after the Romans had left and the Anglo-Saxons arrived. In church environments, of course, Latin never stopped being used, which led to it acquiring the cachet of 'educated speech'. Latin words were used for plants and animals, domestic goods, business matters, law and medicine. As monks began to need new words for new areas of study, over 60 per cent of the later imports from Latin were specifically scholarly or technical, while native Anglo-Saxon words were vaguer and much better, therefore, for poetry and metaphorical speech. The Latin word *sol* became **sun**, so the Anglo-Saxons gradually extended it to words such as **sunshine** and metaphorical uses, such as **sunstruck**. *Sol*, meanwhile, took on a strictly technical usage in words such as **solar**.

For these reasons, the illogical, anti-rational and purely emotive terms in English are predominantly drawn from Anglo-Saxon sources. Such English words as **murder, kill, steal** and **lie** are all direct, even brutal. Latin, meanwhile, the language of authority and discipline as opposed to the language of the street and the tavern, gives us the rather judicial-sounding **homicide** and **mendacity**. Similarly, compare Old English **sweat** with Latinate **perspiration, shit** with **defecation, fucking** with **copulation** and it's clear which word-base has a well-earned reputation for earthiness, directness and rudeness. The word **woman** is from Old English, as is the word **man**, but their stories are more intertwined than that. *Man* is common in Germanic languages and means both a 'human being' and a 'male person'. In addition, Old English had two words – **wer** and **wif** – which meant 'male human' and 'female human' respectively. 'Wer' lives on only in **werewolf** (man-wolf), but is a cousin of the Latin word *vir* for man (see Virtue, page 53). In Anglo-Saxon times 'man' and 'wer' were used interchangeably. The idea, then, that it is sexist to use the word 'man' to describe both men and women is etymologically incorrect since 'man' was originally a root word that implied all humankind.

The word 'wif' is still used today, of course, as **wife**. In Anglo-Saxon usage, however, 'wif' was a much more general term and meant any woman, not just a spouse, and words such as **midwife** are derived from this usage. Coming as it did from the Anglo-Saxon rather than the Latinate **dame** or the later, Anglo-Norman **mistress**, it was a distinctly lower-register term. It was most often applied to women who worked in humble occupations, such as **ale-wife**, **fish-wife**, **apple-wife** or **oyster-wife**. And these women told stories that became known as **old wives' tales**. Meanwhile, the Old English word **wæpman** meant a 'human with a weapon', and **weapon** was coarse slang for the penis from about 1000 onwards (and probably long before). The female equivalent to 'wæpman' was **wifman**, and from this Anglo-Saxon root we get the modern 'woman'.

Originally a Germanic tribe, the Angles settled in Britain and formed the kingdoms of Northumbria, Mercia and East Anglia, eventually giving their name to the whole 'English' people. When King Alfred used the Old English word **rad** in the year 888, it meant 'the act of riding on horseback' or a 'journey on horseback'. From 900 to 1600 it meant 'incursions', in the same sense that **inroads** still carries, and from 1300 for a good 500 years it had the sense of a 'sheltered piece of water', somewhere near the shore, where ships could be anchored safely. It was not until the seventeenth century that the word began to take on its present meaning of a channel down which people, horses or carriages could pass. And many Anglo-Saxon words have had a similarly long journey to get to their present point. It is a tribute to the patience and curiosity of generations of lexicographers that we can trace these words back to their earliest origins.

The Danish presence was felt here as long ago as the eleventh century and also made its mark on the English language. When King Canute (actually Cnut, since he was a Dane) sought to prove his humanity by failing to stop the waves, it would not have been surprising if the word **drown** had flashed across his mind, since that word may likely have come from Old Norse. Caring little for the monasteries, the Danes came to be known by the Gothic word **heathen,** meaning 'heath-dweller', or non-Christian. It may also be related to the Greek word *ethnos*, meaning 'nation'.

It is not always easy to decide whether a word is Norwegian or Danish in origin, but linguists are reasonably certain about their early Scandinavian origins (see Chapter 6, page 170). **Addle** used to mean 'stinking urine' – something to consider the next time you call someone **addle-headed. Boon** meant a 'prayer', and **busk** meant 'to prepare oneself' or 'get ready'. Other than that, the great Danish linguist Otto Jespersen reckoned that Danish and Norwegian or Old Norse were pretty inseparable at the time. It is worth noting, for the tone of the vocabulary, that Old Norse gives us **raid** and **ransack,** as well as the word **Viking** (*vik* means a 'creek', rendered into Old English as 'wic' (a settlement), which is still visible in place names such as Greenwich.

The Vikings

The received wisdom about the Vikings is that they were brutes. They sacked the holy island of Lindisfarne in 793, razed the Venerable Bede's own monastery at Jarrow in 794 and generally set the tone of the period known as the Dark Ages. The best known of the English kings who tried to oppose these murderous, pillaging Danes (and the only one who achieved some measure of success) was Alfred the Great, who reigned from 871 to 899. His best battleground triumph was in 878 at Edlington in Lincolnshire, and in that same year, in the Treaty of Wedmore, he handed over to the Danish chief Guthrum an area northeast of Watling Street, which was thereafter ruled by Danelaw. In Yorkshire, therefore, a large proportion of place names now end in the Old Norse suffix of –*by*, which denoted a town or settlement (e.g. Grimsby, Derby, Rugby, Whitby and Denby – 'town of the Danes').

Norse terms were also used to make geo-political divisions, such as the *thridings* (third parts) found in Yorkshire, now called the **Ridings**. The Watling Street line worked well as a linguistic separator, and its effects are still noticeable. North of it, hay is still raked into **stacks**; south of it, they are called **ricks**. The Old Norse *stithy* is an Anglo-Saxon *anvil*. Old Norse children *lake*, while Anglo-Saxon children *play*. North it's **mun**, south it's **must**. Northern lads and lasses have **lugs**; southern boys and girls have **ears**.

The Normans

The next invaders were the Normans, who came over with William the Conqueror in 1066. These Normans had once been Vikings who settled in the Pas de Calais and around Normandy. They immersed themselves so deeply in the local language that almost no Norse words survive in northern French, apart from some remaining place names. Just as Lancashire has Breck and Iceland has Laugarbrekka, both from the Norse word *brekka* meaning 'a slope', so too does Normandy have Bricquebec. Boothby in Cumbria and Lincolnshire is derived from the word *búth* meaning shelter. Compare Búthir in Iceland, and Elbeuf in the Seine-Mar. Then there's Fulby in Denmark, Lincolnshire's Fulbeck, and northern France's Foulbec, all of which come from the Norse word *full* (foul). *Sund* means 'strait', still visible in the French Sund de Chausey, or Haraldssund in the Faroe Isles. The word *cliff* gives us Cleethorpes and the French Clitourps. There are at least thirty such places, at a conservative estimate.

The French nobility very quickly became the English nobility too, not least through a process of cross-Channel marriages. Their influence on the English language has been enormous, but the strain of French they spoke was not Parisian French. Linguists call it Anglo-French, and it was one of the most successful linguistic imports ever conceived: three-quarters of the 10,000 words that sprang up during the Middle English[1] period are still in use. In fact, it was not until Henry IV came to the throne in 1399 that England had a king whose mother tongue was English. The Normans had engineered a complete cultural takeover.

In England at that time there was almost no middle class. Either you were a member of the French-speaking nobility, or you were a peasant who spoke Old English. Therefore, common trades, such as **miller, blacksmith, cobbler, ironmonger** and **shoemaker**, have Old English names, whereas the more skilful jobs, such as **tailor, painter** and **carpenter**, are Anglo-French. And the Anglo-French **butcher** originally meant someone who dealt in he-goat, from the Old French for he-goat, *boc*.

---

1 A translation of the term coined in 1819 by the great German linguist Jacob Grimm, to denote the English language between Old and modern English, i.e. from 1100–50 to about 1450–1500.

King and **queen** are native English words, but almost all the appurtenances of royalty, including the word **royalty** itself, are on long-term loan from the French, in recognition of the fact that French was the language of the court – which is another French word.

Titles at Court	
Anglo-Saxon	**Norman**
King	
Queen	
	Prince / Princess
	Duke / Duchess
	Marquess / Marchioness
Earl	Count / Countess
Lord	
Lady	
	Viscount / Viscountess
Baron	
	Baronet

The word **crown** is an Anglo-Norman formation, on loan from *corune, coroune* or *corone*. The word *real* (royal) lingers on in such terms as **real estate**, **real tennis** and **Real Madrid**. Other words that we adopted include **realm** and **country**. The original meaning of 'country' sounds so far-fetched as to be speculative, but the *OED* states that it comes from the Middle English 'contre(e, cuntre(e' and that the Old French *cuntrée, contrée* took that meaning from the Latin preposition *contra* (against), as in 'contrary'. And the country is precisely what lies opposite when you look out at it.

French also permeates our government. The word **exchequer** comes from the Old French *eschequier*, which derives from *scaccarium*, the medieval Latin word for a **chessboard**. This is believed to be because the accounts were originally kept using counters on chequered tablecloths that resembled chessboards.

The head of state in Great Britain still uses an old French form of words, 'La Reyne le veult' (The Queen wishes it), when giving assent to an Act of Parliament.

Government, regulation and arbitration all became definably French, even when satisfactory measures had been in place before. The word **thing**, for example, one of the most basic words imaginable, had an original meaning far more nuanced than today. The general assembly of Iceland, the oldest parliament in Europe, was called the Althing, and most Scandinavian countries or their settlements, such as England prior to the Norman Conquests, gave that name to their assemblies, public meetings or legislative council. In Old English a 'thing' was a meeting or an assembly, such as a judicial assembly, court or council. By the year 1000 it was the case itself, a matter brought before a court of law. Then it became a cause or a reason, but even from 897 onwards it could mean 'that with which one is concerned'.

As long ago as the seventeenth century, the grammarian John Wallis (1616–1703) made the point that animals are English in life, but become French upon death.

Alive	Dead
ox, cow, calf, sheep, swine, boar, deer (all Anglo-Saxon words)	beef, veal, mutton, pork, bacon, brawn and venison (all loans from French)

The standard explanation for this duality is that the ordinary people were busy looking after the animals, so they used everyday terms to refer to them, while the nobility used their own language to describe what ended up on the table in front of them. The poor folk looked after the live animals and so named them in their own tongue, while the nobility got to eat them at banquets and feasts, and so named them in theirs; hence the split.

The list of French words that relate to cooking is huge, from **boil** and **fry**, to **sausage**, **soup** and **jelly**. 'To boil' – not to be confused with the impeccably Old English 'suppurating tumour' sort of boil – means 'to pass from liquid into a gaseous state' and has been around since at least the early thirteenth century. And **toast** comes from the French *toster*, meaning 'to roast' or 'grill'. The humble **breakfast** is English. The more sumptuous **dinner** and **supper** – as well as 'feast' – are loans from French.

Anglo-Norman, the French which the first invader barons spoke, eventually died out, to be replaced by a more courtly, Paris-influenced French. But the linguistic hierarchy maintained itself, with French still being used by the upper classes, and Anglo-Saxon or Old English words with approximately the same meaning being used by those lower down the social scale. In fact, almost the entire class system of aristocratic Britain was imported from France, including many of the titles (see page 49). It also gave us words for the sorts of behaviour that might be expected in such an environment, such as **courteous**, **noble** and **refined** (from the French *raffiner*).

The Old French word *dangier* means the sovereignty of a *dominus* or 'lord', so if you wrote in 1450 'I am gretly yn your danger', that meant you were at someone else's disposal. Although it had existed as early as 1225, the word evolved during the fourteenth century to mean the 'power to inflict damage'. A 1611 translation of the Book of Matthew talks about being 'In danger of the judgment', with the sense of 'liability', but within the same decade (1300–10) the word is capable of meaning any of a dozen slightly different things. Not until William Caxton became the first person to set up a printing press in England in 1476 (and thereby began to standardize language) does **danger** come to mean 'exposed to peril', and later the peril itself. The new rulers became the new generals too. The words **war** and **peace** are from French, as are 'battle', 'arms', 'officer', 'soldier', 'navy', 'lieutenant' and 'sergeant'.

In the earliest version of the poem *Sir Gawain and the Green Knight*, dating from around 1400, the English is as follows:

> *And alle his **vesture verayly** watz clene **verdure**,*
> And all his clothing truly was completely green,
> *Both the **barres** of his belt and other blythe stones,*
> Both the bars of his belt and other bright gems,
> *That were richely **rayled** in his aray clene*
> That were richly arranged in his elegant dress
> *Aboutte himself and his sadel, upon silk werkez*
> About himself and his saddle, upon silk embroidery
> *That were to tor for to telle of **trifles** the halue*
> That were too hard for to tell of details the half
> *That were **enbrauded** abof, with bryddes and flyzes,*
> That were embroidered upon it, with birds and flies,
> *With **gay gaudi** of grene, the golde ay inmyddes.*
> With bright verdant hue of green, the gold always in the middle.

A comparison of these two extracts shows that the English poem contains numerous words deriving from French: **clothing** *(vesture)*, **truly** *(verayly)*, **green** *(verdure)*, **bars** *(barres)*, **arranged** *(rayled)*, **details** *(trifles)*, **embroidered** *(enbrauded)*, **bright** *(gay)*, **verdant hue** *(gaudi)*. What is interesting is that even though the translation has opted to take most of these words back into Anglo-Saxon, they live on in other forms, such as **vestments**, **verily**, **verdure**, **gay** and **gaudy**.

Words such as 'clergy', 'romance', 'sport', 'beauty' and 'authority', demonstrate the dominance of the French language in terms of power, religion and the arts in England at that time. And these words have continued to define British life and culture for centuries. The English word **mercy** and the French *merci* (thank you) both come from the early Latin *merces*, meaning 'payment' or 'wages', which by the sixth century came to mean 'pity', 'favour' or 'heavenly reward', and eventually 'thanks'. It is interesting that a word that started out with commercial overtones acquired religious connotations as life became more Christian, then once again became secular. In a more domestic context, the Old French *cloke* or *cloche* (**bell**) is the source of the word **cloak**, the two objects having a similar shape. The same word is also the root of the English word **clock**, when time was measured by the sound of a bell.

Virtue has a similarly intricate history. It began life as a manly sort of word derived from the Latin *vir* (**man**) and hence *virtudo* (**manliness**, valour, worth), and more specifically the power inherent in a supernatural being. Over the years it began to denote the idea of chivalry and 'a secular sense of moral attainment' at a time when the Church was the self-appointed guardian of all pastoral, intellectual and spiritual matters. Gradually, virtue became associated with honour and, eventually therefore, with maidenliness and virginity. The Latin word for 'man' had thus switched sexes in English, and had now become specifically associated with women.

But it was with the adoption of classical Latin words that Middle English became a truly expressive medium. During the fourteenth and sixteenth centuries, Latin words, and Greek words that had been incorporated into Latin, flooded into the English language.

With the start of the Renaissance (a revival of art and learning according to classical models) in fourteenth-century Europe, the vocabularies of the various European languages exploded across the Continent, and English was particularly receptive to them. Having already adopted many French words, England showed little resistance to adopting other foreign words. It isn't always clear whether words such as **consolation, solid, infidel** and **infernal** came direct from Latin or were imported via French.

Streamlining

As Middle English accelerated away from its Alfredian roots, its grammar changed too. Although our concern here is not with grammatical developments, it is worth looking very briefly at the effects of these changes. One was that the English language began to lose its inflections. These are the endings that every verb or noun required in Latin and Greek, and without which their meaning is lost. It is generally considered that this process began when the British started trading with the Anglo-Saxons and they needed to be able to understand each other quickly. It didn't really matter if you got the wrong ending; as long as you picked the right root noun or verb, everyone could understand you, so word endings began to disappear. Suddenly, English grammar was relatively easy. Non-native speakers could do business even if they got their words in the wrong order – people knew what they meant and that was the main thing. English had become a language of communication rather than perfection, and this was to add an important new dimension to its history.

Compared to the grammar of most other European languages, English grammar is a model of simplicity, and this gives our words much greater mobility. If you were to ask what part of speech the word **work** is, the answer could be any of the following:

> **Verb:** 'I work very hard.'
> **Noun:** 'I love my work.'
> **Adjective:** 'The meeting was work-related.'

The flexibility that the single word form offers to English users is immensely valuable. In previous ages three separate spellings would have been needed to reflect the word's different role within each sentence. Those spellings were therefore liberated, and free to be used in more creative ways.

There are whole categories of words that can be used in two if not three ways. Somehow, English has liberated many words from their original meanings and given them functions that are subtly different from their strict application as nouns. Take one group of words: animals. People have been **taking their dogs for a walk** since the year 1050, and they have been **dogged by scandal** since before Shakespeare – 1519 is the earliest citation in the *OED*. The media can **hound** a celebrity to distraction (usage first recorded 1528), or a chess player could be **foxed** (1611) during a game. Some people **parrot** what they hear (1596), and in 1632 Philip Massinger asked, 'Why should you **ape** the fashions of court-ladies?'

Similarly, many parts of the body can also be used as verbs:

To arm (1205)	**To thumb** (1593)
To shoulder (*c*.1300)	**To elbow** (1605)
To head (*c*.1300,	**To hand** (1610)
originally to decapitate)	**To stomach** (1523,
To eye (1583)	originally to be offended)

This usage, which is called 'conversion', lent ever greater flexibility to English language writers, but this would be anathema[2] to a Greek or Latin scholar since classical language is all about rigidity of grammar. There are, of course, many Latin words that have been retained in their original forms – **gratis, genius, prima facie, et cetera, memento** and **limbo** – unlike those earlier words – cheese, wine, pound and inch – that were refashioned and partially de-Latinized. Thousands of other words show what linguists call **assimilation** (a Latin word). **Allegory**, for example, from the Greek *allegoria*,[3] entered English via Latin. The Venerable Bede described Britons at one point as a *perfida gens* when they refused to accept the teachings of St Augustine. **Perfidious** entered the language in the second half of the sixteenth century, when it meant 'deliberately faithless; basely treacherous' and led to the eighteenth century phrase 'Perfidious Albion', of which, no doubt, Bede would have approved.

Geoffrey Chaucer

The poet Geoffrey Chaucer (*c.*1342–1400) is notable for his sensitivity to the different registers of Middle English. The beauty of his language was that while he drew primarily from native words, he could also plunder French or Latin words when required. Proof of his popularity is that he was the first commoner ever to be buried in Westminster Abbey. His wit was admired by all the educated classes, despite the fact that his verse was plugged with profane and obscene words: **fart, arse, piss, shit, queynte** (cunt) and **swive** (an old version of 'fuck', see Chapter 9). Chaucer was sensitive to changes

---

2 A Greek word, originally meaning 'Anything accursed, or consigned to damnation' (1526).
3 *Allegoria* ('speaking otherwise than one seems to speak') – *allos* (other) and *agoria* (speaking).

in language ('*and wordes tho / That hadden prys, now wonder nyce and straunge / Us thinketh hem*' '…and words which previously had prestige, now seem odd and unfamiliar to us' – *Troilus and Criseyde*, Book II, 21–4), and his was one of the last voices of Middle English, but he was also one of the first writers in the language to use the various registers of it selectively to create mood and character. He understood that the newly formed, hybrid English could now reach a range of expressions that would have been previously unimaginable. He uses words such as **governaunce** and **plesaunce**, which had only just joined the English language, while also managing to incorporate French borrowings and, in the finest tradition of the new English language, simply made up words when he couldn't find anything suitable. He gave us **autumn, edifice** and **ignorant**, but he also took advantage of the sheer fluidity of the English language and its new grammatical flexibility to experiment with words like 'beblot', 'achatour' and 'acheck', which haven't survived the test of time quite so well. Chaucer knew that he could bend the language almost any way he liked and his audience would simply enjoy it more.

It was also true that a variety of words in southern English would still not be comprehensible to someone in the north of the country, and in 'The Reeve's Tale' Chaucer becomes the first-known Englishman to ridicule a northern accent in writing. 'Ham' says the character when he means 'home', 'gang' for 'gone' and 'na' for 'no'. The wealthy southerner's mockery of the rustic northerner had begun, and confidence in the use of English as a medium of expression was running high. Despite his mocking of the comic north, Chaucer was particularly concerned that everyone in his native country should be able to read or understand what he had written, despite the immense regional diversities in the language.

His final words in Troilus and Criseyde were the rather tremulous:

And for there is so gret diversite
In Englissh and in writyng of our tonge,
So prey I God that non miswryte thee...

The fifty remaining handwritten copies of *The Canterbury Tales* attest to the fact that Chaucer was well known during his lifetime; even the future King Richard III was familiar with his work. *The Canterbury Tales* has been in print constantly ever since the first two editions produced by Caxton at the end of the fifteenth century, and it would, no doubt, have alleviated Chaucer's fears to know that a mere hundred years after his death the elements of the language had come together to such an extent that they were more or less recognizable as modern English.

chapter two

DR. JOHNSON'S BIG IDEA

A VORACIOUS reader, it was said that he "TORE THE <u>HEART</u> OUT OF BOOKS" — often handing them back to the owners BADLY mauled.

Dr Johnson's Big Idea

We are surrounded by dictionaries these days. You can buy a
dictionary of just about anything, from insults to Igbo,[1] but 250 years
ago the choices were not quite so broad. Dictionaries[2] tell us a great
deal about how language is evolving. The process is continuing
today, and, if anything, is happening faster than ever.

The publication of a dictionary is a rite of passage for a language,
and English was no exception. For centuries the English language
had been a snotty-nosed child, running around the room shouting
anything that sounded funny. It had taken massive liberties with
spelling, and if you had asked it for the etymology of a particular
word, it would have stared at you as if you were mad. But with the
passing into print of the first dictionaries, a different mood set in.
Those early lexicographers must have surveyed the mess and
decided that enough was enough.

Dictionaries proper are of two kinds: they either translate from
one language to another, or they define words within the language
itself. The second category is the more recent.

Given the reputation of the English language, you might have
thought that Britain would have taken to dictionaries as willingly
as it embraced hearty breakfasts, dogs and imperialism. In fact,
compared to our Continental cousins, Britain was a bit slow off the
mark. Even though there were some 642 books known as dictionaries
in print before 1746, the standard was, at best, questionable. One
of the more authoritative efforts was *A Table Alphabeticall of Hard*

---

1 One of the languages of southern Nigeria.
2 Dictionary, *n*. 1. a. A book dealing with the individual words of a language
(or certain specified classes of them), so as to set forth their orthography,
pronunciation, signification, and use, their synonyms, derivation, and history,
or at least some of these facts. First recorded use 1526.

Usual English Words, written (or, more accurately, compiled) by a schoolteacher called Robert Cawdrey. Published in 1604, it contained 2521 'headwords' or main word entries, and is considered the first single-language dictionary ever to be written in English.

Many more compilers were prompted to follow Cawdrey in drawing up a guide for 'Ladies, gentlewomen, or any other unskilfull persons', in which were gathered and explained the mass of strange or 'hard' words that literature, science, medicine and the arts were introducing into the language. Cawdrey also wrote about 'far journied gentlemen' coming home from their travels who then 'pouder their talke with over-sea language'. It may have been in response to this that the dictionary was written.

Despite his pioneering work, some of Cawdrey's definitions don't quite pass muster. His definition of **allude** as 'to speake one thing that hath resemblance and respect to another' is masterful, but would the explanation of 'allegation' as 'alleging' have shed much light? Among other dictionary-makers, simple definition proved even more elastic, with one defining **dog** as 'a common animal, known to all'. That definition, inadequate though it is, goes to the heart of the difficulty in compiling a dictionary. How do you define a dog? (See Chapter 1, page 43.) The idea must have seemed impossible to most people. Why should anyone need to define a dog, for goodness' sake? You'd know what a dog was even if you'd never been bitten by one.

But as lexicography took shape, people began to feel that a word was not properly dressed unless it had been defined, or **spelled**, or perhaps we should say 'spelt', since the issue of a universal spelling model arose after William Caxton brought the printing press to Britain in 1476 and the paths of written and spoken English began to diverge. In speech, most people from the same area pronounced **wife** (see Chapter 1, page 45) the same way, but it could be spelled – and frequently was – as either 'wyf' or 'wif'. The same goes for **little**, which could be written 'lytyl' or 'lityl', or 'good' as 'goode'. It was the emergence of printing that created a need for a standard, but not necessarily simplified, system of spelling words.

As to the other function of a dictionary – once we know what a word is, we can also say what it isn't. We can prise apart words with related meanings – **fierce** and **savage**, for example. How do they differ? A dictionary makes us think hard about the job that words do. It is also a form of word census: by naming the words in use, you also count them.

Across the Channel, other countries were doing just that. The Accademia della Crusca, which is still the national language academy of Italy, was the first such institution in Europe, and the first (in 1612) to produce a record of the words then in use in its national language. The Académie Française, created by Cardinal Richelieu under Louis XIII in 1635, was charged with 'defining the French language'. The French language police are still at it. In July 2003, concerned that the English word **email** was becoming too widespread in the French tongue, they chose the Québécois word *courriel* instead. It is now government policy that this be used. Wish them luck, or read about their progress online, on what the French, with impeccable spelling, refer to as *'un blogue'*.

The Italian and French efforts at recording their languages – the *Vocabolario* and the *Dictionnaire* respectively – were nothing if not thorough. Each was the product of intense scholarship. The French, for example, used an army of forty word-pickers, who agreed the spelling for 5000 words – around a quarter of the words then in use. By contrast, Cawdrey had produced just over 2500. Both the French and Italian dictionaries were bigger than ours. Clearly, something had to be done.

It is somehow appropriate – and very British – that the work that came to represent the best of British lexical scholarship was cobbled together in eight years, on the cheap, in a rush, and was largely the work of one man with five or six helpers. And yet it was immediately acclaimed as a work of genius, and still is to this day.

Another virtue of a dictionary is that it represents a contemporary snapshot[3] of the language – overlooking for now that the word snapshot did not come into common use until the latter half of the nineteenth century. It distinguishes between words that are in common usage, and words that are on the way out. In the process, it tells us a lot about who we are. And in eighteenth-century Britain, a lot of people were interested in finding out. The question was: who would do the best job?

Cometh the hour

Samuel Johnson (1709–84) defines **genius** as 'a man endowed with superior qualities'. He later defines **monster** as 'something out of the common order of nature'. In truth, he was better qualified than most to define those words, since he was both. Born in the Staffordshire town of Lichfield, which also gave us Erasmus Darwin, the polymathic grandfather of Charles, and, more recently, the M6 toll road, Johnson may not seem like an obvious choice for what is now regarded as one of literature's most serious and high-minded commissions. His father was a bookseller, and the young Samuel suffered from poor eyesight and trouble with his ears. A voracious reader, it was said that he 'tore the heart out of books', often handing them back to their owners badly mauled. After attending Lichfield Grammar School, where he was beaten repeatedly by John Hunter, the Latin master, he went up to Pembroke College, Oxford in 1728, but came down

---

3 Snapshot, 1808: 'A quick or hurried shot taken without deliberate aim, esp. one at a rising bird or quickly moving animal.' 'An instantaneous photograph, esp. one taken with a hand-camera.'

fourteen months later when his money ran out. Like many writers and journalists, financial crises came very easily to Samuel Johnson.

Arriving in London, he began to make friends with his impressive wit. Many of his verbal exchanges were collected by his trusty biographer James Boswell (1740–95), whose *Life of Samuel Johnson* (1791) extended to 1500 pages. Johnson was a grandiose, clubbable man, dining with other heroes of the age, such as the great actor David Garrick, whom, incidentally, Johnson had taught at the school he founded in Edial near Lichfield. In 1764 Johnson helped found the Club, later renamed the Literary Club, whose members included other A-list[4] writers, such as Edmund Burke and Adam Smith.

In company, Johnson was vastly entertaining, with enormous social stamina and the endless curiosity of the self-taught intellectual. But he also drank more than was wise, wore himself out with late-night carousing, and suffered frequent bouts of depression, especially during the course of his not-often-consummated marriage to the ailing Tetty. Hard-working and meticulous, from 1738 onwards he had contributed to almost every edition of a publication called the *Gentleman's Magazine*, writing foreign and domestic news and book reviews. These articles had gone down well in literary London, establishing him as a man of letters whose scholarship was beyond doubt.

He received another step up towards his great challenge when, in 1740, he was employed by a bookseller called Thomas Osborne, who had paid the vast sum of £13,000 to buy the library of Robert and Edward Harley, the first and second Earls of Oxford. The library contained 50,000 books, 250,000 pamphlets and 7000 volumes of manuscripts. Johnson worked alongside Edward Harley's personal librarian, William Oldys, and the two men produced a catalogue

---

4 A-list, *n.* 1. The first in a series of lists, esp. lists ranked in order of preference or significance. (1890). 2. *n.* orig. *U.S.* Any (notional) list comprising only the most celebrated, sought-after, or high-ranking individuals, esp. in the entertainment industry or the media; a social, professional, or celebrity elite.

of the collection. According to another of his biographers, Sir John Hawkins (1719–89), 'while he was engaged in so servile an employment [he] resembled a lion in harness'.

Osborne was not terribly interested in reading the books he had bought, but he had a shrewd idea that they might fetch him some cash. Johnson and Oldys busied themselves in documenting the thousands of volumes being put up for public sale. In fact, the auction itself was a disappointment, but Johnson must have been able to study just about every important dictionary that European scholars had produced until then. Of the many lessons Johnson learnt, one was that a proper English dictionary ought to illustrate its definitions with quotations so that readers could see the context in which a word had been used. Second was the good lexicographical habit of arranging words into 'headwords' by taking a main word and then giving its various definitions. If it sounds surprising that anyone should not have organized a dictionary in that way, bear in mind that most dictionaries until then were not arranged in alphabetical order, and that some were alphabetized only by the first two letters of each word.

His career and ambition were both advancing equally when he was approached by a small committee of publishers and booksellers, and asked if he would undertake to compile – though Johnson preferred to use the verb 'write' – a dictionary of the English language. In three years. The committee members' motives were varied, but all agreed that its main purpose was to standardize the language. English was becoming unregulated: it was time to bring it into line. The historian of the Royal Society, Thomas Sprat, had expressed a wish to see a 'mathematical plainness' about the language. Gentlemen also tabled their desire to guard 'propriety' against the advance of 'elegance'. Some felt or hoped that the dictionary would prevent slippage of the tongue. Already the language of Chaucer was almost unrecognizable to some speakers, and the writer and essayist Alexander Pope (1688–1744) was not the first to voice the fear that if steps were not taken, his books might be incomprehensible to future generations. So self-interest played a part in bringing about the work. The enthusiasts knew that it would be their writings that would benefit most directly from the coverage. When Johnson defined the word **opulence**,[5] for example, he added an illustrative quotation from the works of Jonathan Swift, the creator of *Gulliver's Travels*. Even though the two men had their differences, Swift must have been delighted to see himself thus **name-checked**.[6] The branding opportunities were almost endless.

To most learned minds, the Latin dictionary was the main source of reference for English words; they found nothing odd in seeking definitions of English words in Latin. Indeed, Latin was a valuable reference point for writers, since spoken Latin was a finite entity and could thus be studied under a microscope.[7] Johnson, though, rejected Latin as being insufficiently inclusive. He wrote his dictionary in English, though he agreed that the English language should be purged of 'solecisms and improprieties, and made as unchanging and authoritative as Latin'.

One by one, the country's top writers had lent their weight to the idea of a new national dictionary. For the former poet laureate John Dryden (1631–1700), a dictionary would restrain some writers who 'corrupt our English idiom by mixing it too much with French'. Johnson's approach would have pleased Dryden, as he wrote in the

---

5 Opulence – defined by Dr Johnson as 'Wealth; riches; affluence', 'There in full opulence a banker dwelt,/Who all the joys and pangs of riches felt;/His sideboard glitter'd with imagin'd plate,/And his proud fancy held a vast estate.' (Swift)

6 Name-check, v. *trans*. To mention or acknowledge by name. 1986 *City Limits* 16 Oct. 42 'Namechecking The Cat In The Hat gets you no hipster points at all once the club has closed down.'

7 Microscope – defined by Dr Johnson as 'An optick instrument, contrived various ways to give to the eye a large appearance of many objects which could not otherwise be seen.' (Attested from 1651)

preface that he had taken the decision not to include any proper names, nor foreign words that any authors may have introduced through 'ignorance of their own, by vanity or wantonness, by compliance with fashion, or just of innovation...'

The great essayist Daniel Defoe (1660–1731), author of *Robinson Crusoe* and *Moll Flanders*, traveller, dissident, satirist and failed civet-breeder, had in 1697 condemned the proliferation of lewd terms. Johnson doubtless agreed with him. There is no **fuck** in the dictionary, nor **cunt**, **shit** or **wanker**. We are permitted a discreet **fart** ('Wind from behind'), as well as the respectable **piss** (it's in the Bible) and **bum**, **arse** and **turd** (which aren't). But there is no room for **penis** or **vagina**.

Johnson was offered £1575 to write the dictionary. As his annual income at the time was £100, much of it swallowed up on medical bills and opium for poor Tetty, a grand and a half was a fortune (and still more than some publishers pay their authors 250 years later). Johnson signed the contract on 18 June 1746. Then, in true writer's style, he blew much of the cash by moving his wife and servants into a comfortable, three-storeyed house in Gough Square, off Fleet Street, and settled down to his task.

One up on the French

Around the time that Johnson embarked on his labours, he had an exchange with the Revd Dr William Adams, the former master of his old college. 'This is a great work, Sir,' said Adams. 'But how can you do this in three years?' Johnson replied that he was confident that he could. 'But,' said Adams, pressing him, 'the French Academy, which consists of forty members, took forty years to compile their dictionary.'

Johnson's reply is a classic of its kind, and one that should not be repeated south of Dover. 'Sir, thus it is. This is the proportion. Let me see; forty times forty is sixteen hundred. As three to sixteen hundred, so is the proportion of an Englishman to a Frenchman.'

Johnson's working methods were scrupulous, and he hired six fact-checkers. The work must have been tiring, for Johnson throws us a playful hint of this when he gives an example to define the word **dull**: 'To make dictionaries is dull work'. And yet he was passionate about it. When he had finished the work, he wrote in the preface that 'The English dictionary was written with little assistance of the learned, and without any patronage of the great; not in the soft obscurities of retirement, or under the shelter of academic bowers, but amidst inconvenience and distraction, in sickness and sorrow.' It sounds almost like 'in sickness and in health'. For those years, it must have seemed to Johnson as if he were married to the English language.

Boswell described the great man's working methods, though the two men did not meet until after the dictionary had been published, by which time Johnson's reputation was secure. His own library had proved inadequate, so he begged and borrowed volumes from booksellers or friends. This supply of goodwill began to erode when the volumes were returned in a generally worse state than they had been received. On one occasion, for example, his friend Garrick lent him his very rare quarto edition of Shakespeare. When Johnson returned it, it had been torn to shreds.

Johnson began by consulting and rewriting entries in existing dictionaries. But at some point he changed his approach, and instead sought out individual works of literature. It was from these that he assembled his list of words, which he then defined. He marked vertical lines against passages that he wanted to cite, underlined in black lead pencil the word that each passage was illustrating, and wrote in the margin the letter of the word. Then one of his trusty amanuenses would copy out the relevant passage and score through the letter to indicate that it had been included. When friends objected to finding marks in their books, Johnson is said to have claimed that they could remove the marks by rubbing them with breadcrumbs.

The struggle to finish

It was not long before Johnson began to run out of money. Of the various members of the nobility who were tapped with a view to providing funds, the most promising was Philip Dormer Stanhope, fourth Earl of Chesterfield, with whom Johnson enjoyed reasonably good relations. In August 1747 Johnson published his *Plan of an English Dictionary*. This was his manifesto in which he set out his credentials and his aims for the work. It was also intended to warn off anyone else who was considering something similar; this would give Johnson more time in which to complete his work, which, it was now clear, would not be completed within the three-year deadline. The new lexicographer sought to challenge the foundations of previous works. He criticized the lack of authority in the selections and definitions of words in existing dictionaries, and announced his ambition to standardize the spelling and pronunciation of words. The dictionary's 'chief intent', he wrote, must be 'to preserve the purity, and ascertain the meaning of our English idiom'.

A dedicatory note to Lord Chesterfield praised the Earl's 'vicarious jurisdiction'. In describing his aims for the dictionary, he promised to select 'words and phrases used in the general intercourse of life, or found in the works of those whom we commonly style polite writers'. He goes on, 'My idea of an English dictionary [is one] by which the pronunciation of our language may be fixed, and its attainment facilitated; by which its purity may be preserved, its use ascertained, and its duration lengthened.' Johnson seemed to believe that he was ensuring the very survival of the English language.

Noting the illogical way in which **fox** and **ox** become **foxes** and **oxen** in the plural, he acknowledges that 'English poses some peculiarly stubborn problems.' Among the most intractable are an irregular spelling system, which only began to be standardized in the fifteenth century. Twenty-first-century foreign language students may share with eighteenth-century lexicographers a sense of shell shock (see Chapter 8, page 212) at our profusion of synonyms. We also have numerous examples of polysemy, a word which could net you an extra fifty points if used judiciously during a game of Scrabble, but which means 'the phenomenon of a single word with numerous meanings', as in 'bear' (to carry) and 'bear' (large, hugging, furry animal).

The *Plan* was published and immediately provoked a storm of interest from critics. Johnson was encouraged by this, but his funds were running low, so he went to see his patron, Lord Chesterfield. Unfortunately, in one of those administrative cock-ups that persist to this day, the noble lord was out when Johnson called, and thus unable to advance him the cash. Johnson did not take this well. To make things worse, some months before the dictionary was about to be published, Chesterfield wrote a rather insipid endorsement of Johnson's efforts, languidly stating that 'I hereby declare, that I make a total surrender of all my rights and privileges in the English language, as a free-born British subject, to the said Mr Johnson, during the term of his dictatorship'.

The gesture was not appreciated. Johnson fumed to a friend, 'I have sailed a long and painful voyage round the world of the English language; and does he now send out two **cock-boats**[8] to tow me into harbour?' On 7 February 1755 he composed and sent a letter to Lord Chesterfield that, even now, makes one wish the floor could open up and let the unfortunate peer disappear inside it.

---

8 Cock-boat – a small ship's boat, esp. the small boat that is often towed behind a coasting vessel or ship going up or down river. Often used typically as the smallest or lightest of floating craft.

Seven years, My Lord, have now past since I waited in your outward rooms or was repulsed from your door, during which time I have been pushing on my work through difficulties of which it is useless to complain, and have brought it at last to the verge of publication without one act of assistance, one word of encouragement, or one smile of favour. Such treatment I did not expect, for I never had a patron before…

Is not a patron, My Lord, one who looks with unconcern on a man struggling for life in the water and when he has reached ground encumbers him with help? The notice which you have been pleased to take of my labours, had it been early, had been kind; but it has been delayed till I am indifferent and cannot enjoy it, till I am solitary and cannot impart it, till I am known and do not want it.

When his dictionary came out, the word **patron** was defined as 'one who countenances, supports, or protects. Commonly a wretch who supports with insolence, and is paid with flattery.' Patronage cuts two ways.

A warm reception

The first, two-volume edition of Dr Johnson's *Dictionary* was published in 1755. The title-page reads: 'A Dictionary of the English Language: in which the words are deduced from their originals, and illustrated in their different significations by examples from the best writers.' It seems obvious these days, but back then it was still novel to define a word by tracing it back to its first verifiable example. Even more, to source each word by citing an example from the body of literature was revolutionary for its time.

'It is the fate of those who toil at the lower employments of life, to be rather driven by the fear of evil, than attracted by the prospect of good, to be exposed to censure, without hope of praise, to be disgraced by miscarriage, or punished for neglect, where success would have been without applause, and diligence without reward.' So begins the preface to Johnson's *Dictionary*. Long on commas, short on full stops, it reveals the extraordinary combination of swagger and self-pity that defined its author. Johnson continues: 'Among these unhappy mortals is the writer of dictionaries; whom mankind have considered, not as the pupil, but the slave of science, the pioneer of literature, doomed only to remove rubbish and clear obstructions from the paths of Learning and Genius...'

Removing rubbish from the paths of Learning and Genius. If the task demanded the skills of a thoroughly professional street-cleaner, it was lucky for the English language that Johnson had been born with a broom in his mouth. We do not know the full list of all the authors that he consulted, though he made no secret of his admiration for the Bible, Shakespeare, Pope and William Law (1686–1761). Quotations abound, though some contain slight inaccuracies, which suggests that Johnson swottishly inserted them from memory without bothering to double-check. But he must have used other dictionaries and encyclopedias. 'I have been cautious lest my zeal for antiquity might drive me into times too remote, and croud [*sic*] my book with words now no longer understood,' writes Johnson, justifying his decision not to search too far back in history. He decided to go no further than the works of the poet Sir Philip Sidney (1554–86), who died in Holland, aged a mere thirty-two, but achieved immortality through works such as the *Arcadia* and his *Defence of Poetry* – and through being Johnson's **back-stop**.[9]

Johnson's *Dictionary* may have provided the basis for all subsequent works, but it also differs significantly from them. For one thing,

---

9 Back-stop – originally a mound of earth or a now obsolete fielding position in cricket. First recorded use, *Suffolk Chronicle* 1819: 'They were deprived of two of their best bowlers, and a back-stop.' First figurative recorded use in *Lady Sings the Blues* (1956), the memoirs of Billie Holliday: 'Tony kept my job open. He offered to backstop me with the money I needed.'

Johnson himself is a constant presence, often using the word 'I' in a manner that would never be tolerated today. The noun **spot** is defined first as 'a blot', then as 'a taint'. For the third definition, Johnson writes: 'I know not well the meaning of spot in this place, unless it be a scandalous woman, a disgrace to her sex.' Johnson had no editor but himself. His five Scottish researchers were unable to prevent him defining the word **oats** as 'a grain, which in England is generally given to horses, but in Scotland supports people'.

Johnson was sending himself up when he defined **lexicographer** as 'a harmless drudge' (see Introduction, page 18). Drudge he may have been, but he was no slouch. He and his team produced some 42,773 definitions, with approximately 110,000 quotations to back them up. Not quite the whole language: the letter X was ignored on the grounds that 'X is a letter, which, though found in Saxon words, begins no word in the English language'. **Bourgeois** and **champagne**, being foreign words, suffered a similar fate: besides, Johnson was always more of a 'port' man. His entries are also notably scant on areas in which he was less than interested: the word **sonata**, for example, is dismissed merely as 'a tune'. He acknowledged the efforts of scholars such as Francis Junius (1589–1677) and Stephen Skinner (1623–67) for their work on 'Teutonick' (German dialects), though he was not exactly filled with praise for them. 'Skinner is often ignorant, but never ridiculous,' he writes. 'Junius is always full of knowledge; but his variety distracts his judgment, and his learning is very frequently disgraced by his absurdities.'

As an example, Johnson cites, with much derision, Junius's attempt to relate **dream** to **drama**, 'because life is a drama, and a drama is a dream'. Of his own (better) efforts, Johnson comments approvingly that 'My search, however, has been either skilful or lucky; for I have much augmented the vocabulary.' The book contained errors too, of course. Boswell noted that **windward** and **leeward** were both defined as 'towards the wind', and that **pastern**[10] was described as 'the knee of a horse'. When a woman once challenged Johnson as to how he could have made such a mistake, his reply was refreshingly forthright: 'Ignorance, Madam, pure ignorance.'

Given Johnson's character, some might have expected every page of his *Dictionary* to reflect his boisterous nature. In fact, he reins himself in. With his emphasis on usage, he starts with the most practical and accessible meaning before advancing towards the more far-flung or metaphorical. Words such as **cant, hypocrisy, judge** and **bookseller** – in which he might have let off a few fireworks – are defined with a straight face. Where derivations elude him, he confesses, 'I know not whence derived'. At other times, though, his caustic nature emerges. A **stockjobber** is described as 'a low wretch who gets money by buying and selling shares in the funds'. **Excise** is 'a hateful tax levied upon commodities, and adjudged not by the common judges of property, but wretches hired by those to whom excise is paid'. A **fortune teller** is 'one who cheats common people by pretending to the knowledge of futurity'.

At times the *Dictionary* is a medical source book, which reflects the concerns of its time: **colick**, for instance, is accompanied by a 228-word description by John Quincy, a member of the Royal College of Physicians around 1721, which ends 'most commonly to be treated by nephriticks and oily diuretics, and is greatly assisted with the carminative turpentine injection in the anus'. Then again, he can sound almost tender when he defines **embryo** as 'the offspring yet unfinished in the womb'. See also, however, a **pessary**, defined as 'an oblong form of medicine made to thrust up into the uterus upon some extraordinary occasions'.

---

10 Pastern, pre-1400, though attested earlier in the now obsolete sense: 'A shackle attached to the foot of a pastured animal, esp. an unbroken horse.'

Johnson's definitions and quotations tell us something of his political and religious views.

Leader: '4. One at the head of any party or faction: as the detestable Wharton was the leader of the Whigs.'

Popery: 'For corruptions in doctrine and discipline…the most absurd system of Christianity.' (Quotation from Swift)

Protestant: 'One of those who adhere to them, who, at the beginning of the reformation, protested against the errors of the Church of Rome.'

Royalist: 'The old Church of England royalists, another name for a man who prefers his conscience before his interests, are the most meritorious subjects in the world, having passed all those terrible tests, which domineering malice could put them to, and carried their credit and their conscience clear.'

Tory: 'One who adheres to the ancient constitution of the state, and the apostolical hierarchy of the Church of England, opposed to a Whig.'

Whig: 'The name of a faction.'

Spreading the words

Johnson congratulates himself for including a great many compound words formed with prefixes, such as **after, fore, new, night** or **fair**, for which, he says, 'I have endeavoured to make some reparation for the universal negligence of my predecessors'. At other times, thirty-three in all, he even quotes himself as source material for quotations. Some he labels, while others are ascribed to 'Anonymous'. One quotation, listed as Johnson, is actually lifted from Pope's *Essay on Man*, and another quotation seems to have been made up entirely. In his preface, Johnson is bracingly honest about the difficulties under which he laboured, and it is hard not to feel sympathy for him. Describing his undertaking 'to pierce deep into every science' and 'enquire the nature of every substance of which I inserted the name', he concludes with regret that 'these were the dreams of a poet doomed at last to wake a lexicographer'. With such words, he seems to be waving farewell to the body of work that he would leave behind, whether drama, fiction or biography. 'The work, whatever proofs of diligence and attention it may exhibit, is yet capable of many improvements,' writes Johnson. And yet he seems to have reconciled himself to the notion of change. Later, he writes:

> When we see men grow old and die at a certain time one after another, from century to century, we laugh at the elixir that promises to prolong life to a thousand years; and with equal justice may the lexicographer be derided, who being able to produce no example of a nation that has preserved their words and phrases from mutability, shall imagine that his dictionary can embalm his language, and secure it from corruption and decay…

There was no sign of corruption or decay in the language that he so famously delivered just over 250 years ago. Indeed, to judge from his inclusion of words such as **giglet** (a wanton), **fopdoodle** (a fool), **dandiprat** (an urchin) and **jobbernowl** (a blockhead), he may have sought out persons of questionable character, such as market traders or cardsharps, to discover the **chav** vocabulary of the times (see Chapter 5, pages 147–8).

There is also the famous story of Johnson being rebuked by two respectable old ladies for including obscenities in his *Dictionary*: 'Ah, my dears,' he teased, 'so you have been looking for them!'

The publication of Johnson's great work was an undoubted success. As James Boswell wrote thirty years later, 'The world contemplated with wonder so stupendous a work achieved by one man, while other countries had thought such undertakings fit only for whole academies.' Johnson was for a while able to bask in a certain amount of adulation. His friend David Garrick wrote a congratulatory poem to him in the *Public Advertiser*, which described Johnson as 'a hero of yore'. *The London Magazine* and his own *Gentleman's Magazine* – the latter across eight pages – were positively gushing. There were critics, including the economist Adam Smith, who felt that the *Dictionary* was insufficiently grammatical. But even he had to concede that 'when we compare this book with other dictionaries, the merit of its author appears very extraordinary'.

It had been Samuel Johnson's original intention to 'fix' the English language. In the process, however, he himself was, to some extent, 'fixed'. Inevitably, the book changed his life, turning him into a celebrity. His most recent biographer, Henry Hitchings, reports that whereas his name was being mentioned once or twice in the English press during the 1750s, by 1765 it was occurring between ten and fifteen times a month. Johnson went on to produce a valuable edition of the works of Shakespeare, and to take his place in London society as one of its most esteemed wits. He was given an honorary doctorate by Trinity College, Dublin in 1765, having only, and somewhat grudgingly, been awarded a retrospective degree by his old university (after much politicking by his friends) in 1755. His biographical work *The Lives of the English Poets* (1779–81) was his final literary achievement, but his *Dictionary* provoked dozens more to publish books on grammar, language and etymology. Johnson triggered a printing craze, and not just in Britain. His *Dictionary* was translated into French and German, and it was essential reading for lexicographers in the Netherlands, Sweden and Portugal. A friend of his called Giuseppe Baretti even modelled his own Italian dictionary of 1760 on Johnson's work.

In 1855, just over a hundred years after Johnson's *Dictionary* was published, the first moves were made towards compiling what would eventually become The *OED*. The first edition of the *OED* retained just over 2000 Johnsonian quotations, which were marked (J.). As part of the ongoing revision of the *Dictionary* for its third edition (currently underway), the accuracy of each one of Dr Johnson's literary quotations is being checked, just in case the good doctor's pen – or imagination – might have got the better of him. On its website, the *OED* notes that its own first edition made considerable use of Johnson's *Dictionary of the English Language*, quoting at length both from the first and from subsequent editions. 'These were accepted on Johnson's authority, but we are now checking the quotations in their original sources,' states the *OED*, quietly acknowledging that not all of Johnson's 708 quotations are equally reliable. The *OED* editors have once again asked the British public for their help in tracing quotations. So far, it has been a huge success: at the last count, only nineteen quotations remained to be identified (see box, page 80).

A volume of Johnson's *Dictionary* was famously flung through a shop window in Chiswick by an outraged Becky Sharp in Thackeray's *Vanity Fair* (published 1847–8). References to it appear in Laurence Sterne's *Tristram Shandy* (1759–67), Elizabeth Gaskell's *Wives and Daughters* (1866) and Herman Melville's *Moby Dick* (1851), and in several works by Charles Dickens, Wilkie Collins and Jane Austen.

Compared to Johnson's *Dictionary*, most modern lexicographies are sober, severe, maybe a trifle bloodless. Johnson's book, into which he poured so much of his legendary energy, is a work of literature in itself, and a revealing commentary on his own times, which is ironic, given Professor John Carey's description of him as 'the only famous writer who is better known for what he said than for what he wrote'. More than 250 years after it first appeared, Johnson's *Dictionary* remains a publishing phenomenon. It also contains a great deal more jokes than its French or Italian counterparts.

Are they accurate?

Here are some quotes from Johnson's *Dictionary* for which The *OED* is seeking verification. Can you help? (The 'a' before some dates is for *'ante'* – 'before')

1. **1727** J. Arbuthnot, *Tables Anc. Coins*, The Romans had the art of gilding ... but some sort of their inauration, or gilding, must have been much dearer than ours.
2. **a1626** Bacon, The chymists have a liquor called water of depart.
3. **a1682** Sir T. Browne, The fullest good ... the most beatifying of all others.
4. **1651** Ld. Digby, *To Sir K. Digby*, The slightest part that you excel in is courtliness.
5. **a1714** Geddes, In some monasteries the severity of the Clausure is hard to be born.
6. **a1676** M. Hale, Some will have these years to be but months ... yet that reduction will not serve.
7. **a1661** B. Holyday, All that are recusants of holy rites.
8. **a1661** B. Holyday, In a superexaltation of courage, they seem as greedy of death as of victory.
9. **a1661** B. Holyday, Is it the purity of a linen vesture, which some so fear would defile the purity of the priest?
10. **a1640** H. Peacham, A blue stone they make haver or oatcakes upon.
11. **?a1602** W. Perkins, If a man be lopping a tree and his ax-head fall from the helve...and kills another passing by; here is indeed manslaughter, but no voluntary murther.
12. **a1700** Salmon, The pine-apple is one of the tropical fruits.
13. **a1586** Sir P. Sidney, Euryalus taking leave of Lucretia, precipitated her into such a love-fit, that within a few hours she ghosted.
14. **a1698** W. Temple, A lady said of her two companions, that one was more amiable, the other more estimable.
15. **c.1675** A. Walker, The two great aims which every institutor of youth should mainly and intentionally drive at.
16. **?16..** White, It is not an idol ratione termini, in respect of termination; for the religious observation thereof is referred ... to the honour of God and Christ.
17. **1676** R. Wiseman, *Several Chirurgicall Treat.*, Either anasarcous or ascitical.
18. **a1728** J. Woodward, *Attempt Nat. Hist. Fossils*, Another was very perfect...and more sinuated.
19. **1711–14** *Spectator*, He carves, displays, and cuts up to a wonder.

chapter three

FROM 0800 NUMBER INTO NO ZYXXT

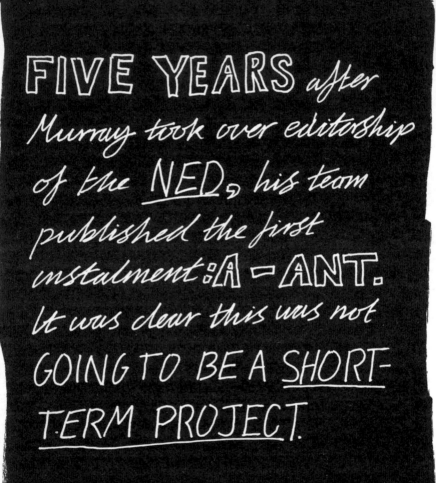

FIVE YEARS after Murray took over editorship of the NED, his team published the first instalment: A - ANT. It was clear this was not GOING TO BE A SHORT-TERM PROJECT.

From 0800 Number to Zyxt

The following paragraph contains some recent additions to the grandest literary project currently being undertaken in the English language:

> I'm having a **bad hair day**. I was **surfing** in this **chat room** and when
> I **logged on** I got a load of **spam**, and it's, like, **24/7**, what is wrong with
> you? And there was this **webcam**, some guy was giving it the **full monty**
> and I thought, I don't know, this really makes me feel **cyberphobic**.
> But then, **doh!** Time's up.

Meet some of the new recruits to *The Oxford English Dictionary*, the ongoing publication that is, according to the Oxford University Press, 'the accepted authority on the evolution of the English language over the last millennium.' The word 'doh' is defined as 'expressing frustration at the realization that things have turned out badly or not as planned, or that one has just said or done something foolish', which pretty well fits how Homer Simpson uses it in the cartoon series that spawned him. The *OED* adds: 'also (usu. mildly derogatory): implying that another person has said or done something foolish'. This illustrates, in a nutshell, what the *OED* does. It watches, notes, quotes and defines. It can take years for a word to be accorded recognition, but when, in July 2001, the *OED* added such phrases as **acid jazz**, **zero tolerance** and **snail mail** to its pages, it was the official sign that they had passed into the language.

The *OED*, which currently begins with an entry for **0800 number**, is a true twenty-first-century creature, but it was once a grand

Victorian project. It did not, however, begin in Oxford. By the mid-1850s, the jaunty, even somewhat pompous, self-assuredness of Dr Johnson's *Dictionary* was no longer appropriate for a more scholarly age. In June 1857, three linguists – Herbert Coleridge, Frederick Furnivall and the Rev. Richard Chenevix Trench, Dean of Westminster – all frustrated with the dictionaries of English then available, formed an 'Unregistered Words Committee' under the auspices of the London Philological Society, and, with the help of a few dozen other interested scholars, set about identifying the words and meanings that even the best of the dictionaries then available failed to cover. Before their findings could be reported to the society, however, Trench delivered two devastating papers on the subject of 'Some Deficiencies in Our English Dictionaries', eloquently setting out the true nature of the problem under seven headings:

* Incomplete coverage of obsolete words
* Inconsistent coverage of families of related words
* Incorrect dates for earliest use of words
* History of obsolete senses of words often omitted
* Inadequate distinction between synonyms
* Insufficient use of good illustrative quotations
* Space wasted on inappropriate or redundant content

The challenge of addressing these problems could best be tackled, Trench argued, with the help of the public. He envisaged a vast army of readers combing the pages of all the available published works, searching for quotations to back up definitions, just as the German reading public had done for the brothers Grimm – Jacob and Wilhelm – with their dauntingly authoritative *Deutsches Wörterbuch*, a dictionary that they had produced in 1852 when they weren't trawling for their other obsession: folk tales such as 'Rapunzel', 'Hansel and Gretel' and 'Rumpelstiltskin'. Once again, it was keeping up with our Continental cousins that stung the British into action.

Within a few weeks of Trench's papers, the Philological Society decided to widen the scope of the project enormously: the aim was now to collect evidence not merely for words previously 'unregistered' by other dictionaries, but for *all* the words of the English language, past and present. Readers would be encouraged to copy out passages that illustrated the actual uses of certain words, and to send these quotation slips to the editor. The work would be called *A New English Dictionary (NED)*, and it amounted to a call for a complete re-examination of the language from Anglo-Saxon times onward.

The new dictionary would comprise four volumes and 6400 pages. It would include all the English language vocabulary from Early Middle English (AD 1150) to the present day, as well as any earlier words that earned a place. The dictionary's supporters were confident that the task could be completed in ten years. That, it soon emerged, was somewhat naive.

Founding fathers

The Rev. Richard Chenevix Trench was central to the project in its infancy, but he had a calling, and his ecclesiastical sense of duty took him to Dublin. Instead, Herbert Coleridge, grandson of the poet Samuel Taylor Coleridge, became the dictionary's first editor. A brilliant man, full of radical ideas, he published his plan for the work on 12 May 1860. He wanted to divide the dictionary into three parts: one for common words, including **slang** and **Americanisms**; the second for technical and scientific terms; the third to consist of an etymological appendix.

Coleridge's home became the *NED*'s first editorial office. A grid of fifty-four pigeon-holes was arranged that could accommodate 100,000 quotation slips. In April 1861 the first sample pages of the dictionary were published. It would have been fascinating to see the rest of Herbert Coleridge's dictionary, but that hope – together with the three-part plan – was cut cruelly short when he died, aged only thirty-one, in 1861. As in life, his death owed much to his beloved Philological Society, since he had attended a meeting after having been caught in a downpour. A chill set in and turned to consumption, from which he did not recover. He never stopped working, though. His last words were said to be, 'I must begin Sanskrit tomorrow'.

The mantle of editor passed to Frederick Furnivall, then aged thirty-six. He was a great linguist and passionate about language, but lacked the grafting temperament needed for such a job. Furnivall took his eye off the ball, frequently resting it instead on an ever-increasing number of highbrow, literature-related societies, and on an army of young female admirers, whom he cultivated with great energy. For a while, the project began to founder. He was not good at keeping in touch with his assistants, and some of them gave up on him, or assumed that the whole undertaking had run out of steam, or money, or both. Furnivall lost track of the whereabouts of hundreds of thousands of contributors' slips. One complete set of quotation slips for words starting with H was eventually traced to Florence, taken there by an American scholar who thought he would like to work on them there and in his house in the Tuscan hills. There were other close shaves. Q turned up in Loughborough and Pa in a stable in County Cavan, where some of the slips were assumed to be waste paper and burnt.

Furnivall also introduced a young man called Kenneth Grahame to the joys of rowing. This inspired Grahame to write his immortal tale of waterborne life, *The Wind in the Willows* (1908), about the friendship between a mole, a rat and a toad. Aged eighty-two, Furnivall, that ever-youthful, bright-eyed pedant – the inspiration for Grahame's Ratty – was still sculling up to 30km (20 miles) on the river every day.

Knowing that the *NED* could never come to fruition with himself at the helm, Furnivall approached some other scholarly men – Henry Sweet and Henry Nicol – in the 1870s, but they said no. Finally, though, in 1879, the Philological Society struck lucky for two reasons. It found a suitable publisher – Oxford University Press (OUP) – and an editor, called James Murray.

Editor extraordinaire

Murray was born near Hawick, Roxburghshire, on 7 February 1837. A compulsive reader, he was more or less fluent in Italian, French, Catalan, Spanish and Latin. He also spoke Portuguese, Provençal and Vaudois (as spoken by the inhabitants of Vaud, Switzerland). He was 'tolerably familiar' with Dutch, Flemish, German and Danish, knew a little Celtic and some Slavic languages, had obtained 'a useful knowledge' of Russian, and could manage some Persian, Sanskrit and Hebrew. He was also familiar with the thirteenth-century dialect of Aramaic known as Syriac, and could decipher the ancient script of Mesopotamia.

In 1870 he became a teacher at Mill Hill School in North London. In 1876 he was approached by Macmillans, the publishers, to edit an English-language dictionary. This came to nothing, but his name was then put forward as a potential editor of the Philological Society's dictionary. In 1879 – by which time he was also president of the society – contracts were signed, and it was then that the dictionary really began to take shape.

The complexities of the English language made the task formidable, involving as it did the examination of seven centuries of the language's development. Five years after he took over, Murray's team published the first instalment of the *NED*: A–Ant. It was clear that this was not going to be a short-term project.

Murray was able to conceive the project on the grand scale that befitted it. He also took seriously the task of organizing the thousands, and ultimately millions, of quotation slips, enlisting the assistance of his wife and their eleven children. Murray worked not from home, but from an iron outbuilding that he called ('first in sport, and then in earnest') the Scriptorium.[1] It contained a lot of bookshelves, 1029 pigeon-holes, but no pigeons.

Murray issued an appeal, asking readers to report 'as many quotations as you can for ordinary words'. He felt that readers who had taken up the Philological Society's invitation to join in the Reading Programme and send in quotations had concentrated too much on esoteric vocabulary. (For instance, readers had collected about fifty examples of the word **abusion**, but only five examples of the much more widely known and used word **abuse**.) Murray's 1879 'Appeal to the English-speaking and English-reading Public' was much broader in scope than previous appeals. It was printed in newspapers, and some 2000 copies were widely circulated to bookshops and libraries, not just in Britain but in North America and the British Colonies. 'Anyone can help,' he wrote, 'especially with modern books.'

There were numerous other knowledgeable, enthusiastic and dedicated contributors upon whom Murray could call, and many of them submitted thousands of quotations. James Platt Jr, for example, was a prolific philologist who, although he worked in London, spoke

---

1 Scriptorium: 'A writing-room; specifically the room in a religious house set apart for the copying of manuscripts.'

many non-European languages. He had said that anyone who could learn twelve languages would have little difficulty in mastering a hundred, but he was so famously shy that he was said to be a man who had 'learnt a hundred languages and forgotten his own'.

He must have had some capacity for speech, though, because he often visited London's opium dens in search of linguistic variants – and only that, we are assured – as well as offering himself as a guide to foreigners on the streets of London, just so that he might soak up some of their language and usages. He worked in the City, and visited the library of the British Museum every day to take out a book – in those innocent days when the British Museum library lent some of its stock. He would return it the next day for another title. When Platt died in 1910, aged forty-nine, Murray was distraught. 'I know no one, and cannot hope ever to find any one,' he wrote, 'to whom I can send any strange alien word and say "What language can this belong to?" with a very sure and well-founded expectation that in a day or two there will come an illuminating answer.'

Several women became champions of the 'Big Dictionary', as the project was informally known. Miss Jennet Humphreys of Cricklewood personally sent in 18,700 quotations, somewhat ahead of Miss E.F. Burton of Carlisle's 11,400, and the extraordinary Thompson sisters, Edith and E. Perronet, who sent in over 15,000 and did invaluable work on the proofs. All these were pored over and sorted by Murray's team of helpers, or, in many cases, opened first by his children, who all developed prodigious vocabularies as a result of their association with the project. Some of the lady contributors found it quite bracing even to correspond with a gentleman.

Another of Murray's principal contributors was Dr Fitzedward Hall, a professor of Sanskrit who had lived in India. After his return to London he had an argument with Professor Goldstücker of the

Philological Society, and allegations were made that he was a foreign spy and a drunkard. Piqued, he went to live in Suffolk, where he accused a local clergyman of ruining his marriage, and became a virtual recluse. But he spent between four and six hours each day proofreading the *NED*, adding comments gleaned from browsing in his own extensive library. When Hall became ill, Murray broke the habit of a lifetime's formality by ending his letters to him 'yours very affectionately'. In the preface to the published work, Murray acknowledged the important part Hall had played: 'there is scarcely a page to which he has not added earlier instances of words or senses'.

Trials and tribulations

Murray had frequent and spirit-sapping arguments with the Oxford authorities, which are discussed in *Caught in the Web of Words* (1977), a book written by his grand-daughter Elisabeth. But a more recent book, *Lost for Words* (2005), by the Oxford academic Lynda Mugglestone uses previously unseen documents to throw more light on the struggle over the compilation process. Decisions about what to include and what to exclude, as well as how to define what was included, were the source of much grief among the editorial team. Murray antagonized his colleagues, and was on notoriously bad terms with some of the loftily named 'delegates' of OUP, the university dons who oversaw the press's business and who were effectively his bosses. Some had no time for scientific terms, and many took a dim view of the slang, **jargon** and Americanisms that many readers were contributing. They wanted to limit the range of definitions and the illustrative quotations he sought, and they wanted the work finished sooner rather than later.

Elisabeth Murray and Lynda Mugglestone both describe the constant battle between Murray's perfectionism and the more commercial and pragmatic instincts of his publishers. The delegates, who were senior academic staff from Oxford University, had, in today's parlance, a very hands-on[2] attitude towards the dictionary. To the dismay of Murray, many got close – too close, in his opinion – to the text itself. Murray records arguments with them in which he pleads that there is no such thing as a 'good' or 'bad' linguistic source. And yet they were not placated. Complaints of 'too many scientific words' arose at a Delegates' Dictionary Committee on 10 May 1883. 'Should not the quotations illustrative of modern literary words be taken from great authors,' they asked, 'and the language of newspapers banished?' It's a commonly heard complaint. One wonders whether the speakers had in mind the lofty pronouncements of *The Times*, or was that, too, fair game? Lynda Mugglestone quotes an apoplectic note from Murray's colleague, the phonetician Alexander Ellis, that 'The delegates contracted to print the dictionary – not to edit it'. Murray and his more enlightened contemporaries were running ahead of the bull of academic opinion, and being roundly gored in the process.

Murray's problems were not merely with the dictionary's content, however. The project had begun slowly, with less than one letter being published in five years. At that rate, it could be decades, if not several centuries, before the whole work was complete. Speed was important, especially to the publisher – whether they expected to make a profit on the venture or not – and yet the work was such a serious undertaking that its pace could not be hurried. Murray was almost inventing the process of modern lexicography. He and his team were nothing less than pioneers – nothing this ambitious had been attempted before. No wonder it was slow going at first.

---

2 The phrase 'hands-on', meaning to take part directly in something, is sourced by the *OED* to a *Sunday Times* article from 1969 that refers, in fact, to a computer training scheme in schools.

The delegates' frustration was, in part, due to their desire to present the academic world with a work they knew was eagerly awaited. Learned journals and popular newspapers alike were united in their praise of each fascicle[3] that appeared, hence the unconstrained impatience in notes sent to Murray, such as, 'The dictionary is *wanted* by students *now*' (January 1887). No doubt the announcement that the work was in preparation had aroused a frenzy of anticipation. All they had to do now was to produce the book and the prize would be theirs, yet it was a long time coming. The delegates were aware of Noah Webster's masterful *American Dictionary of the English Language* (1864), a work against which Murray's work was, at times, larger by a proportion of 16:1. OUP had decreed that the proportion should be no more than 6:1, but that was an impossible demand. By drawing an arbitrary line, some words would inevitably be ruled out, yet the original intent had been to include a biography of every word in the language. A compromise was eventually reached: they would proceed at eight times the size of Webster's dictionary.

Thanks to scholars such as Lynda Mugglestone, who in her research had access to the *OED* archives, we too can stumble on the quotations that were, perforce, invented by Murray on rare occasions. The illustrative quotation 'Such responsibilities are not **abdicable** at will' was written to support the word 'abdicable', and came not from literature but from Murray's own pen. The reason? The researchers knew its meaning, but could not find a text to back it up. 'He gives good dinners, but I don't think much of his **cellar**' performs the same function under the heading 'cellar', where the word stands for 'wine-cellar'. But such cases, like really good wine, are rare – and in any event, the word existed and must therefore be dealt with. But what happened when a word's very existence was debated? On one occasion, Murray entered into correspondence with a reader

---

3 Fascicle, 1647: 'A part, number, "livraison" (of a work published by instalments).'

who upbraided him on his use of the ungainly word **advertisemental**. Murray hit back that although the reader might not like it, he personally liked it as much as **testamental, ornamental, monumental** 'or any other –mental'. His point was that 'The dictionary does not advise you to say so, it merely records the fact that such has been said.'

The matter of subjectivity is, of course, a crucial issue for an editor of dictionaries. Murray coined his own term, **nonce-words**, for words apparently used 'only for the nonce', i.e. once. A similar term as used by the Greeks, who had a word or two for most things, is *hapax legomenon* (a thing once said), though the one-off word **graiomania** (a mania for all things Greek) never made it. Murray was happy to dispatch many of these singularities to the paper-bin, even when he met them in proofs. Questions of Victorian taste determined other choices. The word **condom** (see Chapter 8, page 204) was omitted on grounds of taste, and the word **clap**, for 'venereal disease', was labelled 'obsolete in polite use'. **Bloody** was defined by Murray in 1887 as 'now constantly in the mouths of the lowest classes, but by respectable people considered "a horrid word", on a par with obscene or profane language, and usually printed in the newspapers (in police reports, etc.) "b——y"'. We should not point mocking fingers at Victorian prudishness: a classical scholar wrote to Murray about the word **cunt**, 'It must in any case be inserted.' Other scholars, including the headmaster of Murray's old school in Roxburghshire, felt it should be included because it was a good old English word of Teutonic origin. And yet Murray had the final word: the first edition contained no entry for 'cunt'.

The original pioneering voice behind the dictionary, Richard Chenevix Trench, had deprecated scientific terms, seeing them as mere 'signs' or 'tokens' and not relevant to a work of literary reference. Murray did his best to include as many as he could, but the dictionary could not keep up with the rapid pace of scientific advancement in the nineteenth century. Murray frequently complained that he was being asked to make judgements, often on matters of spelling or pronunciation, forcing him to protest that 'I am not the editor of the English language'. And yet, when push came to print, he had to cast his vote.

Raw ingredients

The procedure for getting quotations into the *New English Dictionary* remained standard for over a century. The first step was for quotations to be collected by readers participating in the Reading Programme. Initially, they were asked to produce quotations for 'remarkable' words, although this was changed in time to accommodate the specific needs of the editor (known by Murray as his **desiderata**[4]), to reflect a concern that there must surely be an earlier reference that would give a fuller history of a particular word. After these were submitted to Murray each quotation was written out on a small (6 × 4-inch) index slip, and a reference added to explain the source of each quotation. Each slip was then filed alphabetically according to the word noted by the reader so that the lexicographers could refer to them as they worked on the dictionary. The Scriptorium was soon receiving around 1000 slips per day. By 1882 its shelves were groaning with a combined total of 3.5 million slips.

For a while, OUP had been pressing Murray to move to Oxford to be closer to the heart of the project. Somewhat reluctantly, Murray finally conceded, and the family moved to Banbury Road in 1885, together with the Scriptorium – which he got builders to half-sink into the ground so as to minimize noise and disturbance to the neighbours. The Post Office obligingly installed a new letter-box

---

4 Plural of Desideratum, 1652: 'Something for which a desire or longing is felt.'

outside his house. OUP also felt Murray needed the help of a deputy. Henry Bradley, a man who was reputed never to have uttered an ungrammatical sentence, was appointed as an assistant in 1886. He became an independent editor in 1888, working in a room of the British Museum in London, and later in Oxford.

The Scriptorium became an essential stop on the tourism trail for a certain type of visitor. Victorian celebrities, such as the writer Mark Twain, asked to visit the Murray residence in Banbury Road, as did Lord Gladstone. The great Victorian statesman was somewhat surprised to find the door opened by a young man clutching a knife, but there was no cause for alarm: it was just one of the Murray children, who happened to have been helping his mother in the kitchen.

Mad about words

When 2000 copies of Murray's first appeal to readers were distributed to bookshops and news-stands, one came to the attention of a retired assistant surgeon of the American army called Dr William Chester Minor. Minor was a lover of books, and he wrote to Murray offering to help. The work he sent in was exemplary, and from around 1880 or 1881 he became one of the Scriptorium's most valued, efficient and prolific correspondents. Minor had plenty of money, which he put to good use in buying parcels of rare and historical books, but it was not until after several years of regular and cordial correspondence that James Murray asked permission to visit him at his home in Broadmoor. However, the extraordinary and uncomfortable fact was that Minor was an inmate of Broadmoor's criminal lunatic asylum, having shot dead a man in Lambeth in 1872. They met several times after that, becoming close friends, and Minor did much invaluable research for the dictionary.

Rational by day, at night Minor's mood changed and he suffered dangerous delusions about his own safety, being convinced that he was at risk of injury from murderous Irishmen. He also suffered terribly from sexual fantasies, which he did his best to cure in 1902 when he cut off his own penis with the penknife that he normally used for slicing open uncut pages. Minor eventually returned to Washington DC, and died in 1920.

The reason the dictionary took so long to finish is that James Murray insisted on having the phrase 'on Historical Principles' in the title. Far from listing merely a guide to pronunciations, definitions and Latin, Greek and other roots where applicable, and not content with listing just those words that stretched back to AD 1150 – which would have been a monumental enough undertaking – Murray undertook to cite passages that illustrated how every term had been used in a given sense over the centuries, including the earliest known record of each word's appearance.

The material that became *The New English Dictionary*, subsequently known as *The Oxford English Dictionary*, was drawn largely from the 5 million examples of words and phrases that had been sent in via the Reading Programme. These included extracts from novels, newspapers, magazines, scientific and philosophical treatises, manuscripts and other documents covering written English from Anglo-Saxon times until the early twentieth century. In its scope, ambition, confidence, thoroughness, seriousness, dedication and determination, it was a truly Victorian undertaking.

First edition facts

Proposed extent: Initially 4 volumes, 6400 pages
Actual extent: 10 volumes, 15,490 pages
Proposed completion time: Ten years
Actual completion time: 70 years (from approval date)
Publication date: 19 April 1928
Pages edited by James Murray: approx. 7200
Number of entries: 252,200
Word forms defined and/or illustrated: 414,800
Contributors (readers): est. 2000
Quotations submitted by contributors: approx. 5 million
Quotations used in dictionary: 1,861,200
Authors represented in quotations: 2700
Works represented in quotations: 4500

Murray never lived to see the project through to completion. He died in 1915, having overseen the publication of A–D, H–K, O–P and T, nearly half of the finished dictionary. Bradley died in 1923, having edited E–G, L–M, S–Sh, St and W–We. Two additional editors, who had been working alongside Murray and Bradley, ensured that the work continued smoothly. William Craigie had joined the staff in 1897, becoming editor in 1901, and was put in charge of N, Q–R, Si–Sq, U–V and Wo–Wy. C.T. Onions joined in 1895, becoming editor in 1914. He oversaw the remaining pages, Su–Sz, Wh–Wo and X–Z.

If Murray was the Moses who didn't live to see the promised land, Onions and Craigie were the joint Joshuas who led the tribe in. The last fascicle of *A New English Dictionary on Historical Principles* was published in April 1928 and cost twelve shillings and sixpence. The full set, consisting of 125 fascicles, sold for between fifteen and fifty guineas, depending on the binding. Here, at last, was the English language complete. Well, not quite. The word **bondmaid** (a slave girl) went missing from the 1887 fascicle (Batter–Boz) in which it should have appeared after its paperwork was lost. This embarrassing omission was amended in the next edition.

And yet, bound or unbound, the English language was far from being – in the words of Samuel Johnson – 'fixed'.

Keeping it fresh

Even as the first edition was being prepared for publication, it was clear that new information was becoming available all the time and deserved to be incorporated into the great work. But how to include it when the book was already published? In 1933 OUP published a single-volume supplement to the dictionary, containing new words, and new meanings and senses of words already listed. Alongside this, the original dictionary was reprinted in twelve volumes and formally given the title that it still holds – *The Oxford English Dictionary*. But a living language never stops evolving. The harsh fact is that a dictionary is antiquated on the day of its publication. It had been forty-four years since A–Ant had been published, and though ants had not in themselves undergone fundamental structural change, the editors knew that the updating had to begin immediately. To some, this might make the job of compiling a dictionary seem Sisyphean.[5] But lexicographers are made of sterner stuff.

The background to the second edition is that a decision was made to expand the 1933 supplement, since it was recognized that the dictionary was now in great need of updating. At that time, according to the *OED*'s present-day team, no thought was given to a new edition. The man chosen to oversee this, in 1957, was Robert Burchfield. Onions was still around, although he was eighty-four that year. The work was expected to take seven to ten years. Once again, this proved wide of the mark. Burchfield's new supplement took twenty-nine years and spanned four volumes, which were published between 1972 and 1986.

Supplementary facts

The following figures relate to the supplement produced between 1972 and 1986.
Proposed extent: 1 volume, 1300 pages
Actual extent: 4 volumes, 5730 pages
Proposed completion time: 7 years
Actual completion time: 29 years
Publication date: Vol. 1, 1972; vol. 2, 1976; vol. 3, 1982; vol. 4, 1986
Number of entries: 69,300
Number of quotations: approx. 527,000

---

5 Sisyphus was a character in Greek myth who had to roll a rock up a mountain. Every time he got near the top, the rock rolled down again and he had to start from the bottom. It was a thankless task.

In 1989 the *OED* combined the first edition with the 1933 supplement and the 1972–86 supplementary volumes, and added about 5000 new entries. Some light revision across the alphabet was also done. The second edition of twenty books contained just over 615,000 definitions and 2.4 million quotations. This edition contained a greatly enhanced selection of twentieth-century vocabulary – hardly surprising since the century had only just got going as the first edition was nearing completion. The dictionary maintained a Reading Programme so as to monitor modern English, and many more scientific and technical terms were added. The work also took on a more global aspect, reflecting the increased interest in and significance of words from North America, Australia, New Zealand, South Africa, Asia and the Caribbean.

Second edition facts

All the figures below relate to the 1989 edition and should be regarded as approximate.
Proposed extent: 20 volumes
Actual extent: 20 volumes, 21,730 pages
Publication date: 1989
Weight of manuscript: 62kg (137lb)
Ink used to print complete run: 2830kg (6243 lb)
Words in entire text: 59 million
Number of printed characters: 350 million
Different typographical characters used in text: 750 (660 special, plus 90 on regular keyboard)
Equivalent person years used to key in text: 120
Megabytes of electronic storage required for text: 540
Number of entries: 291,500
Longest entry: The verb 'set', with over 430 senses explained in 60,000 words
Number of etymologies: 219,800
Number of quotations: 2,436,600

In 1971 OUP published the entire thirteen-volume 1933 *OED* in a compact edition of just two volumes, housing them in a sturdy box. Each page reproduced four pages of the old edition, so the magnifying glass that was supplied in a pull-out drawer at the bottom of the box was essential, even for those with good eyesight. The second edition (*OED2*) went on sale in 1991 in a compact edition, with nine original pages to one page, and a stronger magnifying glass.

The digital dictionary

The second edition became available on CD-ROM in 1992, whereupon more than 60kg (132lb) of paper were replaced by about 550 megabytes of text on a disk weighing just a few grams. The *OED* was now increasingly becoming an electronic product. Paper editions were still in demand, but new realities were coming into play.

In March 2000 the *OED Online* became available to subscribers as part of the £34 million revision programme that began under chief editor John Simpson in 1993. Since then, on any given day, some seventy scholars, research assistants, systems engineers and project managers, as well as about 200 specialist consultants and readers, have worked on this project. Estimates of a completion date for what will be *OED3* are conservative, which is probably wise, given how wide of the mark all the earlier dates were. There is at present no estimated end date, as this depends on a number of factors. New technology, new evidence and new developments in the worldwide use of English are rapidly changing the picture. But the rate at which revised and new words are being published has risen by 150 per cent since online publication of the third edition began.

With the revision process starting in earnest in 2000, the online database that contains the whole of *OED2* is being updated quarterly. Every word and every definition – most of which have been left unchanged since they went into the first edition – will eventually be subjected to the intense scrutiny of Oxford's team of lexicographers. The online revised text is an ever-expanding third edition, in continuous publication until completion. Revision started at M because by mid-alphabet the original editors were sure of their style, and had enough quotation evidence as well. 'As editors who were learning how to revise the dictionary,' writes Penny Silva of the *OED*, 'we felt that we needed a secure base for our work on the text. Also, M is a representative letter: it includes large, old words (such as make, man, may and might), and also many words borrowed from other languages.'

It is possible that the *OED3* will never be printed conventionally, but will only ever be available electronically. That will be a decision for the future, when it is nearer completion. The *OED* went online in March 2000 to rave reviews. Writing in the *Observer* newspaper, literary editor Robert McCrum welcomed it, excitedly describing his first encounter with the *OED*'s cyber version as 'a vivid reminder that we are living through a second Gutenberg revolution'.[6] There are two sides to *OED Online*. First is an open-access information site that contains news, history, educational resources and a generalized help area. Second is a closed, subscription-only area that houses the internet version of the dictionary, known as *OED3*.

The main, open site is the public face of the *OED*, and would take several days or weeks to explore properly. Schoolchildren will be drawn to its educational site, which contains word stories, links and

[6] Johannes Gensfleisch zur Laden zum Gutenberg (c.1398–1468), a German metal-worker and inventor, developed a printing press with moveable type. Books could then be printed at a rate never known before and resulted in an information explosion in Europe.

quizzes. General readers might want to scroll through the history and significant facts of the *OED*, or read through one of the many newsletters that the dictionary has been producing since January 1995. The policy of openness suggests confidence and accessibility, and the striking design of the pages complements, albeit electronically, the grandeur of the original Victorian project. Indeed, it's difficult to stay on one page without the eye being distracted by a link to another, just as consulting the 'hard copy' of the *OED* inevitably led to a paper-chase from one word to another.

But it is the dictionary itself that is the shining star of the *OED Online* project. The current annual subscription rate is £195 plus VAT, so for about £50 per quarter readers can see for themselves how the *OED* has entered the twenty-first century. Aside from the bells and whistles of technology, this is a work that has wholeheartedly grasped the opportunity to revise its original definitions, and to present an English language that is truly global. Lynda Mugglestone, in *Lost for Words*, recollects William Craigie's original definition of **white man** as 'a man of honourable character such as one associates with a European (as distinguished from a Negro)'. Ouch. *OED2* rephrased that as 'a man of honourable character (such as was conventionally associated with one of European extraction)'. The original entry for **negro** referred to 'black skin, black woolly hair, flat nose and thick protruding lips'. The draft revision from September 2004 takes us on a condensed historical journey through the word's meaning, touching on the **black power** movement of the 1960s, organizations such as the United Negro College Fund, and 'positive contexts', such as baseball's Negro Leagues. One comes away with a sense, more than ever before, of having learnt something. Now, the *OED* can expand to fill all the available space necessary to encapsulate a word's meaning. They also have all the time in the world.

OED3 is a versatile and adaptable tool. If you approach it with one thing in mind – let's say to look up a word such as **justice** – you can find a response within seconds. The search brings up both the noun and verb senses of the word. The noun page opens up to reveal the headword on the right. On the left, you can choose whether to display an alphabetical list of those words that precede and follow it, or you could show a date map of all the other words that came into the English language in the same year – 1137. The only other word from that year is **crucet-hus**, which means 'a house of torment'. The following year, 1138, gave us the noun **letch**. The entry for 'justice' has a good many quotations. If the author of the quotation is underlined, a simple click will take you to a bibliographical chart containing all that author's works, once again surrounded by alphabetical forebears and successors. The overall impression gives the reader, scholar, researcher or idle browser a powerful sense of immediacy. Here we are, with our noses pressed right up against whole generations of words. Although the original bound edition of the *OED* had charm and authority, it had become unwieldy, and pages became creased and damaged with use. There can be few scholars who would not welcome the functional flexibility that *OED3* offers.

The Simple and Advanced search buttons allow readers to search with pinpoint accuracy. You can check spelling and punctuation, look for a word within a definition, an etymology or a quotation, or search for a word within a particular year. You might want to see all the quotations used from a particular author in the *OED*, or to see which quotations have been used from, say, *Hamlet* (sixty-three in total). All these features are available at the click of a mouse. The result – a twinning of nineteenth-century meticulousness with twenty-first-century computer sophistication – is a mouth-watering prospect for anyone who has ever wondered how words fit together. The *OED Online* is a serious research tool that has been made available to the ordinary reader.

Oxford University Press has not abandoned the paper-based dictionary. The idea of a concise dictionary was first mooted by Frederick Furnivall in 1862. As with other planned works, it took a long time to materialize, but finally, in 1911, the first edition of *The Concise Oxford English Dictionary* (*COD*), edited by H.W. and F.G. Fowler, was published. This popular volume has since passed through two editions and reached its eleventh printing in July 2004. It contains more than 240,000 words, including over 2000 *COD* debutantes, such as **plasma screen, speed dating** and **sexing up**, which reflect the smaller dictionary's responsiveness to developments in the English language. It also has an expanded list of words from around the English-speaking world, as well as boxes offering advice on usage and a section of 100 special word histories.

Another OUP project, *The Shorter Oxford English Dictionary*, is one of the great oxymorons of publishing because it's still longer than most other dictionaries. Its two volumes are a tenth of the size of the first *OED*, but as the entries are shorter it contains a third of its words. It was prepared for publication by William Little, H.W. Fowler and Jesse Coulson and revised by C.T. Onions. The first edition was published in February 1933 after work had begun in 1902. The aim of *The Shorter OED* was to gather together all the words that have been in general use in English since 1700, as well as the language of Shakespeare, the Authorized Version of the Bible and works by Edmund Spenser (*c.*1552–99) and John Milton (1608–74); two-thirds of the entries in the great *OED* were removed. The fourth edition was published in 1993 and the fifth in September 2002. It contains many new words yet to be added to the full *OED*, such as the modern usage of **text message**. The list of people whose works have been quoted includes Helen Fielding and Quentin Tarantino.

Other reduced dictionaries include *The Pocket Oxford, The Large Print Dictionary, The Oxford English Reference Dictionary* and *The Visual English Dictionary*, and there are also children's dictionaries, such as *The Oxford School Dictionary of Word Origins*. OUP publishes over 4500 books a year, so somewhere within that mass of information is the right title for every taste.

Meanwhile, *OED Online* pushes on. It aims to clear up the discrepancies of the past and to incorporate an ever-increasing number of new words – approximately 900 a year entering the language at present estimates. All printed sources are currently acceptable, which modern readers will recognize as a thoroughly contemporary attitude towards the printed word. Few dictionary editors would have to face the concerted hostility to journals and periodicals against which James Murray battled, and readers might be surprised to see that some supposedly topical words have an older lineage than they imagined. At last scholars have the technology to take on these challenges. The benefits are immediate, enormous, wide-ranging and fun.

It would take a while to piece together all the quotations sourced to our most famous playwright. A search on William Shakespeare brings up 3566 entries, and the abbreviated '*Shakes.*' – abbreviations were used for some particularly well-known authors – produces even more: 26,106. It's certainly true that Shakespeare's influence has been felt far and wide across the English language, but could any other work match his? Possibly the Bible. The next chapter looks at them both.

chapter four

DESERT ISLAND TEXTS

SHAKESPEARE

coined many words that we use to this day, as well as many – <u>ACTURE</u> <u>ANTHROPOPHAGINIAN</u> <u>BEPRAY, FUSTILARIAN</u> <u>IRREGULOUS</u> – that have not lasted quite so well.

Desert Island Texts

Considering how much is said about how dumb we are all meant to be getting, it is amazing how much we quote the Bible and Shakespeare – those staples of any visit to a desert island – in daily life. If you have ever talked about the **promised land**, if you have occasionally felt **bloodthirsty**, said that someone had **iron in their soul** or felt **at death's door**, you will have been quoting straight from the Old Testament. If you have ever **licked your wounds**, if you have **suffered fools gladly**, been **in fear and trembling**, suspected that something could be a **double-edged sword**; if you imagined yourself in a **bottomless pit** or thought your outfit covered a **multitude of sins**, then you are quoting the New Testament. Phrases like **high-minded**, to be **beside oneself**, **old wives' tales** and **a sting in the tail** were not originally in the Bible, but gained much popularity from being repeated therein. And if you have ever **held up a mirror to nature**, been **hoist with your own petard**, given the **devil his due**, or **stood on ceremony**, then you have been spouting pure, unadulterated Shakespeare. Perhaps we are all far better read than we thought we were.

By the Book

The early history of the Bible in translation – both the Old and New Testaments – is a tale of overlapping re-translations. In the early years of the first millennium after Christ, extracts were translated by the monk Caedmon and the Venerable Bede. Some psalms were rendered into English in the ninth century. The flowering of scholarship in northeast England towards the end of the tenth century produced the Lindisfarne Gospels. A similar flowering in Winchester produced Aelfric's translation of the first seven books of the Old Testament.

John Wyclif (c.1330–84) was born in Richmond in North Yorkshire and studied at Oxford. The two translations from Latin of the Bible associated with his name (1382 and 1388) are the first complete English versions of the Scriptures, though scholars disagree on how much was Wyclif's own version. The second version is both cleaner and clearer.

William Tyndale (c.1495–1536) studied at both Oxford and Cambridge. His translation of the New Testament is the first based on the Greek text. His 1530 translation of the Pentateuch (Genesis to Deuteronomy), which he followed with the Book of Jonah, were made, at least in part, from the original Hebrew, though other classic texts, such as the Vulgate, Erasmus's Latin version and Martin Luther's Bible were also consulted.

Miles Coverdale's translation of the Bible – from Luther, the Zurich Bible, the Latin Vulgate (c.404) and with some debt to Tyndale – was printed in 1535 and reissued in 1537. Amid an explosion of interest in translations of the sacred text and the development of the printing industry, other versions include Matthew's Bible (1537), Taverner's Bible (1539) and the Great (or Cranmer's) Bible of 1539, which was sponsored by Henry VIII.

The Authorized Version, the most famous English translation and generally known as the King James Bible, was commissioned in 1604 and published in 1611. Although it was meant to be based on the Bishops' Bible of 1568, it is, in essence, Tyndale's text, with an occasional nod to Wyclif. Much of the wording that became famous through the King James Bible was Tyndale's own, including 'Let there be light', 'Am I my brother's keeper?', 'The powers that be', 'Blessed are the peacemakers', 'The signs of the times' and 'Eat, drink and be merry'. Tyndale was conservative: only 120 of our words owe their first recorded usage to him. Nevertheless, we are also indebted to Tyndale for his first-time use of compound phrases, such as 'broken-hearted', 'fellow-soldier', 'house-top', 'long-suffering', 'rose-coloured', 'sea-shore', 'stumbling-block', 'two-edged' and 'wine-press'.

But let's start at the beginning. When we think of the Book of Genesis, most of us remember the Adam and Eve story, the Garden of Eden, the Tree of Knowledge and, of course, the **apple** that Eve ate, gave to Adam… and the rest was downhill all the way. The problem is that apples are unjustly maligned, since apples were not specified in the text itself. The guilty couple merely ate of the tree's fruit. The specification of the tree is thanks to generations of painters, who must have sensed that 'Eve handing a generic fruit to Adam' or 'Eve tempting Adam with a satsuma' lacked a certain something.

Moses referred to apples in a poetic passage near the end of Deuteronomy (32:10) when, in a sentimental mood on the bank of the Jordan river, he reminds the tribe of Israel that the Lord cared for them and kept them as the **apple of His eye**. Here, the apple has nothing to do with Granny Smiths or Coxes. From Old English onwards, the word 'apple' had another, purely biological meaning, as in the **pupil** of the eye. This phrase is repeated in the book of Zechariah (2:12), when God assures Israel of His divine protection by assuring them that 'He that toucheth you toucheth the apple of His [i.e. God's] eye'. The same Hebrew word, you might think, but no. This time, the writer uses a different Hebrew word for 'pupil' or 'apple', and one that occurs only once in the entire Old Testament. *Bavah* shares a sense with the Arabic word *bab*, which means 'gate', as in *Baby*lon. The meaning is the same, though: the 'eye' – or the 'pupil', which is its direct translation – is the gate to the soul. Bear in mind also that those early English translators were translating from the Latin, with no reference to the original Hebrew text.

There is more fruit in the book of Ezekiel (18:2), though this prophet's tastes were rather sharper: 'The fathers have eaten **sour grapes**, and the children's teeth are **set on edge**.' In fact, Ezekiel has borrowed verbatim a turn of phrase coined by his senior partner in prophecy, Jeremiah (31:28), though it seems that even then the phrase had achieved proverbial status.[1] The verb originally used for 'to set on edge' means literally 'to blunt or dull', which is certainly what sour grapes – mentioned in the original version – do to the teeth. These days 'to eat sour grapes' means to deride something that you can't enjoy, in such a way that no one else will want to enjoy it either: a somewhat self-defeating operation.

In his seminal work on language and translation, *After Babel* (1975), the literary critic George Steiner, during a discussion of 'the innocent finality' of ancient poetry, writes almost enviously about how ancient texts such as the Bible and the writings of Homer could use such metaphors because – although he doesn't quite put it like this – they had got to the metaphor cupboard first. 'To them, metaphor and simile had been novel, perhaps bewildering suppositions. That a brave man should be like a lion, or dawn wear a mantle the colour of flame, were not stale ornaments of speech but provisional, idiosyncratic mappings of reality.' For a modern equivalent, imagine, in the very early days of football commentary, saying admiringly, 'Well, at the end of the day it's a game of two halves,' and being loudly applauded for your eloquence.

---

1 We also owe the phrase to Aesop (sixth century BC) in one of whose fables, 'The Fox and the Grapes', a fox could not reach some grapes and so declared them to be sour – to prevent anyone else enjoying what he himself could not eat.

As well as fruit, the Bible is full of words for dangerous predicaments. One is to **escape by the skin of one's teeth**, which comes from the Book of Job (19:20). The King James translation reads: 'My bone cleaveth to my skin and to my flesh, and I am escaped with the skin of my teeth.' Some have suggested that Job's teeth had been ground down to his gums, or that this was the very barest form of escape, rather like surviving by a **hair's breadth**, almost tantamount to not escaping at all – which was clearly the predicament that Job felt he was suffering from.

The Bible had its share of grumpy old men. 'Can the Ethiopian change his skin, or the leopard his spots?' asks the prophet Jeremiah (13:23) in one of his (many) deeply pessimistic moments. Jeremiah, you felt, was not one of life's cheerier types, which is perhaps why Victorian wine merchants, hunting for colourful names to give their outsize and novelty bottles, chose the name of a different biblical figure – evil King **Jeroboam** – to denote a large bottle that holds four normal bottles of sparkling wine or six regular ones.[2] He may have been a byword for depravity, but at least he knew how to throw a party, as did evil King **Rehoboam** (six bottles of champagne) and the not-at-all-evil **Methuselah** (the equivalent of eight standard bottles).

There are more **lions** in the Book of Daniel, prompting one of the most long-lasting images in the Bible, when Daniel's friends Shadrach, Meshach and Abednego are cast by the Babylonian king **Nebuchadnezzar** (twenty bottles, still or sparkling) into a fiery furnace for refusing to bow down to his image. Three chapters later there is more trouble when Daniel himself is cast by King Darius into a lion's pit. (Not Darius's fault, say his spin-doctors – see Chapter 7, page 180 – Daniel was the victim of a palace coup, and Darius the innocent party.) In any event, Daniel survived without a

---

2 Although the *OED* quotes *The Daily News* from 27 July 1889 to the effect that a Jeroboam contained 10 or 12 ordinary bottles.

scratch, and even changed places with the plotters, who met the bloody end that they had intended for him. So a more accurate definition of **to be in the lions' den** should really be 'to emerge triumphant, against apparently impossible odds, and to turn the tables on your former pursuers'.

Daniel is not quite out of trouble yet. His next challenge was Belshazzar's feast, at which the equivalent of a good many jeroboams, rehoboams, methuselahs and nebuchadnezzars were drunk. Belshazzar was in fact Nebuchadnezzar's son, and the party he threw – let's not mince words, it was an orgy – was famously interrupted by a hand that suddenly appeared and wrote with one finger upon the wall. In fact, the words **writing on the wall** are nowhere mentioned in the text, but the biblical commentaries are confident that the inscription, which was all Greek[3] to Belshazzar's wise men and enchanters, but which was actually in Hebrew letters, was displayed as follows, to the confusion of the king's interpreters:

S U T M M
Y PhK N N
N R L E E

Start in the top right-hand corner and read down to the E. Then move up to the adjacent M and read down again, and so on.

You need to add a few vowels because Aramaic letters are mostly consonants, but what you should end up with (Daniel 5:25) is MENE MENE TEKEL UPHARSIN. The phrase has been used in full by authors such as Charlotte Brontë, William Gladstone and D.H. Lawrence in the sense of an obscure omen or a warning of impending disaster for the following reason. The Aramaic word *menë* is a play on the word

---

3 SHAKESPEARE, *Julius Caesar* (1601): 'He spoke greeke ... those that vnderstood him, smil'd at one another, and shooke their heads: but ... it was Greeke to me.'

manneh, which is a coin. *Tekel* is the Aramaic for the Hebrew word *shekel*, also a coin, and the noun *pharsin* is the plural of *peres*. A *peres* is worth half a *manneh*, but also signifies the word *peris* (divided) and *paras* (Persia). No wonder the enchanters and the astrologers were scratching their heads. Daniel's interpretation was as follows. The repeated word MENE means 'God has numbered your kingdom and brought it to an end'; TEKEL means 'you have been weighed in the scales and found wanting' – another memorable phrase that we still use today; and UPHARSIN means 'your kingdom is to be divided between the Medes and the Persians'. Not surprisingly, we don't often use the words MENE MENE TEKEL UPHARSIN to describe the imminent demise of a regime of which we disapprove, but the phrase 'the writing on the wall' has come to mean, as the *OED* puts it, 'warning signs of impending disaster'. As for Belshazzar, he tried to change his ways. He clad Daniel in the finest clothes, and doubtless the party died away and the guests made their excuses and left. And later that night Belshazzar learnt what Daniel's interpretation meant when he was slain. Still, he achieved wino-immortality, since a **balthazar** (a corruption of his name), contains sixteen bottles, still or sparkling, which must be some consolation.

As a source book for unfeasibly large bottles of wine, the New Testament is disappointing, but a treasure trove in all other respects, especially phrases involving minerals. In the Sermon on the Mount in the book of Matthew, for example, in a passage thickly studded with ringing phrases, Jesus declares to his followers 'Ye are the salt of the earth…' (5:13). **Salt** was a crucial substance in the ancient world, ever since Lot's wife turned to look at the destruction of Sodom and Gomorrah and found herself transformed into one half of a condiment set. The line continues, '…but if the salt loses its flavour, how shall it be seasoned?' But how can salt lose its flavour?

One way is by being spilt and mixed with other things. In other words, Jesus is telling his believers to keep themselves pure in thought.

In its biblical use, the phrase **salt of the earth** implied a select group of people. It evolved, perhaps inevitably, to refer to the powerful and wealthy, those who gave the world its flavour. Salt has also been used for thousands of years as a preserving agent, and that usage was applied to a class of people who were seen to preserve life on earth by their wealth and power: namely, royalty and aristocracy. In the twentieth century, though, it has been democratized, and its original moral qualities reinserted. It now means, in effect, a **geezer**,[4] a decent person from any class. **Down to earth**, you might say, though that phrase dates from the early twentieth century, perhaps from a time when the possibility of flight had become stronger. Salt also recurs in phrases such as **to be worth one's salt**, though you might want to take that one with a **pinch of salt** – or at least, you would have done since the first recorded (non-biblical) use of the phrase in 1647.

Matthew also contains the famous declaration 'You are the light of the world' – same idea – and follows this with another memorable turn of phrase: 'Neither do men light a candle, and put it under a bushel, but on a candlestick.' This means that if you were to hide your light under a bushel, you wouldn't be able to see it, which would be a bad thing. But what is a **bushel**? It certainly has nothing to do with a bush, since if you hid your candle under one, the whole thing might go up. A bushel is a measure, approximately 36 litres (8 gallons), or a container for that same amount – and not a drop of wine. The modern usage came into common currency in the sixteenth and seventeenth centuries, so whenever someone tells you that you're **hiding your light under a bushel**, they're quoting from the book of Matthew.

---

4 An 1885 dialect pronunciation of 'guiser' (chiefly Scotland and the north) 'one who guises' (1488), a masquerader or mummer. As geezer, 'A term of derision applied esp. to men, usu. but not necessarily elderly; a chap, fellow.'

The imagery of flames and light – not surprisingly from a man who said 'I am the light of the world' – fills the New Testament. Matthew again (15:14) tells us that Jesus said 'if the blind lead the blind, both shall fall into the ditch'. **Blind** is a common Teutonic adjective. (Ask any Latvian and they will tell you that the verb *blendu* means 'I do not see clearly'.) A crude contemporary version of **the blind leading the blind** is a T-shirt bearing the slogan 'I'm with this idiot…'.

On a not dissimilar theme, we might note that President George W. Bush quoted the book of Matthew when declaring his **war on terror**. 'He that is not with me is against me', was Jesus's uncompromising message in Matthew (12:30). George Bush said much the same on 6 November 2001, when he said 'You are **either with us or you are against us** in the fight against terror.' Of course, the president was hardly the first politician to dip into his Bible in search of a suitable sound bite. 'We've gone the **extra mile** in arms control, but our offers have not always been welcome,' said President Ronald Reagan on 14 November 1985, with reference to the nuclear arms race that the Unites States and the Soviet Union were still fighting. He wasn't the first to talk about mileage in this way. The British comic actress Joyce Grenfell, in her 1979 autobiography *Turn Back the Clock*, wrote of 'Working like a beaver / Always with a smile / Ready to take the rough and the smooth / To **go the extra mile**.' But it seems unlikely that the president's speech-writers had studied the works of Joyce Grenfell. In fact, the phrase occurs in odd writings from the mid-nineteenth century onwards, but it was with Reagan that the phrase 'extra mile' entered the political vocabulary and never really left it. Again, the inspiration comes from the book of Matthew (5:41), in which Jesus says, 'And whosoever shall compel thee to go a mile, go with him twain.' Jesus was talking about the requirement to love your enemy. It was a Christian response to provocation and violence, suggesting that one should be prepared to go to any length to secure peace.

This, incidentally, is just two verses after the injunction to **turn the other cheek**, which was not a policy option favoured by the Reagan administration, nor any US government since. And in between those two verses, Jesus also advises that the response to someone who takes away your coat is to let them have your cloak.[5] The Scottish novelist Tobias Smollett, in *Humphrey Clinker* (1771), as well as coining the non-biblical phrase **not room enough to swing a cat**, also wrote 'He would **give away the shirt off his back**', which was the exemplum for those who can't help giving until it hurts.

On the subject of politicians, it is worth pointing out that when Neville Chamberlain returned from Berlin on 30 September 1938 to a country gripped with war panic, he told them that he had brought them **peace in our time**. That phrase, as many people in those days must have known, was borrowed from the Book of Common Prayer. Just under a year later, he was announcing that Britain was at war. 'Beware of false prophets, which come to you in sheep's clothing, but inwardly are ravening wolves,' says Jesus (Matthew 7:15). The idea of a **wolf in sheep's clothing**, with or without false prophets, is as much in use now as ever. And as the gospel of Matthew reaches its climax, we meet Pontius Pilate, the Roman governor of Judea from AD 26–36. Pilate made his decision about the fate of Jesus and then famously **washed his hands**, saying, 'I am innocent of the blood of this person' (27:24). Since then, the imputation of guilt has, to some extent, melted away, in that you can say 'I'm washing my hands of the whole business' without it being inferred that you have thereby sentenced an innocent man to an agonizing death. And when we say

---

5 'And if any man will sue thee at the law, and take away thy coat, let him have thy cloak also.' (Matthew 5:40).

something will **all come out in the wash**,[6] it implies that the truth will eventually emerge, which at least represents some sort of ethical vindication for the whole laundering process.

The book of the Apostles contains that memorable phrase **kicking against the pricks**. This has a remarkable history, far from the brief burst of schoolboyish sniggering that it might occasion. The remark was made, twice in the same book (9:5), by Jesus to Saul, later Paul, who, because he didn't know any better, had been persecuting Christians. A **prick** is actually a 'goad' – a wooden shaft, sharply pointed at its end – which is used by tillermen to keep oxen walking in a straight line. The oxen might try to deviate from the course by 'kicking against the prick', but the more they did so, the more the tillermen, working in the field, would drive it against the poor beasts' skin. The expression originally meant to resist authority even if you harmed yourself in the process. These days it means, more generally, to be **recalcitrant** or just plain **bolshy**. Kevin Mitchell of the *Observer* newspaper got that sense of futile aggression about right in May 2005 when he described Manchester United fans burning an effigy of their new owner Malcolm Glazer as an example of 'to kick against the pricks'.

Have you ever said **in the twinkling of an eye**? That's from the Bible too. In 1535 the priest and translator Miles Coverdale (1488–1568) published the first complete Bible to be printed in the English language, which contained the line from Psalms 30:6, 'His wrath endureth but the twincklinge of an eye.' Ever since the early fourteenth century it had meant not just the action of blinking, but a tiny amount of time too. Geoffrey Chaucer (see Chapter 1, pages 56–8) had used it for the same effect, and Shakespeare would return to it in *The Merchant of Venice*.

---

6 Kipling, actually. 'An' it all went into the laundry, / But it never came out in the wash.' (*Five Nations*, 1903).

Corinthians, written by the arch spin maestro Paul, abounds with drop-dead[7] phrases. It is, for example, one of the first places where you would find the phrase **puffed up**. It's there in Tyndale's translation of Colossians 2:18, 'puft vppe with his flesshly mynde', and Coverdale wrote, 'Knowlege puffeth a man vp, but loue edifyeth' (1 Corinthians, 8:1).

The saying **My body is a temple**, so beloved of health faddists, has a holier origin than most Reiki practitioners might have imagined. Jesus said it first, or Paul wrote it, anyway, in 1 Corinthians 6:15. The Authorized Version gives 'Know ye not that your bodies are the members of Christ?' But more modern versions prefer 'temples' – and that seems to strike the right chord. And, of course, your body cannot be said to be ready to **fight the good fight** (1 Timothy, 6:12) unless it is in peak condition. One way to do this is to **gird your loins**. This expression is everywhere in the Bible, both Old and New Testaments. To **gird** means 'to put a belt around the waist', in other words, to prepare for exertion, the loins being the part of the body between the pelvis and the ribs.

St John's Gospel reminds us what to do when we're being judgmental: 'He that is without sin among you, let him **first cast a stone**.' (8:7) In fact, the last two words are missing from this quotation, which should end 'at her', since Jesus was arguing with a crowd who wanted to stone an adulterous woman. From one stone to an even bigger one: Paul, in 1 Corinthians (13:2), wrote the memorable exhortation: '…though I have all faith, so that I could (re)**move mountains**, and have not charity, I am nothing'. Moving – or removing, depending on the translation – mountains is an enviable occupation, and one that still exists, as then, in the imagination.

---

7 Drop-dead, American, colloquial: 'Stunning, striking, exceptional; breathtaking, heart-stopping.' First cited in 1962 in the *New York Herald Tribune*: 'Fashions from Florence not drop-dead… For almost the first time in history Simonetta failed to deliver an absolutely drop-dead collection.'

And for those trapped under the relocated mountain? A painful death, probably, that will lead them to **give up the ghost**. The Bible translators may not have been the first to put it this way, but in 1388 the scholar John Wyclif (*c*.1330–84) translated Matthew 27:50 as, 'Jhesus eftsoone criede with a greet voyce and gaf vp the goost'. Jesus also 'gave up the ghost' in Mark, Luke and John. Another ghostly phrase that post-dates the Bible is 'Williams hadn't the **ghost of a chance** with Tom at wrestling' from *Tom Brown's Schooldays* (Thomas Hughes 1857).

By the Bard

Whereas Wyclif, Tyndale, Coverdale and the other great Bible translators were rendering sacred texts into the most formal language, to be spoken in church at births, marriages and deaths, Shakespeare's linguistic daring was created for that most despised of settings – if you were a Puritan – the popular theatre. At the end of the Anglo-Saxon period of British history – before about AD 1100 – the size of the lexicon (the total number of words in use) was around 50,000. By the end of what is known as the Middle English period it had doubled, and it would double again in early modern English. The current *OED* has about 400,000 **lexemes** – 'a word in the most abstract sense, as a meaningful form without an assigned grammatical role; an item of vocabulary' – in actual use (and 100,000 marked as obsolete or obsolescent). Shakespeare's output ran from 1588 (*Love's Labour's Lost* and *Titus Andronicus*) to *Henry VIII* in 1613. During this amazing, life-long burst of creativity, he coined many words that we use to this day, as well as many – **acture, anthropophaginian, bepray, besort, conceptious, fustilarian, irregulous** – that have not lasted quite so well.

Shakespeare, like Chaucer, gave vent to a full range of dialect voices, and he likewise made much of the contrast between learned and common speech. Shakespeare's word play was endless, not least because of the lack of grammatical inhibition that English was beginning to show. When Cleopatra said of Antony, 'He words me, girls' (V.ii), we understand that she is being chatted up. This is the first recorded use of **word** as a verb (1608). Similarly, and again for the first time, Antony talks of being **windowed** (IV.xv), in the sense of being shown off or exhibited. (It was thirty years before a different writer would use it to mean 'to furnish with windows'.[8]) Many of these words enter the dictionary as one-offs, as if only Shakespeare's daring or **pedantry** – he invented the words **pedant** and **pedantical** – could have put them there. But many more phrases have lodged themselves permanently in our mental phrase books, so much so as to appear at times almost clichéd. We may not know the original context in which the phrases were used, but there are so many in daily use that it **beggars**[9] **all description**, to quote again from *Antony and Cleopatra* (II.ii).

How much Shakespeare is there in daily English? 'Thereby hangs a tale' we could say, quoting from Act Four of *The Taming of the Shrew* (1596) (IV.i), where the phrase first appears. He evidently liked this turn of phrase, as he used it again two years later in *The Merry Wives of Windsor* (I.iv). At moments of heightened emotion, it seems, we often reach for a phrase of Shakespeare's. If you're feeling happy, you might echo Pistol, the friend of Sir John Falstaff in *The Merry Wives of Windsor*, when he says, 'Why then **the**

---

8 That man was the Earl of Essex's favourite spy Sir Henry Wotton (1568–1639), the man who defined his job of ambassador as 'an honest man sent to lie abroad for the good of his country.'
9 The origin of the word 'beg' could come from a thirteenth-century order of friars called Beghards or Beguins, who carried no money and relied on charity. They were known as 'mendicants', from the Latin *mendicare*, meaning 'to beg'.

world's mine Oyster, which I, with sword will open' (II.ii), perhaps hoping or expecting to find a pearl lying within.

Someone who rarely felt so benevolent in that same play was Mistress Page, who at one point splutters 'I cannot tell what the dickens his name is' (III.ii), invoking an old name for the Devil. If there was an earlier devilkin or deilkin from which this is derived, none has turned up, but later in the seventeenth century the word is used to curse, as in the dickens take you or go to the dickens, and if someone has played the dickens, they have caused mischief or havoc. Falstaff is the cause of raised tempers in *Henry IV Part Two* (1597), when an exasperated Mistress Quickly demands that Falstaff be arrested. 'For what sum?' asks the Lord Chief Justice. 'It is more than for some, my lord,' she says, misunderstanding, 'it is for all, all I have. He hath eaten me out of house and home: he hath put all my substance into that fat belly of his.' (II.i) To eat someone out of house and home passed rapidly into the language, but the two words 'house' and 'home' have somewhat different CVs. Both are Old English, and first recorded – in the Anglo-Saxon poem *Beowulf* and the Lindisfarne Gospels – within a hundred years of each other at the turn of the first millennium AD. House could be connected to the verb 'to hide': both have a sense of private space. 'House' was used in *Beowulf* to mean 'a building for human habitation; esp. a building that is the ordinary dwelling-place of a family'. But we also find other formations, such as almshouse, lighthouse and workhouse. Home, by contrast, meant 'A village or town' in the year 900, or 'a collection of dwellings; a village with its cottages'. A home from home, as used in the 1400s, is cosier than a house could ever be. 'England is my home,' someone might say emotively. They wouldn't say, 'It's my house,' unless they didn't speak English very well.

And if the Lord Chief Justice had lost his temper with both Falstaff and Mistress Quickly, he might well have said **a plague on both your houses**, which were almost the dying Mercutio's last words in *Romeo and Juliet* (III.i) (1592). Having been struck under the arm, he repeated that curse three times, while admitting that he was **peppered** (i.e. not long) for this world. 'Plague on't,' wrote Jonathan Swift (1667–1745) in one of his pamphlets. The word **plague** is Greek (*plaga*), meaning 'stroke' or 'blow'. The *OED* cites it as a borrowing from Latin, reinforced by French. **Plague, pestilence** and **infection** all came into the English language via the Latin Vulgate translation of the Bible of AD 405.

We noted earlier that apples bob up all over the Bible. They feature in Shakespeare too. If anyone has ever been described as a **rotten apple**, the reference is to *The Taming of the Shrew* (I.iii). 'Faith, as you say, there's small choice in rotten apples,' says Hortensio, referring to the rather poor choice between marriage to Katharina the shrew, and being whipped at the high cross every morning. And Antonio in *The Merchant of Venice* refers to Shylock as **A goodly apple rotten at the heart** (I.iii). (Apples can be good too, of course. New York has prided itself on being the **Big Apple** since 1921, when horse races were held in the city, and the 'big apple' became the term for the prize, which later spread to mean the city itself.)

There are plenty of other such expressions in *The Taming of the Shrew*. The word **shrew** is believed to be related to the shrew mouse, which was held to be unlucky, as a manual from 1545 which is quoted in the *OED* suggests: 'a kynde of myse called a shrew, whyche yf it goo ouer a beastes backe, he shall be lame in the chyne'. There is an old German[10] word *schröuwel*, which means 'devil', and Chaucer may have used it in that sense too, but 'shrew' did not originally imply 'woman'. Around the year 1250, and for centuries after, it meant

---

10 Middle High German, to use the proper linguistic description.

'a wicked, evil-disposed, or malignant man; a mischievous or vexatious person; a rascal, villain'.

We know that Chaucer also used the term 'shrew' to denote a scolding wife, but another strange transformation in the word's meaning came in the sixteenth century, when it drew near to the word **sheep** in an unflattering sort of way. A country writer called Thomas Tusser wrote in a 1573 husbandry manual, 'Now be she lambe or be she eaw, Giue me the sheepe, take thou the shreaw'. Another writer, John Lyly, wrote in 1580 that 'although the virgin were somwhat shrewishe at the first, yet in time she myght become a sheepe'.

Cleopatra, another feisty woman, invokes lettuce rather than apples in *Antony and Cleopatra*, when she refers to 'My **sallad dayes**, When I was greene in iudgement, cold in blood' (I.v). Just like a good fresh lettuce should be. Professional wordsmith Michael Quinion, in his word column on Salad Days, writes: 'for Shakespeare a salad wasn't just lettuce with some dressing, but a much more complicated dish of chopped, mixed and seasoned vegetables (its name comes from the Latin word for salt)'.

But, as we know, Shakespeare can be **hot-blooded** too. 'Now the hot-blooded Gods assist me!' shouts Falstaff in *The Merry Wives of Windsor* (V.v), as he springs on to the stage with horns on his head and ready for love. And, sure enough, within minutes he was in trouble of his own making, which is a somewhat different way of saying what was described by Alonso and Trinculo in *The Tempest* as being **in a pickle**, a reference to drunkenness (V.i).

'What's here?' says Arragon in *The Merchant of Venice* (1596). 'The portrait of a **blinking** idiot.' (II.ix) At that time this epithet simply meant 'winking' or someone with weak eyes. A 1914 edition of the *Scotsman* newspaper oversaw the word's transition into a minor swear word: 'One Guardsman … declared … that His Majesty seemed to carry the "blinking Army List in his 'ead".' More famously, in *The Merchant of Venice*, the Jewish moneylender Shylock demands his 'pound of flesh' (IV.i), a phrase that has come to stand for the unjust and relentless pursuance of any debt. No wonder that Antonio, from whom he sought repayment, was unwilling to satisfy the debt, but would the word 'sorry' have **stuck in his throat**? If it had, Antonio would have been quoting from *Macbeth* (1605), when the eponymous anti-hero returns to his wife in Act Two after she had told him to **screw your courage to the sticking-place** (I.vii) so that he could murder Duncan, King of Scotland. 'I had most need of blessing, and "Amen" stuck in my throat,' says Shakespeare's tormented hero (II.ii). Ever since, more words than ever have been sticking in people's throats.

It all ends rather messily, of course, and there is very little **milk of human kindness** (I.v) in evidence by the time Birnam Wood is relocated in Dunsinane. But still, **Come what come may**, as Macbeth says (I.iii) in one of his many asides, and from which later generations extracted the second 'come'.

Shakespeare was generous with his good lines: he liked baddies to sound well-spoken too, and in *Othello* the dastardly Iago jokes darkly – one could almost say he crows, in the circumstances – 'I will wear my heart upon my sleeve for **daws** to peck at' (I.i). 'Daws' are small crows, more commonly jackdaws. *Othello* has a wealth of other marvellous allusions to the dark side of human nature, such as the **green-eyed monster** of jealousy (III.iii), from green's meaning of 'sickly or bilious'. The play has other famous phrases, such as **pride, pomp and circumstance** (III.iii), from which we have since lost the first word, and **foregone conclusion** (III.iii), though commentators have not been able to agree whether the word 'conclusion', as used here by Shakespeare, means 'a final result', 'an experiment' or 'the outcome of a discussion'.

Hamlet, the play about the University of Wittenberg's most illustrious and ill-starred ex-student, gave more phrases to English than any other play. We could make several paragraphs out of well-known *Hamlet* expressions, from **more in sorrow than in anger** (I.ii) and **to the manner born** (I.iv), to being **cruel to be kind** (III.iv), **in my mind's eye** (I.ii), **suspecting foul play** (I.ii), **holding the mirror up to nature** (III.ii), and being **hoist with your own petard** (III.iv). It's worth noting that a 'petard' is defined in the *OED* as 'a small engine of war used to blow in a door or gate, or to make a breach in a wall, etc.'. The word owes its origin in part to the French word *petard*, which is from the verb *péter*, meaning 'to break wind'.

The tide of change

The works of Shakespeare and the books of the Bible represent a high point – perhaps a 'golden age' – in a language that is, for the most part, more or less recognizable as modern English. They wrestle with great moral issues, but they are also full of the most fantastic stories. On the BBC Radio 4 programme *Desert Island Discs*, castaways are invited to choose a favourite book, 'as well as the Bible and Shakespeare', as if there might not be enough to keep them occupied with just those two works alone. There are 791,328 words in the King James Bible, and 884,647 in Shakespeare. That's a grand total of 1,675,975 words, which should be enough to keep most readers gripped between the time it takes for a potential rescue boat to get from one side of the horizon to the other. And yet, of course, the marooned guests of *Desert Island Discs* always ask for one extra book – and they would probably light a fire and wave if they looked up and saw any chance of rescue. Why? Because human beings are curious and they always want something more.

But language did not stop evolving just because it had reached a stylistic high point, so we continue our exploration of English, not in the hands of great writers, but with snuff merchants, carpet traders, fabric printers, roof tilers, circus promoters, vegetable packers and make-up appliers. And if there's a boat on the horizon, it'll just have to wait.

chapter five

LOCAL LINGO

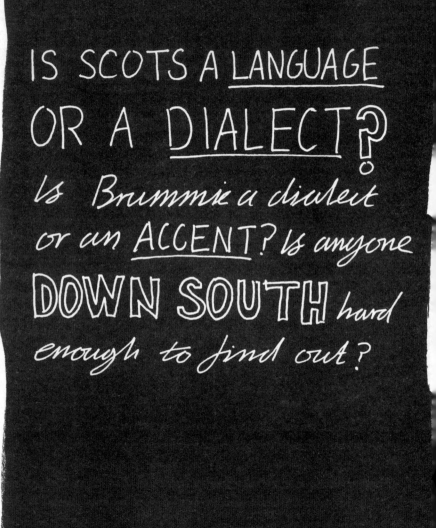

IS SCOTS A <u>LANGUAGE</u> OR A <u>DIALECT</u>? Is Brummie a dialect or an <u>ACCENT</u>? Is anyone DOWN SOUTH hard enough to find out?

Local Lingo

Volume one of Joseph Wright's *English Dialect Dictionary*, containing the letters A–C, was published in 1898. The sixth volume, T–Z, came out in 1905. In between the first proper word **aam** (chill) and the last, **zwodder** (drowsy) is the most comprehensive attempt ever made to bring together the dialect words of the English language, and it is reasonably clear what was at the back of Wright's mind. In the introduction to the first volume he explains that the book is intended to be a museum for dialect words, but also, to some extent, a mausoleum. 'It is quite evident from the letters daily received … that pure dialect speech is rapidly disappearing from our midst,' he wrote, 'and that in a few years it will be almost impossible to get accurate information about difficult points.' He obviously hadn't met any 'chavs'.

Wright cannot have anticipated the upsurge in regional pride that took place in the latter years of the twentieth century. Regional speech is now regarded as one of the glories of the British Isles. A few generations ago, if you travelled the length of the country, you would have been exposed to a pick-and-mix selection of independent strains of speech, in which words and phrases, accents and emphases differed from place to place, sometimes from street to street. The BBC Voices Survey (www.bbc.co.uk/voices) keeps track of our changing English language, recording people from all over the country and charting the many different ways of saying different things. For example, Professor Paul Kerswill of Lancaster University has a page in which he describes the changing accent of Reading, whose older citizens have the Berkshire accent, which, as he says, sounds West Country to many people, while young people reflect the influence of the London accent.

In a sense, the survey is carrying on the tradition established by the *Survey of English Dialects*, an information-gathering project that was created by Harold Orton and Eugen Dieth in 1946. By October 1950 they were ready to take their model questionnaire out on the road and put their carefully composed queries to local people in a wide variety of places. In all, 313 localities were chosen, usually not more than 25km (15 miles) apart, in villages with a fairly stable population base. Those interviewed, says *The Cambridge Encyclopedia of Language*, 'were natives of the locality, mainly male agricultural workers, with good mouths, teeth and hearing, and over sixty years of age'. The interviewees were asked up to 1300 questions about farming, animals, housekeeping, weather and social activities. Over 404,000 items of information were recorded.

The *Survey of English Dialects* was published in four volumes between 1962 and 1971, culminating in *The Linguistic Atlas of England* (1978). As an example, they were asked what word they would use for **snack**. The answers were traced in all their dizzying variety across England from Cornwall to Northumberland: in all, forty-two alternatives were offered, from 'progger' (around Dover or Felixstowe) to 'ten-o'-clock(s)' on the Scottish border. Around the Wash the most common word was 'lunch'; in the southwest tip of Cornwall it was 'crust', but further north in the county they found 'crib'. In Devon they came up with 'nammet(s)'. Other words offered around the country included 'bagging(s)', 'bait', 'beaver', 'dew-bit', 'docky', 'dowen', 'jower', 'lowance', 'minnin-on', 'nummick', 'snap', 'tenses' and 'tommy'. All this in a country just larger than the US state of Pennsylvania.

Has all this diversity disappeared, or resurfaced in another form? Walk into any shopping centre today (having remembered to take off your **hoodie**) and you will see how **dialect**[1] has to some extent given way to **sociolect**.[2] Whereas dialect is geographically specific, sociolect groups people together not by where they live but by how they speak. Sociolects are linguistic subcultures: groups of kids right across the country could all be saying 'ayrie' if the word catches on.

We should note, though, that the word 'dialect' is a disputed term, and that languages, as well as people, can make war. Before Yugoslavia dissolved into anarchy, Serbian and Croatian were regarded as dialects of the Serbo-Croatian language. Several years later, after hundreds of thousands of deaths and some hasty paper shuffling, they were carefully regarded as separate languages. You might even call 'dialect' a dirty word, though we might use **reasty** as a Black Country substitute for 'dirty', or a wonderful Orcadian (Orkney) word **skyuimy**. These days the word **variety** is preferred to 'dialect', as if the d-word were perjorative: is Scots a language or a dialect? Is Brummie a dialect or an accent? Is anyone down south hard enough to find out? The dialect map is shrinking, but it is still a tapestry of the English tongue.

---

1 Dialect, 1577: 'One of the subordinate forms or varieties of a language arising from local peculiarities of vocabulary, pronunciation, and idiom.'
2 Sociolect, 1972: 'A variety of a language that is characteristic of the social background or status of its user.'

North, south, east and west

Henry Higgins, the professor of linguistics in George Bernard Shaw's *Pygmalion* (1913), was fascinated by accents in the same way that rubber-neckers[3] can't help staring at car crashes. 'Hear a Yorkshireman, or worse, hear a Cornishman converse, I'd rather hear a choir singing flat,' he harrumphed in *My Fair Lady*, the film based on the play. And yet all of us speak some form of dialect English, even when we don't know we're doing so. Take **grockles**, a perjorative term for 'holidaymakers'. Many of us may have used the word ourselves. It is

---

3 US slang. As verb: 'To crane the neck in curiosity, to gape; also, to look around, to sight-see' (1896). As noun: 'Someone who stares; an inquisitive person; a sight-seer, a tourist' (1899).

marked in the dictionary as 'origin uncertain', but its first recorded use in the *OED* was in the October 1964 magazine *Films & Filming*, which mentions 'life's drifters who wend their way down to these resorts to make an easy living off the "grockles" (holidaymakers) during the four months of the summer season'. Since that appearance, it has blossomed, along with caravans, until the *Daily Telegraph* in August 1986 could poke fun at **grockle fodder** (fish and chips), **grockle bait** (the merchandise sold in souvenir shops), and **grockle nests** (camp sites). That same paper got the summer of 2004 off to a typically bilious start by describing the queues of caravans on the road in the West Country as the start of the **grockle-hutch season**. Meanwhile, Norfolk was described as 'an unusual mixture of the trendy and **grockle-ridden,** alluding to tasteful bungalows shoved next to caravan sites virtually falling off cliff-tops.

Of course, there's no use grizzling over a bad press. **Grizzle** originally meant 'to show the teeth; to grin or laugh, especially mockingly'. The following examples, gathered from the *OED*, make it pretty clear that the word was a West Country coinage:

> Grizzle: 1746 *Exmoor Scolding* Tamzen and Thee be olweys … stivering or grizzling, tacking or busking. 1837 Mrs Palmer *Devonian Dialects* The ould man grizzled: No sure, lovy, zed he, I ne'er had the leastest inkling for such a thing. 1880 *West Cornwall Glossary* 'What's the g'eat bufflehead grizzling at?' 'He grizzled at me; he was as vexed as fire.'

One hundred years after the first reference to 'grizzle', it has moved away from its local base, and its meaning. By 1842 it means 'To fret, sulk; to cry in a whining or whimpering fashion' and has made it into a book of Kentish dialect.

Heading up towards Wales, in Hereford, you might still hear someone say 'Have you heard the **charm** in the garden?' Trace that one back a few hundred years and you would find a reference to Milton's *Paradise Lost*: 'Sweet is the breath of morn, her rising sweet, / With charm of earliest birds' (IV:642). *The New Shorter OED* also lists the noun or verb **chirm** as, for example, 'the sound of birds singing or children chattering': the two sounds are probably more easily distinguishable these days, since birds – lacking thumbs – have not yet acquired the skill of using a Gameboy.

For almost every area of Britain there is a dictionary of local dialect. Many of these were compiled during the nineteenth century, and are smaller, localized versions of Joseph Wright's *English Dialect Dictionary*. Anticipating Harold Orton and Eugen Dieth's *Survey of English Dialects*, they paint a unique picture of a landscape that was still largely rustic but must have been disappearing almost as fast as the book was being completed. A good linguistic guide to the area might tell you that in Ludlow, for example, 120 square metres (144 square yards) of coppice wood make a **lugg**. And an old farmer might be able to point to twenty-four sheaves of corn and describe them as a **thrave**.

But dialect words do not have to be obscure, still less obsolete. Many, with very specific regional origins, now enrich all our tongues. One reason that we have so many words is that we freely use synonyms from all over the UK. In the Midlands, for example, the young William Shakespeare might once have played in a **yard** as opposed to a **garden** or **garth**; the last of these is still used in some eastern and northern parts. (In fact, they are all connected at the roots. The ancient word *gard* or *gart* means 'an enclosure'.) 'Yard', from the same word root, meant 'a twig' in Old English (*c.* AD 950). Then around AD 1000 it meant 'a staff' or 'walking stick' and, during the same period, the stick was laid on the ground and used as a measurement. The French word *verge* also means 'stick' or 'cane', and was introduced by Edward III in 1353, when French units were all the rage, but the English word came back into fashion, and **verge** (which originally, before 1400, meant 'penis') went on to mean a sceptre. Its sense of 'edge' or 'margin' is fifteenth-century.

The *OED* has **manky** meaning 'skittish horse', from **mank** ('a hesitation; a fuss, to-do'). It also has 'manky' meaning 'bad, inferior, defective' and notes that it is 'of uncertain origin', but it might be connected to the Brummie word meaning 'heaving with maggots'.

Brummies also claim **conk** as their own, perhaps as a figurative application of the word 'conch', which comes from the French *conque* (shell). 'Conk' has a spirited literary ancestry stretching back to the early nineteenth century and means 'nose' or 'face', though these days it has comic book associations, being the word that accompanies custard pies and pratt-falls. During the nineteenth century **to conk someone** was to punch them on the nose. In the twentieth century – and perhaps in response to such an assault – **to conk out** meant to faint. In the Midlands, however, **to conk** means to talk, chat or gossip, from an eighteenth-century verb meaning 'to cackle like geese'. And **chelp** is the Midlands or northern term for impudence, as in 'I want you on your best behaviour when the grandma and grandpa get here; any of your chelp and you'll be grounded for the week.'

From Lincolnshire to Cumbria, in parts of Britain that were occupied by the Danes and Norwegians, **beck** means a 'brook' or 'stream'. But there are other rivulets of meaning attached to 'beck'.[4] You could make a sign or nod your assent to someone in Scotland by **becking**, a shortened form of the verb 'to beckon', which led to the expression about being at someone's **beck and call**. Scots writer John Arbuthnot (1667–1735), who came to be Queen Mary's personal physician, used it to mean 'curtseying': 'I must stand becking and binging'.[5] He was

---

4 'Beck' is also the name of an agricultural implement used for dressing turnips and hops, and a large shallow vessel or tub used in brewing and dyeing.
5 From *Law Is a Bottomless Pit* (1712). 'To binge' meant 'to fawn' right through to the nineteenth century.

a friend of writers such as Alexander Pope and Jonathan Swift, and wrote a satirical pamphlet called 'The Art of Political Lying'. Dr Johnson described him as 'The most Universal Genius'.

Central Northamptonshire fifty years ago was no place for a left-hander. The word **cack-handed**, which means 'clumsy', was reserved for them. This disgraceful slur starts badly and gets worse, since the word **cack** means 'shit' in most Germanic languages – as in the sentence, 'I was so nervous I was cacking myself' – so 'cack-handed' is the equivalent of saying that one had shit on one's hands. In the same region, **clod-hoppers** was a rather deft play on the word 'grass-hopper', and is an example of many instances where country life was an easy target for mockery. These days a nasty newspaper critic might describe a rather **leaden-footed** performance of Beethoven's *First Symphony* as **clod-hopping**, but around 1690 'clodhopper' was a slightly mocking word for a ploughman. The *OED*'s first definition is 'one who walks over ploughed land; a ploughman or agricultural labourer; a country lout; hence, a clumsy awkward boor, a clown'. By 1836, 'clodhoppers' had come to refer to the ploughman's shoes. The word implies a yokel making slow progress across a field of clods or lumps of earth. Charles Dickens in *Martin Chuzzlewit* (1843) writes of 'A common, paltry, low-minded, clodhopping, pipe-smoking ale-house'. **Clod** is a fourteenth-century variant from 'clot', the word for 'a lump of anything, especially blood'. What a difference a 'd' makes.

The past will out

It may be news to some that the first official female police constable in the country came from Grantham. Her name was Edith Smith and she joined the force in August 1915. More familiar is the name of another public servant supplied by Grantham: Margaret Thatcher.

In April 1983 in the House of Commons, the Labour MP Denis Healey tried to goad the prime minister by asserting that her plans for a June election proved her desire to **cut and run**. The Iron Lady cut him down with the following retort: 'Oh, the right honourable gentleman is afraid of an election is he? …"Fraid, frightened, **frit**!' This last word was pure Grantham – dredged up from her roots in a moment of high emotion.

The most familiar northern English dialects are those spoken in Yorkshire, Lancashire, Cumbria and Tyneside. These make much greater use of original Angle vocabulary – about 80 per cent, as opposed to the more diluted 30 per cent down south. Yorkshire is still the place to go to hear the second person singular pronoun **thou** used with a degree of regularity, and words such as **aye** and **nay** are still heard a lot when 'yes' and 'no' are standard. Family words are different: northern speakers, and Scots especially, will say bairn for 'baby', and you'll find a **lad** or **lass** (boy or girl) playing, again in the yard (not garden) – at least in those houses that had yards. Scandinavian agricultural vocabulary survives in words such as **pike** (a small stack of hay).

In York it must be reassuring for visitors from Denmark, Norway and Iceland to see streets called Walmgate, Coppergate, Stonegate and Skeldergate, since the word for 'street' in those countries is *gata*. **Skeldering** – 'a cant term of obscure origin' attested from 1601 – means 'to live by begging, especially by passing oneself off as a wounded or disbanded soldier', which gives you some idea of the quality of folk who used to congregate in that street. York's **gates** should not be confused with its gateways, which are called bars; nor should its **bars** be confused with its pubs, which, reassuringly, are called pubs.

Modern northern writers are not scared of taking traditional language and making dialogue that manages to be both antiquated yet recognizable to a contemporary reader. In, for example, *The*

Blackpool Highflyer by Andrew Martin (2004), every page emits an unmistakably Yorkshire flavour. 'You look **all-in**,' says one character. 'Will you **give it here** for a moment?' says another. Someone else says, '**Frame** yourself, man!' in the sense of **pull yourself together**. One truculent character says, 'I was **blowed** if I was going to tell him the truth'. When people don't believe something, they say, '**Get away**.' And when something good happens, they say, 'You must be **chuffed**.' With that last word, Martin is visiting the sight of a 1960 literary skirmish, since two novels, published in that year, contained absolutely contradictory definitions. Auberon Waugh's *The Foxglove Saga* used it to mean 'pleased': 'He was chuffed at this new monumental skive he had discovered.' Whereas in David Storey's *This Sporting Life*, when Frank Machin says, 'I felt pretty chuffed with myself,' he means the complete opposite: displeased or disgruntled.[6] Despite the classic status of Storey's novel, Waugh's positive meaning has won through. During the nineteenth century a **skive** was a hard-working tool, used for cutting or polishing diamonds. In 1829 a **skiver** was a 'person who split leather' – there are references to this profession from Newcastle-upon-Tyne and Ayrshire. But 'skiver' came to mean 'one who avoids work; a shirker; a truant' in military slang from the early twentieth century, perhaps from the French *esquiver*, meaning 'to dodge or slink away'.

In Lancashire and many other areas, a comical euphemism for 'dying' is to **pop one's clogs**. We have written evidence of **clog** meaning 'wooden shoe' from the fifteenth century. In the seventeenth century **to clog** meant to put wooden soles on shoes, as a blacksmith shoes a horse. The *OED* says it was common in the north of England and the south of Scotland during this period for people to take their shoes to the **clogger**, who would 'clog' them for the winter.

---

6 Why not gruntled? Because the verb 'to gruntle' means 'To utter a little or low grunt. Said of swine, occas. of other animals; *rarely* of persons.' In use 1400–1855.

To this day in Scotland a 'clog' is a 'heavy block, especially of wood, fastened to the legs of a person or animal to impede motion'. (We can be certain that clog-dancing owed nothing to this definition.) That notion of impeding motion now applies to traffic getting **clogged up** during peak periods, which might cause some people to start 'mithering'.

According to the *OED*, to **mither** means 'to complain or moan'. It's related to the word **moider** from the Irish *modartha*, meaning 'dark, murky, morose'. In 1587 'mither' meant 'to confuse', but confusingly, by 1828 it meant 'to work very hard', which is pretty confusing. Then it meant 'to babble or ramble', and by 1847 meant 'to smother, muffle up; to encumber, burden'. A year later it had the meaning 'to bother, pester, worry, irritate'. Then it meant 'to ramble, be delirious; to "go on"; to complain, make a fuss, whine', as in this 1998 example from the *Observer* newspaper: 'The throng of pale grey Brummie lawyers sipping champagne and mithering … about how poor they are.'

In Liverpool, the affectionate appellation **wack** as a familiar term of address, like 'pal', was attributed to Ringo Starr when it first appeared in a 1963 Beatles fan magazine (this was at a time when Merseyside speech still needed subtitles in some parts of the country). If you were feeling **chordy** anywhere near Merseyside, you would be feeling 'moody' elsewhere. The derivation is uncertain, and surely not derived from the eighteenth-century word **chordee**, defined by the *OED* – though they have more sense than to try to make a connection between the words – as 'a painful inflammatory downward curving of the penis', which would put anyone – or most men – off their chips. The same city gave us **scally**, which is defined by the *OED* as 'a young working-class person (esp. a man); *specifically* a roguish, self-assured male (esp. from Liverpool), typically regarded as boisterous, disruptive, or irresponsible'.

New dialect words are coming into the language the whole time, but some are not as new as we might think. After Liverpool's dramatic win on penalties against AC Milan in May 2005, their inspirational captain Steven Gerrard expressed his delight at goalkeeper Jerzy Dudek, whose goal-line antics – wobbling his knees and swaying from side-to-side – had evidently psyched out the AC Milan penalty takers. Gerrard said he was **made up** (see Chapter 1, page 36) for the thousands of fans who had travelled to Istanbul. That expression[7] has been in use since at least 1956, when it meant 'assured of success or happiness…'. A long time before, it meant 'of a person: consummate, accomplished' as used by Shakespeare in Timon of Athens (1616): 'Know his grosse patchery … Yet remaine assur'd that he's a made-up Villaine' (V.i).

In the north of England if you feel 'tired' you'll say you're **jiggered**. The noun form, jigger, has two separate meanings in the *OED*. The first means 'someone who dances a jig' and the second is a type of tropical flea. Perhaps when the flea had stopped jigging it

---

7 Which the *OED* says is 'Irish English and British regional (esp. Liverpool) English.'

was exhausted – hence the word 'jiggered'. In other parts of Yorkshire you might use the word fligged for the same purpose.

From battleground to boardroom

Does anyone still use the word **slughorn**? You might hear it if you were eavesdropping on military leaders, since it is a variant of 'war cry', which goes back to at least 1513. The cry usually included someone's name, as in 'Advance, McDonald!' and was known generically as a **slogan**. Since the eighteenth century it has lost some of its belligerent overtone, and is now used in advertising – odd bedfellows perhaps, not unlike a redundant miner who has found employment in the fast-food industry.

Over to the northeast, Geordie and Northumbrian words are more than 80 per cent Angle (Danish) in origin, so, for example, the Geordie phrase **gannin yem** (going home) would be perfectly understood by a Norwegian. The phrase **Ah wes pelatick**,[8] meaning anything from 'I enjoyed myself' to 'I was completely smashed, bladdered, pissed, etc.', may not yet have travelled far outside the city walls, but *Viz* comic, which is still produced in Newcastle upon Tyne, has popularized such sayings as, 'Join the army cos all the birds are **gagging** for squaddies'. Even better if they are **bonny** (good-looking), but less likely if they're **canny** ('knowing, sagacious, judicious, prudent; wary, cautious').

Present-day Scottish writers have proved themselves to be among the most dynamic and exciting writers today. Liz Lochhead, A.L. Kennedy, James Kelman and Irvine Welsh have all explored their Scots heritage differently. 'Sae the Kirk Assembly are makkin' a mountain oot o' a **mowdie**-hill,' writes Lochhead in *Mary Queen of Scots* (1989), using the Scots word for 'mole'. She also used the term 'fuck-me shoes' in her 1985 book *True Confessions & New Clichés*. The only printed predecessor was David Bowie's 1974 album *Diamond Dogs*

---

8 Etymology a total mystery.

which had 'fuck-me pumps'. Welsh, in *Trainspotting* (1993), throws in phrases such as 'Dinnae really ken the boy. Only likesay run intae the gadge a couple ay times since we were **ankle-biters**, ken?' 'Ankle-biter' was first used to mean 'small child' in an 1850 issue of *Harper's Magazine*. And Welsh, who has an honourable forty-one quotations to his name in the *OED*, was on the money again where we find the following: 'I open my overcoat and flap it to see if the **ming** is as steadily rancid as I imagine it to be' (*Filth*, 1998).

Minging, in the sense of 'stinking', (attested from 1970) is one of the twentieth century's less attractive words. It used to be an alternative to **mingling**, which lasted from Old English to the mid-nineteenth century. It was also an Old English alternative to the etymologically distinct warning word **mind**, as in 'Mind you don't do that', and later went from 'looking out' to simply 'remembering', but by the eighteenth century that use had gone too. **Meng** merits an honourable mention in the 1923 *Roxburghshire Word-book*, where it is defined as 'human excrement'. It might be related to another early nineteenth-century word, **ming**, meaning 'the ingredients mixed with or substituted for tar in sheep-smearing', but whether that was its true parentage or not, **minger** ('an ugly or unattractive person, esp. a woman') has come to be a particularly nasty insult, as internet discussion themes such as 'My wife is a minger: should I run away to Thailand?' can attest.

Cockney Rhyming Slang is the romantically preserved language spoken in a small area of East London, historically by people born within the sound of the bells of St Mary-le-Bow. It is spoken by young and old alike. Theories abound as to how the language originated: most likely is that it was a code system devised to keep small-time criminals from having their plans overheard. The word 'head', for example, was referred to as a 'loaf of bread', and then – as sometimes happened to further outfox nosy parkers – just 'loaf'.

In the same way, 'talk' became first 'rabbit and pork' and then just 'rabbit'. Stairs have long been referred to as 'apples and pears', 'trouble (and strife)' is 'wife', and the phrase 'Would you Adam and Eve (believe) it?' has almost slipped into modern parlance. 'Alligator', as in 'See you later alligator' is originally rhyming slang. 'Barnet fair' stands for hair. 'Khyber pass' means 'arse' and 'mince pies' means 'eyes'. Admittedly, few of these words have much to do with small-time crime, though one is the word **scarper**, which has two roots – the Italian *scappare*, to escape, and the rhyming slang 'Scapa Flow', to go.

Modern cockney rhyming slang

Andy Farley – Charlie (cocaine)
Anchor Spreadable – Incredible, e.g. 'That goal was Anchor Spreadable'
Bexley Heath – Teeth, e.g. 'Look at the Bexleys on that'
Billie Piper – Windscreen wiper, e.g. 'Some slag snapped off me Billies'

Britney Spears – Beers, e.g. 'Get us a few Britneys in'
Casablanca – Wanker
Dirty Den – £110
Forty-four swinging door –Whore
Horse's hoof – Roof
Tony Benn – Ten pound note, e.g. 'Shall we call it a Tony Benner?'

From: www.cockneyrhymingslang.co.uk

Evolving English

Regional English has entered a new and vibrant phase. Old English words are now mixing things up with the language of Britain's multicultural communities. 'British Asian adolescents may sound more British than Indians in India, but they just don't sound as British as their white counterparts,' wrote Rashmee Z. Ahmed of the *Times of India* in April 2004. He noted that Britain's second-generation Indians are revelling in their bilingual ethnicity, pronouncing ordinary English words, such as **goat**, **kill** and **face**, in a recognizably Indian way, and that they never go to see a **film**: 'to British Asians, it's always a **fillum**'. Their language is peppered with Indian words such as *gora*, a term for a white person, and *chuddies* (underpants). And wherever large numbers of British Asians live alongside the white community, linguistic co-habitation starts to take place. Asian English is a genuine sub-language, with words such as **innit**, which is short – though not that short – for 'isn't it', often appearing at the end of a sentence, where a full stop might do the same job on paper. The website urbandictionary.com quotes three exemplary snatches of dialogue:

> 'Shane's got that new Nokia phone, innit?'
> 'EastEnders was wicked tonight, innit?'
> '… and then she fell on her arse. That was well funny, innit?'

A recent study for the BBC Voices Survey found that the once traditionally cockney sound of London's East End was being influenced by the area's Bangladeshi community. Young white men in particular are starting to say *nang* (good), *creps* (trainers) and *skets* (slippers) in imitation of their neighbours. Other cultures are feeding into the mix too. Black English is a sub-language of many sources, and much of its vocabulary involves taking English words and, basically, having fun with them. At the beginning of the fourteenth century, **to big** meant 'to dwell in or inhabit', and in parts of Northern England and Scotland 'to big' still means 'to build'. In black British English, though, to **big up** means 'to talk up, praise or promote' something or someone – compare with 'large it' (see Chapter II, page 268). **Irie**, developed from 'all right', is a word with a West Indian lilt, meaning 'nice' or 'good'. The slightly more confrontational **facety** – a more intensive way of pronouncing the

US slang word **feisty** – means 'bold', sometimes 'rude'. Someone who is **dissing** you (being disrespectful) could be said to be 'facety'. And anyone keen to show off their **Bimmer** (a nickname for BMW cars, which may have begun in the black community) will probably have an ample selection of **bling**. 'Bling' is not yet recognized by the *OED*, but rap and hip-hop street fashion have created this 'echoic' word, which mimics the chinking sound made by the wearer of a large amount of flashy gold jewellery.

For anyone who joins a gang, crew or **posse**, the last of these is shortened from the Latin *posse comitatus* (the force of the county), meaning 'a body of men raised and commanded by the sheriff'. As the word edged towards crime, the *OED*'s first sighting of it comes from the *Daily Gleaner*, based in Kingston, Jamaica, which reported in 1986 that 'Police have identified the largest and most feared Jamaican gangs as the "Shower Posse" … and the "Spangler Posse".'

Dialect can become a very emotive subject. **Chav** was named buzzword (see Chapter 11, page 256) of the year in 2004 by the linguistics expert Susie Dent in her book *Larpers and Shroomers*. Its prominence arose in part from the website chavscum.co.uk – 'A user's guide to Britain's new ruling class'. The behaviour of chavs is broadly anti-social. Many are regarded as **council** (on social security). Chavs wear baseball caps, trainers, branded shirts and jackets, preferably Burberry. The Chav Freebies website www.chavfreebies.co.uk offers wristbands, horoscopes and a dating service. Its 'Chav Bling' page – a sublime coupling of two linguistic sub-groups – offers a broad range of high street jewellery, all at the very reasonable prices you would expect.

The word 'chav' has caused huge debate in linguistic circles. It's possible that it comes from the Chatham area of Kent, where a lot of chavs live and don't exactly work. In the opinion of language scholar Michael Quinion, the word probably comes from the Romany *chavi*, meaning 'child', which has been in use since the middle of the nineteenth century. The word then went underground for about 150 years, only to resurface and haunt us all. In Newcastle, chavs are called **charvers**. They too wear fake designer and sports gear, are usually from poor backgrounds, and frequently get into fights with other youth groups, such as **goths**.[9] A website called Charver Central (www.newcastlestuff.com/charver) contains the following urban tale:

> I was on the back seat of a 38 bus heading for the West End, when two charver lasses parked themselves next to me. They were talking about last night, when one asked the other how she'd got on with Scott.
>
> 'He took me behind the Youth Club and we had a snog. Then he put his hand straight up me skort.'
>
> 'He nivva! What did y'dee?'
>
> 'Ah smacked him rund the heed and telt 'im, "Where's your fuckin' manners? It's tits first!"'

'Chav' may not be a beautiful word, but it is very much alive and with us. No doubt Joseph Wright would have been excited to come across it.

Revenge of the regions

Contemptuous of the linguistic anarchy that he observed all around him, George Bernard Shaw addressed the decline of English in his play *Pygmalion* (1913) as Europe was about to dissolve into a different and even more murderous form of anarchy. In the introduction he wrote, 'The English have no respect for their language, and will not teach their children to speak it. They spell it so abominably that no man can teach himself what it sounds like. It is impossible for an Englishman to open his mouth without making some other Englishman hate or despise him.'

---

9 Once a Germanic tribe who invaded the East and West in the third to the fifth centuries. Now the name for someone whose fashion sense and choice of music celebrate a mood of horror, darkness and the supernatural.

Shaw's character Henry Higgins was modelled on the real-life Henry Sweet (1845–1912), one of the founders of the British School of Phonetics. As Higgins hangs around the streets of Covent Garden, he winces at what to his ears are the mangled vowels of the various coster-mongers and barrow-boys. His views had changed little by the time the play was filmed as *My Fair Lady* in 1964. 'Remember that you're a human being with a soul and the divine gift of articulate speech, that your native language is the language of Shakespeare and Milton and the Bible. Don't sit there crooning like a bilious pigeon,' he chides the flower seller Eliza Doolittle. To Higgins, the nearer one's speech was to standard English, the better one's chances of social advancement. 'Hear them down in Soho Square dropping aitches everywhere. Speaking English any way they like,' he chants.

'You, sir, did you go to school?' he asks one man. 'What do you tike me for, a fool?' the man hits back. 'No one taught him "take" instead of "tike",' says Higgins, but the man did learn to speak the way he did, just as Higgins learnt to talk posh. We think very differently about cockney speech these days. We still don't have many top officials in government dropping their aitches and minding their apples and pears, but nor do we have as many old Etonian accents in Cabinet. The main accent down south has become known as Estuary English, and the Mayor of London himself, Ken Livingstone, is a prime example of the species. Higgins observes, 'It's "ohh" and "garn" that keep her in her place. Not her wretched clothes and dirty face.' The faces are cleaner these days, but the accent has not been scrubbed up that much.

The study of linguistics has moved on since the days of Henry Higgins. In December 2000, Australian researchers at Sydney's Macquarie University revealed their findings – in which they had compared the vowel sounds of the Queen's annual Christmas broadcasts over a period from the 1950s to the 1980s. The analysis revealed that the Queen's pronunciation of some vowels had drifted towards what is generally known as Estuary English – the term which comes from the Thames Estuary bordered by Kent and Essex, where this accent predominates. Her Majesty's pronunciation of 'had', for example, used to rhyme with 'bed', but now the 'a' was becoming more prominent and less like the sort of upper-class speech which used to be called 'cut-glass'. Whether this was conscious or not – an attempt by the Queen to 'get down' with the people or merely the inevitable result of fewer people talking that – the verdict seems to be that even the Queen doesn't speak the Queen's English.

Maybe this is a touch sweeping. The Queen's English, along with other similar terms like Oxford English, BBC English and Received Pronunciation (RP),[10] is a specific accent, and Estuary English seems to be influencing them all. But there was nothing pure about the Queen's English: it mangled all sorts of alien vowel sounds, such as 'hice' for house and 'clorth' for cloth. Nor was it enshrined that way for centuries. John Walker, in the 1791 preface to his *Critical Pronouncing Dictionary and Expositor of the English Language*, writes that 'The best educated people in the provinces, if constantly resident there, are sure to be strongly tinctured with the dialect of the country in which they live.' So if Her Majesty has taken to pronouncing investiture 'investicher', or, for that matter, 'Eschery English', it proves how wise Samuel Johnson was when he realized that any attempt to 'fix' the language is doomed to failure.

So far we have been looking inwards, at the development and evolution of English words within the British Isles. But there has been an enormous influence on the English language from other countries and languages, and we need to address that too.

---

10 Received pronunciation – the pronunciation of that variety of British English widely considered to be least regional, being originally that used by educated speakers in southern England.

chapter six

GLOBAL LINGO

IF THE <u>FRENCH</u> HAVE
SEX AND SUGGESTIVENESS,
the GERMANS
have Sausages and
<u>DOUBT</u>.

Global Lingo

Languages don't care which other languages they talk to, and the English language has for long been as chatty as the most up-for-it Club 18–30 holidaymaker, willing and eager to get to know the locals wherever on the globe it pitches up. Part of the trajectory of that journey was caused by imperial swell, as the British Empire gave fresh hope to several generations of red ink suppliers, but, given its promiscuity while abroad, the English language has proved remarkably good at making long-term relationships. Linguistic borders are porous, and the process normally rubs both ways, but English has absorbed enormous numbers of foreign words and phrases, some of which are heard more often on the lips of foreign-born English speakers than in the language of their origin. Our strongest connection is to our European neighbours and occasional enemies. But the other languages form a shadow world map that betrays the thud of British boots – whether military or mercantile – across the world for several centuries.

Arabian nights

What is the connection between a nineteenth-century British officer's off-duty clothing and a legal decision? The clue lies in the Arabic word *fatiya*. In its basic form, that verb means 'to be youthful or adolescent'. But a more complex form of the same verb means 'to give a formal legal opinion' – from this comes *fatwa* – and a personage whose opinions are always listened to is a **mufti** (a legal expert entitled to pronounce on religious matters). From there, British soldiers overseas seem to have been rather struck by the resemblance, in dress terms, between an off-duty officer's wardrobe of dressing-gown, tasselled smoking cap and slippers and the costume of a *mufti*, so they named their non-uniform clothes after this legal grandee.

Another expression used by British Servicemen, but not recorded until the Second World War, was to have a **shufti** (look), which comes from the Arab *shufti*, meaning 'have you seen'.

Arabic has made a huge contribution to English, largely thanks to merchants, who were continually crossing trade routes between Europe and the Middle East, and who brought hundreds of Arabic words into the English language. Another, perhaps stranger, journey takes us from eye-liner to the local pub. The Arabic verb *kahhala*, pronounced with a slightly harder than usual H, means 'to rub, paint or smear with kohl'. **Kohl** was – and still is – used by women in the East to darken the area around the eyelids. Such femmes fatales as Jezebel and Cleopatra must have made use of this bewitching substance to cast their spell over men. In some societies, they even used to throw the substance into their eyes to give them extra sparkle. Arabic verbs can be pressed, squeezed or manipulated into all sorts of shapes, and *kahhala* was moulded into *kuhhūl*, meaning 'spirit'. The spirit in question, which was much in use when attached to the products of distillation, came to be known in medieval Latin as **alcohol**.

Given the prominence of alcohol in British society, it might seem like a slur on our national pride that the word 'alcohol' is not originally British. Consider, furthermore, that the Koran can be read as distinctly ambivalent about – if not downright hostile to – alcohol. But that is an example of what happened when British explorers met people of different races and traditions. Ideas spread, and words were one of the currencies for that encounter.

Another seemingly impeccable English word is **admiral** or the 'ruler of the Queen's Navee', to quote from Gilbert and Sullivan's *HMS Pinafore* (1878). In fact, it's not that impeccable, since it comes from the Arabic words *amiir al-bahr* meaning, literally, 'commander (*amiir*) of the (al) sea (*baHr*)', which was the title that the Arabs created for the leader of their navy after he had conquered Spain and Sicily. This phrase was successively adopted by the French, Genoese and English (under Edward III) who all apparently misunderstood the individual parts of the phrase and thought that the definite article *al* meant 'sea'. Eventually, the English dropped the final word *bahr* – because they didn't know it meant 'sea' – and, around 1500, ended up with a new official title that, somewhat eccentrically, meant 'commander of the', or *amir-al*. And, partly because the letter 'a' often stood for the Latin preposition *ad* (e.g. 'admirable'), the 'a-' soon changed to 'ad-' and we were left with a stump of a word, with nevertheless sweeping powers over an entire fleet.

Many other originally Arabic words retain their original *al*. One example is **alkali**, the salty substance at the other end of the pH scale from acid. The word was anglicized from the French *alcali* and is derived from the verb *qalay*, which means 'to fry or roast in a pan'. You might have guessed by now that **algebra** is ultimately from Arabic, but did you know that in our earliest sighting of the word, from 1541, it means 'bone-setting'? A mere ten years later, however, it refers to mathematics. How so? Algebra was introduced into Italy, and thence the rest of Europe, by the Arabs, who had come across it in ancient Babylon, Egypt and India. Its old meaning continued for a while in Spain, where in medieval times a bone-setter was called an *algebrista*, a 'restorer' of bones, which was precisely the same effect mathematicians were expected to have on jumbled piles of numbers.

Alchemy, which came into the language via Old French and medieval Latin, is that branch of science in which medieval scientists vied to turn base metals into gold. It originally comes from the noun *al-kīmīā*, though there is much dispute as to whether that comes from an early word for Egyptian art, or the Greek verb *cheō*, which means 'I pour', an action that is integral to the pursuit of chemistry. Alchemy was a risky science, or, to put it another way, a hazardous occupation, which is coincidental, since the word **hazard** is ultimately Arabic – again from the French. William, Archbishop of Tyre in old Antioch (*c.*1130–*c.*1185) – the city that gave us beautiful dyes – claimed that the city's name came from the siege of a castle called Hasart or Asart in Palestine. It was used in the sense of a game of dice, played as long ago as 1300, and vulgar Arabic gives us the word *az-zahr* or *az-zār*, meaning 'die', the singular of 'dice'.

The city of Mosul, which came to prominence during the American-led invasion of Iraq in 2003, was once famous for something altogether different – the lightweight cotton fabric that was made there: **muslin**. By the nineteenth century, that term had come to represent the women who were inside the cloth. In his rakish novel *Pendennis* (1850), William Thackeray (1811–63) includes the line, 'That was a pretty bit of muslin hanging on your arm – who was she?'

Iraq's neighbour Iran is another world-famous fabric producer in its own right, and **taffeta** from that country figures in our written records as long ago as 1373. Chaucer, in the prologue to *The Canterbury Tales* (1386), describes 'A Doctour of Phisik … In sangwyn and in pers he clad was al / Lyned with Taffata and with sandal.'[1] In early times it would have been 'a plain-woven glossy silk of any colour'.

---

1 'He wore scarlet and blue/ lined with taffeta and fine linen.'

Shakespeare took it to mean something florid or bombastic in *Love's Labour's Lost* (1588), when Berowne the suitor, trying to impress the ladies, renounces refined speech – 'Taffata phrases, silken tearmes precise' (V.ii) – while using precisely the same refined speech.

Our love of **sugar** is at least partly to blame for the current global epidemic of obesity, and that addictive substance has been around a very long time. Arabic is stuffed with words for sweet things. The verb *shariba* (to drink) gave us **sherbet, sorbet** and **syrup** – all via French. The relationship between the English 'sugar' and the Arabic *sukkar* is clearer in Spanish (*azucar*) and Portuguese (*assucar*). The word 'candy' has also been involved with Arabic at some point, via Persian, since the Arabic *qand* refers to what's left when you boil cane sugar. Alongside all this sweetness it is worth adding that *tabib isnaan* – which has not made its way into English – is the Arabic for 'dentist'.

From dessert we make our way to **desert**, for which the Arabic word is *badu*. *Badawi* means 'desert dweller', of which the plural is the rather better-known *bedouin*. Another plural Arabic word that we know well these days – though with a singular sense in English – is **assassin**. Most word-watchers go along with the *OED* derivation, which puts it all down to drugs.

The story sounds so far-fetched that it might just be true. The *OED* traces it to a tribe of 'Ismaili sectarians, who used to intoxicate themselves with hashish or hemp, when preparing to dispatch some king or public man'. There is certainly a verb, *hhasha*, which means 'to mow' or 'cut'. In a slightly stronger form, it means 'to smoke hashish'. Sure enough, the noun *mah'shash* means 'hashish den'. But the noun mih'ashsha means 'a tool for weeding'. This has nothing to do with smoking weed.

'Assassin' was defined in the *OED* as 'certain Moslem [*sic*] fanatics in the time of the Crusades, who were sent forth by their sheikh, the

"Old Man of the Mountains", to murder the Christian leaders'. The old man in question was Hassan ibu-al-Sabbah, a renegade Persian, who controlled a bunch of Ismaili separatists in the eleventh century, capturing the castle of Alamut, south of the Caspian Sea, in 1090.

Marco Polo visited the area in 1273, about 150 years after Hassan's reign. According to him, the old man sent his followers into a beautiful garden, where he gave them hashish to drink, which knocked them out for three days. 'When these young men woke and found themselves in the garden with all these marvellous things, they truly believed themselves to be in paradise.'

The only problem with these etymologies is that they may not be right. The Old Man of the Mountains was not an Arab, but a Persian, so the word 'assassin' should be Persian rather than Arabic in its roots. Is it possible, then, that the assassins were not followers of hashish, but of Hassan? Also, Hassan's religious views on intoxicants should have barred such narcotic indulgence. Besides, if they believed in the cause, he surely didn't need to drug them. The idea that a mysterious, charismatic, mystical man would take to the mountains and inspire hundreds of followers to risk all, even their own lives, for a cause… well, who would ever imagine that such an unlikely thing could come about?

Indian takeaway

Alongside the British debt to Arabic stands our legacy from the Raj, the name given to the period of British rule in India. Britain's first ambassador, Sir Thomas Roe, presented his credentials to Jehangir, the Mughal[2] emperor, at Delhi in 1615 amid the first stirrings of

---

2 Or, formerly, Mogul: 'The name given to the heads of the Muslim dynasty founded by Zahir-ud-Din Muhammad Babur (1483–1530).' The Mughal empire stretched across much of the Indian subcontinent between the sixteenth and nineteenth centuries.

British interest. History is sparing on the details of their meeting: was the maharaja sitting out on his verandah? Was Sir Thomas wearing jodhpurs? We may never know, though we do know that in the years since then, Britain's Indian take-away included words borrowed from Hindi and the subcontinent's other languages.

There was no doubt that the British and the Indians, though at times at each other's throats over the years, were in a sense spiritually entwined. Many words were coined by the British army, who had distinctly mixed feelings about the whole experience: pleasure at the country and people, horror at the climate, and the fact of being separated from their loved ones by a huge sea voyage. Naturally, one of the things they talked about obsessively was how much they missed Blighty (England), but it says something about the experience of being away that the very word they used for the old country was Hindi/Arabic in origin.

The Hindi word *bilāyati* is related to the Arabic word *wilāyatī*, both of which mean 'foreign', especially European. As usual, the great British Tommy was not adept at pronunciation, but he excelled at adapting foreign words. The famous *Glossary of Anglo-Indian Words and Phrases* by Sir Henry Yule and A.C. Burnell, popularly known as '*Hobson-Jobson*'[3] (1886), records *bilayat pan*, or 'European water', a reference to the usual name for soda water in British-ruled India. Another was *bilayati baingan* for the tomato, at that time unknown in India. Such were the terms used by Indian soldiers to describe the strange things that the 'white devils' had brought with them, and sure enough the compliment was returned. Perhaps the English liked the fact that the Hindi word smacked of that English word 'blighted'.

The present-day word sleuth Michael Quinion maintains that Blighty didn't pass into common usage until the First World War.

---

3 The title derived from an 'Anglicized form of the repeated wailings and cries of Muslims as they beat their breasts in the Muharram procession.'

The music-hall songs of the period have that poignant urgency: 'Take me back to dear old Blighty,' wrote A.J. Mills, Fred Godfrey and Bennett Scott in their famous 1916 song. 'Put me on the train for London town. Take me over there, Drop me anywhere: Liverpool, Leeds, or Birmingham, well, I don't care!' There were other songs from the same period that also hailed Blighty, but these have not stood the test of time so well.

It's also possible that the surprisingly recent word **bloke** – only in use since about 1850 – derives from the Hindi word *loke*, meaning 'man'. We don't talk about taking a **dekko** (look) so much these days, but it is an adaptation of the Hindi *dekho*, which is the imperative of *dekhnā*, to look.

The British loved Indian architecture, particularly the **bungalow**. This word comes from the Hindi *banglā*, meaning 'belonging to Bengal'. It was originally a one-storeyed house, with tiles or thatch on the roof, first in Bengal and afterwards throughout India. According to the authors of *Hobson-Jobson*, it was 'the most usual class of house occupied by Europeans in the interior of India'.

India's less formal dress code was also popular with the British. **Pyjamas**, from an Urdu word, were a form of loose drawers or trousers tied round the waist, worn by both men and women in India, and especially popular with Sikhs and Muslims. Anglo-Indians[4] took to wearing them to sleep in, adding a matching jacket. 'It is probable,' say the authors of *Hobson-Jobson*, 'that we English took the habit, like a good many others, from the Portuguese', who also had a substantial presence in India.[5]

---

4 British people who made India their home, or people with mixed European and Asiatic parents.
5 The Portuguese reached India well before the British. The globe-trotting Vasco da Gama landed in Calicut (now Kozhikode) on 20 May 1498, and trading terms began shortly after. The southern area of Goa remained a Portuguese possession until December 1961 when Indian forces reunited it with the rest of the country.

India was the source of many fabrics. 'Bought my wife a **chintz**, that is, a painted Indian **callico**, for to line her new study,' wrote Samuel Pepys in his diary on 5 September 1663. The *OED*'s first citation dates from 1614. The Hindi word *chint* comes from an even older Sanskrit word *chitra*, which means 'variegated'. 'Calico' itself comes, of course, from the Indian city of Calcutta, from where so many of the fabrics were shipped back to Britain. And the wild goat of Tibet, if you can catch it, gives up its wool – along with that of the Kashmir goat – to be made into the costly fabric known since 1822 as **cashmere**.

Many more words became common currency in Britain, such as **khaki** (dusty), a Persian word that passed into Urdu and became forever associated with the dull, yellowish-brown fabric of the British army in India. Perhaps that dust was also responsible for another import from Hindi – *čāmpo*, which was the imperative form of *čāmpnā* (to press). We anglicized the word into **shampoo**, but in the eighteenth and nineteenth centuries it was much closer in meaning to 'massage'. A 1762 account of the process by a British traveller to the East Indies contains the understandable reaction: 'Had I not seen several China merchants shampooed before me, I should have been apprehensive of danger.' And John Badcock, in his *Domestic Amusements* (1823), writes: 'We had long ago seen negroes employed in percussion upon their Barbadean masters, by whom it is termed "Champooing",' at which time it was part of the Turkish bath process. In 1829 it was described in the journal *Health & Longevity* as 'friction with the hand', but at around the same time, the experience of a shampoo changed from a dry one to a wet one, and newspaper advertisements for 'shampoo liquid' started to appear in British magazines in the 1860s.

Did that shampoo do a **pukka** job? We'll never know, but pukka, in the sense of 'good' has been popularized by the celebrity chef

Jamie Oliver and he is not far off using it in its original sense, since *pakkā* is a Hindi word, meaning 'ripe, mature or cooked'. In Hindi it is most often contrasted with *cutcha* (imperfect, slight), a term that Jamie might perhaps have used to describe just how awful he thought school lunches were.

The British brought back many exotic things from India, though few are more surprising than the expression **big cheese**, meaning 'an important person'. This in fact comes from Persian via the Urdu word *chiz*, meaning 'thing'. According to *Hobson-Jobson*, the phrase was a common one, as in 'These cheroots are the real chiz.' Since people had already been saying 'the real thing' as an expression of admiration, there may have been an element of linguistic interplay. And what of that popular dish, the **curry**? The *Oxford Dictionary of the English Language* cites the Tamil word *kari*, which means 'sauce'.

One of Anglo-India's most famous words, but one that did not come to the attention of the editors of *Hobson-Jobson*, is **doolally**. This is defined by *The Times English Dictionary* as 'out of one's mind or crazy'. But the story of how it came to be so is interesting. The full phrase is **doolally tap**, and is British army slang, originally named after the town of Deolali, near Bombay. There the British bought a military sanatorium in which to treat soldiers who had really seen enough of India. The word *tap* is Urdu or Persian for 'fever'. F. Richards, in his book *Old-Soldier Sahib* (1936), wrote that 'Time-expired men sent to Deolalie [*sic*] from their different units might have to wait for months before a troop-ship fetched them home... The well-known saying among soldiers when speaking of a man who does queer things, "Oh, he's got the Doo-lally tap," originated, I think, in the peculiar way men behaved owing to the boredom of that camp.'

Everybody salsa

From the land of the curry to the land of the tortilla chip, typically topped with melted cheese, linguistics experts have puzzled long and hard over the origin of the word **nacho**, until an enterprising *OED* researcher came across a story about a Mexican chef, Ignacio Anaya, whose name was shortened to 'Nacho'. He lived in a small Mexican town called Piedras Negras, just across the border from Eagle Pass, Texas, and he is credited with creating the first nachos in 1940 for a group of women who asked the chef to make something for them to eat with their cocktails.

Aztec civilization dominated Mexico and Central America for centuries, and Aztecs were growing the *tomatl*, as it was then called in the Nahuatl language, as early as AD 700. The Aztecs of Central America called it *xitomatl*, and wild Central American tribes called it *tomatl*. *Tomatl, xitomatl… xitomatl, tomatl…* let's call the whole thing off: **tomato** emerged as the compromise candidate. At first, people were suspicious of eating it, since it belonged to the same botanical family as deadly nightshade, but once the usual tests had been run and no mothers-in-law, force-fed on nothing but tomatoes for a week, had gone belly up, it became an essential part of our diet.

Before curry became so popular, the British national dish was, of course, chips. The **potato** was said to have been imported by Sir Walter Raleigh (*c.*1552–1618), though these days scholars are leaning more towards Sir Francis Drake (*c.*1540–96) as the importer of this vegetable. Within thirty years of their arrival in Britain, potatoes were such a craze that they had been referred to by Shakespeare in *The Merry Wives of Windsor*. They were, it seems, an older version of Viagra, noted for their power to enhance love-making. 'Let the sky rain potatoes,' declares Falstaff as he attempts to ravish Mistress Ford, 'and hail kissing-comfits and snow eringoes.' ('Kissing-comfits' were like sweet mints, and 'eringoes'[6] were supposedly an aphrodisiac. They also reduce flatulence: just the thing when going on a date.)

West meets East

In a satisfying meeting of cultures, those Aztec tomatoes mentioned above were later used in China to make a sauce that we now all eat with our fries. However, the name of that sauce, **ketchup**, is one of the most disputed words around, and no matter how many times you thump the bottom of the dictionary in a bid to sort out the mess, when you look at the other end, nothing seems to come out. Amid such confusion, one strong possibility is the Amoy (Chinese) dialect word *kôechiap* or *kê-tsiap*, which means 'the brine of pickled fish or shellfish', and which may have been an early ingredient in the sauce. Or was it the Malay word *kēchap*? When the Dutch came to China, they found the sauce, ate it, bought the company and spelt it *ketjap*, which is as near to today's word as you would wish to be.

Following our palates around the world, we say **chin-chin** as a pre-drink toast because we are copying the Chinese, who use the salutation ts'ing ts'ing. The first surviving British reference is from 1795 by a British traveller, Michael Symes. Some thirty-nine years later, in 1834, the *Canton Register* newspaper was recording the use of **chop-chop hurry**, which is pidgin English, from the Chinese *k'wâi-k'wâi*. The same usage survives in chopsticks, since 'chop' is pidgin for 'quick' and *k'wâi-tsze* means 'nimble boys' or 'nimble ones', which no Chinese person could have said if they had seen an English diner struggling to eat gracefully with chopsticks.

---

6 Or eryngo: 'The candied foot of the Sea-Holly, formerly used as a sweetmeat.'

Chinese society had for centuries been highly ritualized, and one of the customs that particularly caught the eye of many a British explorer was the act of prostrating oneself before the emperor or the local bigwig. This involved the supplicants stretching out so low on the ground that their forehead grazed the earth or floor. This act of extreme respect or submission, even worship, is known in Chinese as the *k'o-t'ou*, coming from *k'o* (knock) plus *t'ou* (head). The Greeks tried the same thing, but called it *prosgenesis*. That never caught on as a phrase nearly as well as the English adapted version, which became a noun, first recorded in 1804, then a verb, to **kowtow**. Nowadays it means to be an all-round crawler, but it has nobler roots.

The Japanese and Chinese hierarchy went all the way up to the heavens. When the Chinese brought together the words *ta* (great) and *kiun* (prince), the Japanese reshaped it into *taikun*, meaning 'great lord or prince', the title given to the Japanese shogun. The most famous Westerner to be called a **tycoon** was Abraham Lincoln (1809–65): the name stuck to him for a while, since when it has been popularized, and is now more often applied to people who have amassed huge business fortunes, from Rupert Murdoch to Bill Gates.

Out of Africa

In 1900 the pink parts of the world map, which indicated the extent of the British Empire, included much of Africa, so we have acquired many words from that huge continent. The Swahili word **safari**, meaning 'an overland journey or hunting expedition, especially in Africa' (*Collins Concise Dictionary*), comes originally from the Arabic word *safara*, meaning 'to travel'. At first these (purely hunting) expeditions usually took place on foot in East Africa. Since then tourism has turned them into an opportunity to view or research wildlife in a game reserve. Instead of carrying a dead animal home slung between two poles, the supreme mark of courage is now to sit in your jeep while a curious monkey snaps off your radio aerial.

These days, four wheels are the main form of transport throughout Africa, but the word **trek**, originally from South Africa, came from Afrikaans (the Dutch spoken by early settlers), and in 1849 meant 'to make a journey by ox wagon'. It now means a long overland journey, whether on foot or in a vehicle. Nowadays the word can have more frivolous uses, as in 'I had to trek all the way to the supermarket', where the word 'safari' doesn't have the same comic potential. The original *Star Trek* TV series ran from 1966 to 1969 and featured the first interracial kiss on American network television, in the episode 'Plato's Stepchildren', which aired on 22 November 1968. In this episode, Captain Kirk (William Shatner) kissed Lieutenant Uhura (Nichelle Nichols). The studio at first demurred, wishing to spare the blushes of white people watching in states such as Alabama and Tennessee. It was even suggested that Uhura kiss Mr Spock instead because he was, after all, only a Vulcan, but in the end Kirk and Uhura kissed, which marks the end of an arduous linguistic journey for the Afrikaans word that gave the TV series its title.

Such a kiss would not have been possible on TV screens in South Africa in 1968, where the **apartheid** regime still had twenty-six years to run. The word *apartheid* is Afrikaans for 'separateness', from the Dutch word *apart*. The system of apartheid was imposed by the government in 1948 and referred to the 'segregation of the inhabitants of European descent from the non-European (Coloured or mixed, Bantu, Indian, etc.)'. The *Cape Times* wrote in 1947: 'It is always easy to discern the immediate benefits or comforts conferred on the apartheid-minded Europeans, but impossible to discern the benefits conferred on the non-Europeans.'

Africa was at one time known as the Dark Continent because it was mysterious and little known to outsiders. Part of its mystery stemmed from its cults and rituals, of which **voodoo** is probably the best known. We talk liberally about voodoo these days, but this form of religious witchcraft originated in the Dahomey area of northwest Africa, and was later transported to the West Indies (especially Haiti) and the southern states of America through the slave trade. Since then 'voodoo' has evolved to refer to dodgy practices, such as **voodoo economics** (1980).

Some people, of course, think it's all a load of **mumbo-jumbo**, which seems to derive from the Mandinka word *maamajomboo*, which was, says the *OED*, 'the name of a mask or masked dancer representing a cultic society and participating in religious ceremonies'. It has been terrifying British people ever since 1738. There was also a Haitian Creole voodoo ritual dance – a modified version of the rumba – called the **mambo**. But the after-life of the word **jumbo** is still more extraordinary, since it was the name given to an unusually large elephant that was kept first in Paris and then, for seventeen years from 1865, in the London Zoological Gardens (now Regent's Park Zoo).

This popular, benign, hard-working animal gave rides to thousands of children, and he was still growing when he came to the attention of the American circus promoter P.T. Barnum. In 1882, Barnum bought the elephant for $10,000 and brought him to the United States. Just one year later *Harper's Magazine* was describing a humble cicada as 'the Jumbo of crickets, and just as black'. Jumbo was very popular in the USA and Canada, but after a mere three years he was hit by a train as he was being loaded into a carriage in St Thomas, Ontario, and died. We still remember Jumbo, though, every time we have a **jumboburger** (hopefully never) or fly in a **jumbo jet**.

And another thing: maybe 'jumbo' is linked to *jambo*, the Swahili word for 'hello', which is pronounced: 'jumbo'. *Jambo* is used all over Africa as a kind of slang term for 'hello' in the same sort of way as 'what's up' or ''sup'. Other English words which may have evolved from *jambo* include **jamboree**, a gathering of people all saying 'hello' or 'jambo' to each other. Or is such a party a bit of a **jam** in which everyone is pressed tightly together? Jamborees can be high-brow too, albeit sarcastically, as the thinker and novelist Aldous Huxley wrote in a letter in 1960: 'Meet me in Boston with the Microbus and drive me … to Hanover, where you might stay for all or part of the Jamboree (at which I am to receive an honorary degree).' He could have **commandeered** a driver, which is another Afrikaans word. And Huxley was always interested in the effects of narcotics. Would he have considered smoking some *dagga*, from the Hottentot word *dachab*, a name for 'cannabis' or 'hemp' used as a narcotic?

A fistful of Euros

By some estimates, almost a third of all English words are French in origin, and without French, we would be mighty pushed to find the right words or phrases. You may enjoy going **head-to-head** with someone, but would you prefer to have a **tête-à-tête** with them? The English is an exact translation that has been used in writing since at least the days of the dramatist and architect Sir John Vanbrugh (1664–1726), who used it in 1697, but the French phrase implies none of the competitiveness or aggression of the English. Rugby players or golfers go head-to-head: friends – or potential lovers – have a tête-à-tête.

Time and again, when it comes to getting *intime* (intimate), the English language has preferred to hide behind a tree and let French do the talking. After all, if the tête-à-tête goes particularly well, they might exchange the occasional **billet-doux**, even by text or email. Somehow the phrase 'sweet note', which is the literal translation, doesn't seem to do justice to the French words, as writers from Dryden (in 1673) onwards have noticed. The use of language in such circumstances owes something to the heavens: the Latin word *nubes* means 'cloud', which came into Old French as *nue* and thence to Middle French *nuer*, meaning 'to shade'. In 1380 that shading was restricted to colour, but by 1668 it had spread to language – **shades of meaning** – and to music by 1849. The word they all used, of course, was **nuance**, and it fulfilled much the same role in English, ever since Horace Walpole[7] noted in 1781 that 'The more expert one were at nuances, the more poetic one should be.'

The French verb *nuer* has another connection in that it resembles the Latin verb *innuere*, 'to give a nod to'. The verbal noun or gerund is *innuendum*, and the ablative of the gerund, which means 'by nodding at, pointing to, meaning, intimating', is **innuendo**. In medieval Latin this word was used to introduce a parenthetical phrase in a court case, and came to mean 'an indirect or subtle reference' (*CCD*) often, these days, to something indelicate.

---

7 1717–97, fourth Earl of Oxford, politician, writer, former lover of the poet Thomas Gray and others.

Imports from other European languages

Czech – polka, robot, Semtex
Dutch – coleslaw, cookie, deck, easel, freebooter,
    maelstrom, tattoo, waffle, wagon, walrus, yacht
Finnish – sauna
Hebrew/Yiddish – amen, bagel, cherub, chutzpah,
    cider, hallelujah, kosher, latke, leviathan, messiah,
    sapphire, Satan, schlemiel, schmaltz, schmooze,
    schmuck, schnozz, seraph
Hungarian – biro, goulash, hussar, paprika
Icelandic – geyser
Italian – studio, baloney, fascism, propaganda,
    bankrupt, paparazzi, umbrella, vendetta
Norwegian* – cog, fjord, kraken, lemming, quisling,
    ski, slalom
Russian – babushka, gulag, intelligentsia, mammoth,
    pogrom, agitprop, bolshevik, samizdat, tsar, vodka
Polish – mazurka
Portuguese – auto da fé, cobra, dodo, emu
Spanish – adios, barrio, guerrilla, lasso, machismo,
    peccadillo, renegade, sherry, siesta, sombrero,
    tobacco, vamoose
Swedish* – gravlax, ombudsman, smorgasbord
Turkish – kaftan, doner, minaret

* Some Norwegian/Swedish words share a root

Matters romantic and sexual are notoriously tricky to navigate, so
should we worry about making a **faux pas**? No, comes the resounding
reply, if the alternative is the banality, in straight translation, of
making a 'false step'. But are we being a little **risqué**? If so, we are in
good company, since the artist Aubrey Beardsley (1872–98) was one
of the first to embrace the term in his introduction to *The Yellow
Book* (a quarterly journal, still top-shelf in most good libraries)
of 1894. 'Our idea,' he wrote, in connection with starting the book,

'is that many brilliant story painters and picture writers cannot get their best stuff accepted in the conventional magazine, either because they are not topical or perhaps a little risqué.' Perhaps it was a little affected to go into French at this point, but *The Yellow Book* was the publishing scandal of its time, and it lasted three years until 1897.

If the French have sex and suggestiveness, the Germans have sausages and doubt. Of the vast number of words that have entered the English language through the German portal, few evoke the streets of Berlin and Munich better than *zeitgeist* (spirit of the time) and *angst* (anxiety, guilt or remorse). Germans have not given us as many words for beauty as the French have, but when it comes to feeling a bit down or confused, they are past masters. Thanks to Sigmund Freud[8] (1856–1939) – OK, he was Austrian, but he spoke German – we can all revel in *schadenfreude* at the expense of our friends, who may well wish that they could revel in it themselves, but since the word means 'malicious enjoyment of the misfortunes of others', why should we care? Of course, we might find ourselves weighed down by *angst*. The first English writer to note the phrase was George Eliot,[9] who in a letter from 1849 wrote that 'Die Angst' often brought on a pain at her heart.

Still, the Germans can party too, so much so that their word for party, *fest*, derived from similar Greek and Latin words, can now be tacked on to the end of just about any area of human endeavour, sometimes mockingly, sometimes with better intentions. A **gabfest** is a mocking way to describe a conference, and a **rockfest** is a concert – perhaps a form of escape for ageing hippies oppressed by

---

8 The founding father of psycho-analysis, born in Austria, fled to London in 1938. His theories of the unconscious were perhaps his most impressive contribution to the field of psychology.

9 Real name Mary Ann Evans, 1819–80, amongst the greatest Victorian novelists. Her work combines high intelligence with an ability to engage in political and social debate, and penetrating psychological insight. *Middlemarch* (1871) is her most famous and influential novel.

the modern world. If so, they are suffering from *weltschmertz* (literally 'world pain'), a term dating from 1875 that the *OED* defines as 'a weary or pessimistic feeling about life; an apathetic or vaguely yearning attitude'. And if they can't take all that criticism, the world of aviation has given us a new word for it – *fliegerabwehrkanone* (pilot-defence gun), thankfully shortened to **flak** in 1938. Figuratively, it came to mean 'a barrage of abuse', as in the line from Tom Stoppard's 1976 play *Dirty Linen*: 'Isn't that going to cause rather a lot of flak in the … PLP?' But Tom Wolfe had already coined the term 'flak-catcher' in his 1970 book *Radical Chic & Mau-Mauing the Flak Catchers*: 'And then it dawns on you… This man is the flak catcher. His job is to catch the flak for the No. 1 man.'

Above all, though, no one likes to take the flak for someone else's mistakes. It's not fair. Or, as French president Jacques Chirac put it recently, in faultless French, it's not '*le fair play*'. Now where on earth did he get that from?

chapter seven

THAT'S ENTERTAINMENT

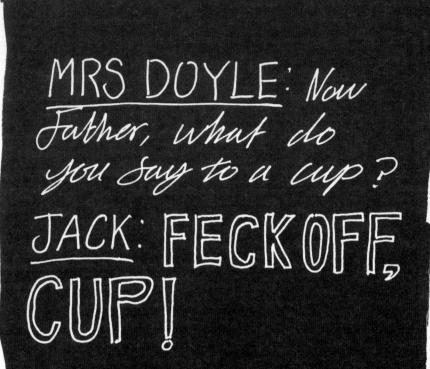

MRS DOYLE: Now Father, what do you say to a cup?

JACK: FECK OFF, CUP!

G. LINEHAN & A. MATTHEWS
FATHER TED (1995)

That's Entertainment

It was the last few days of the 2005 British general election campaign, and the then Conservative leader Michael Howard was staring defeat in the face. With only two days to go, Howard – a lifelong Liverpool football fan – roused his weary troops by claiming that the party was 'two–nil down at half-time'. His chairman, Liam Fox, picked up the analogy by claiming that the election would 'go to penalties' – that, rather than injury time, being the current way to settle a match. The meaning was clear: it wasn't over yet, oh no. In fact, it was, and Labour won comfortably, but the remark shows how often politicians resort to using sporting metaphors rather than – well – political metaphors.

Howard might also have used a metaphor from horse-racing and said that in the **final furlong** he was sure he could find 'an extra yard' or 'catch his second wind', since it was now all **down to the wire** (first recorded use in a horse race, 1901), or that he was predicting a **photo-finish**, a technique first used in a New York horse race in 1936. Of course, he must have been hoping that, in tennis terms, the ball was **in his court,** and that he could now, as if playing rugby, **pick it up and run with it.** Perhaps he could have switched to cricket to say that he intended to **bowl a bouncer** to Tony Blair or even **hit him for six.** What he couldn't admit, in any sporting metaphor, was that he was **on the ropes,** that Blair had him **snookered** and was about to **checkmate**[1] him.

The problem with leadership is that, in the words of Harry S. Truman (US president 1945–53), **'The buck stops here,'** an expression lifted from poker, in which 'to pass the buck' means 'to shift

---

1 Arabic: from *shā-māt*, meaning 'the king is dead'.

responsibility to someone else'. In bridge, on the other hand, you want to be able to play a **trump** card (a sixteenth-century corruption of 'triumph'). Having a **joker** or **trick up your sleeve** doesn't always help.

The English language is blessed with numerous sporting terms, all of which have reached an audience well beyond the comparatively small number of people who partake in these various sports. On the other hand, the worlds of, say, academia and the Church have a rich and complex technical language too, but fewer words have leaked out into everyday use. Our lexicon is drawn not from a particularly highbrow word base: it is drawn from popular culture – leisure, music, entertainment and sport – the worlds in which we are most interested.

What's the upshot?

Tracing the development of the sporting metaphor 'upshot' from its sixteenth-century origins:

1531: The final shot in an archery match; chiefly *figurative*, a closing or parting shot.

1591: A mark or end aimed at. SPENSER: The onely upshot whereto he doth ayme.

c.1580: An end, conclusion, or termination.

1586: The climax or completion of something.

1669: The extreme limit. ABEL BOYER: A gay Coat and a Grimace is the upshot of what he can pretend to.

1604: The result, issue, or conclusion (of some course of action, etc.). In very frequent use from c.1830. SHAKESPEARE, *Hamlet*: So shall you heare… Of accidentall judgements… And in this vpshot, purposes mistooke.

1639: The conclusion resulting from the premises of an argument. See also the phrase 'A fool's bolt is soon shot', common from the thirteenth to eighteenth centuries, a bolt being 'An arrow; especially one of the stouter and shorter kind with blunt or thickened head, called also quarrel, discharged from a cross-bow or other engine. Often *figurative*.'

1811: *Slang*. A riotous frolic.

1837: *Dial*. A merry-making, a feast.

The beautiful game

Football is our national sport, as well as our national phrase repository. To be **on the ball** means 'to be sharpness personified'. **Keep your eye on the ball** is an instruction to concentrate. Football is, in that famously trite phrase, **a game of two halves**, but that wouldn't make much sense to an American football fan because their game has four quarters. The concept of a second half dates from the end of the nineteenth century. Before then, you were more likely to say, 'It's basically a game of all day, or sometimes more'.

The very first written reference to our national game seems to date from 1424 and is suitably vehement, as in this royal instruction: 'The king forbiddes yat na man play at ye fut ball vnder ye payne of iiiid', i.e. 4d, a whopping fine of fourpence, which in those days was about one week's wages for a decent club player. And Sir Thomas Elyot in *The Governour* (1531) writes scathingly of 'Foote balle, wherin is nothinge but beastly furie and exstreme violence'. It was ever thus, it seems. The very first references to football, and already there's crowd trouble.

William Shakespeare liked his football. In *King Lear* (I.iv) the Earl of Kent is behaving as badly as Sir Alex Ferguson at a post-match press conference:

> **Lear:** Do you bandy[2] looks with me, you rascal?
> **Oswald:** I'll not be stricken, my Lord.
> **Earl of Kent:** Nor tript neither, you base Foot-ball plaier
> (tripping his heels).
> **Lear:** I thanke thee, fellow.

---

2 A 'bandy' used to be a way, now lost, of hitting a tennis ball (1578). There was also a hockey-like game called bandy (1693), and from the action of driving a small ball back and forth across the ground comes the verb 'to bandy', as in 'to throw or strike' (1577) or 'to give and take' (blows, words, reproaches, compliments, etc.).

Shakespeare also referred to **foul play** in *The Tempest* ('What fowle play had we, that came from thence?') (I.ii) as well as **fair play**, also in King John ('Shall we upon the footing of our land, / Send fayre-play-orders, and make comprimise [*sic*]?') (V.i). Truly, he would have made a great half-time analyst.

Catches win matches

For a brief period during the summer, the back pages of newspapers yield to **cricket**, another game with an equally illustrious history. The word 'cricket' is mentioned as 'Creckett and other plaies' as early as 1598, fifty years after the death of that great sportsman Henry VIII. It is possible that the game may even have its roots in a French game called *criquet*… But let's not spend too long considering that ghastly possibility.

The names of fielding positions have occasioned many a raised eyebrow, though most seem to derive from the fielder's closeness to the ball and the resultant chances of getting a ball in the shins, or worse, hence 'point', 'cover', 'slip', 'silly mid-on' and so forth. But it's our familiarity with other aspects of the game that gives cricket its unique value. **To keep a straight bat**, for example, which is what you do if you're a good batsman, is defined by *Chambers English Dictionary* (*CED*) as 'to behave honourably'. Failure to do so may lead to the Englishman's harshest condemnation, as noted by *The Times* on 17 December 2004: 'IMF says loan deal is **just not cricket**,' though the *OED* can date the phrase to at least 1851. Quite what the International Monetary Fund knows or cares about the rules of cricket is highly debatable, but we know what the sub-editor was thinking.

Cricketing magic

Bernard James Tindal Bosanquet (1877–1936) came from a famous Huguenot family. He scored 120 runs for Harrow against Eton at Lord's in 1896. Oxford picked him as a fast–medium bowler and he became the university's best all-rounder. But his 'greatest conjuring trick in the history of the game', as it was reported, was the 'googly', a ball which, on leaving the bowler's hand, seems to all intents and purposes to be a leg-break (heading for the off-stump) but instead, cunningly, breaks the other way, towards the leg stump. It shocked cricketers the world over, though it was devised as no more than a party piece to amuse the other members of his side. After a few ordinary leg breaks, he would slip in his googly: the batsmen didn't know what had hit them – or their stumps.

In 1902 Bosanquet was picked for Lord Hawke's team to tour Australia and New Zealand. Thanks to his unplayable new delivery, the tourists won all eighteen of their matches in New Zealand, and it was here that the word 'googly' was first used in print to describe Bosanquet's weird off-break[3].

The delivery became the subject of furious debate when the victorious English team travelled on to Australia, where the Australian team suffered a mass collapse. England beat them by 157 runs and regained the Ashes. Of course, someone asked Bosanquet if his googly might be illegal. 'No,' he replied. 'Only immoral.'

An unsuccessful batsman may well be out for a **duck** (nothing). Why a duck? Probably because a duck's egg is shaped like a zero. Many other cricketing phrases have entered the language so stealthily that we now use them while being only dimly aware of where they come from. If you have ever felt under-confident, be it in a relationship or a meeting, you might say that you were on a **sticky wicket** or **on the back foot** even if you have never picked up a cricket bat in your life.

---

3 1903 C.B. Fry in P.F. Warner *How We Recovered the Ashes* (1904): 'You must persuade that Bosanquet of yours to practise…those funny 'googlies' of his.'

Punchy language

If you have ever been plucked from danger, just as you thought your luck had run out, you might well describe yourself as having been **saved by the bell**. That's boxing talk, and boxing is one sport that has always **punched above its weight**, since the range of boxing terms extends far beyond the ring. Nelson Mandela has often been described as a **political heavyweight**, as have Gordon Brown and Ann Widdecombe, though you wouldn't fancy their chances over fifteen rounds with Lennox Lewis.

If bids were being sought for the new leader of a political party, someone might **throw their hat into the ring** without pausing to consider that this was the way in which boxers used to declare their readiness to fight. Not surprisingly for a sport that pushes its exponents to their physical limits, boxing has a wealth of terms for that state of mind when your brain feels like mush. **Punch-drunk** is one such phrase that has broken free and taken on a life of its own. First recognized in the *Saturday Evening Post* in 1918, the *CED* defines it as 'having a form of cerebral concussion from past blows in boxing with results resembling drunkenness'. The poet Cecil Day-Lewis (1904–72) even attempted to smuggle it into his translation of Virgil's *Aeneid* in 1954: 'So he called an end to the bout, saving the punch-drunk Dares from further punishment.' Nice try, Cecil.

Had you taken a particularly sharp hammering, you probably wouldn't be feeling **up to scratch** either. 'To come up to (the) scratch' means to reach the required standard, though it's more common these days to find it in the negative: not good enough, below par.[4] In the past, boxing was an outdoor sport. A line was scratched across the ring to which the prospective fighters were brought. In the days when boxing had no ropes, and certainly no bell, the smaller of the two men, on seeing his larger opponent, might suddenly remember an urgent reason for being elsewhere, such as it being his turn to clean out the rabbit hutch, and off he would go, having clearly not come 'up to the scratch'.

Boxing does have certain safety requirements. No self-respecting boxer should hit **below the belt**; that's unseemly and unsporting both in the ring and out. One need hardly add that the original meaning was to whack someone in the **goolies** (from the Hindi word *goli*, meaning 'ball'), and very painful that is too. Among other safety requirements is a mouth-guard to protect the teeth, though this cannot prevent what dictionaries may one day refer to as 'doing a Tyson' (chewing off the opponent's ear). If tempted to make a remark that could be described as **near the knuckle**, that's an allusion to the days when fights were allowed to degenerate into such

---

4 The Latin word for equal, e.g. *Primus Inter Pares* means 'First Among Equals'. The 1897 *Encyclopaedia of Sport* describes a 'scratch player' as 'a good player, who receives neither handicap nor penalty.'

savagery that bones were exposed. Of course, at that time boxers fought bare knuckle, so the expression **the gloves are off** in a non-boxing context suggests some really brutal behaviour.

The boxing ring is no place for cowards, which is why it has given society some of its most direct phrases. To **pull one's punches**, for example, is defined by the *Collins Concise Dictionary* (*CCD*) as 'to restrain the force of one's criticisms or actions' or, with reference to boxing, not to use quite as much force in the punch as you could, for whatever reason. The verb **punch** used to have a much sharper meaning when it meant (*c*.1440) 'to stab, prick, puncture'. The closed-fist type of punching came a hundred years later. The *OED* thinks 'punch' might derive 'collaterally' from **pounce**, the etymology of which is obscure.[5] Surely everyone knows that to **take it on the chin** means 'to face squarely up to a defeat, adversity, etc.' (*CCD*). **Throwing in the towel** – which is usually white, except when it's covered in blood – is tantamount to running up the white flag. It's a form of surrender, a way of admitting defeat, more humiliating because it's done on behalf of the protagonist, who might not be in the best position to judge whether it's safe for him to carry on. And it doesn't just happen in the ring.

In boxing, but not necessarily in the wider world, there's always somebody in the middle, who is supposed to see fair play. The word **umpire** comes from the late-twelfth-century French adjective *nonper*, meaning 'peerless, without equal, surpassing all others'. The *OED* says that the word was anglicized around 1350 as **noumpere**, and the 'n' dropped off over the next century (the initial letter 'n' of **adder** and **apron** met a similar fate). **Referees**, on the other hand, who were appointed by parliament in 1621 'to examine and report on applications for monopolies or letters patent', seemed not to have turned their attention to sport until 1840.

---

5 No corresponding noun is known in French or any other Romanic language.

A big song and dance

While the language of sport is mined for expressions to do with moral rectitude, winning and losing, confidence and the lack of it, the language of music is hijacked[6] for different purposes. And we can command a whole orchestra without even being able to play the triangle. To blow the trumpet, for example, means 'to declare or announce', even 'to celebrate something'. But you would not want to be accused of **blowing your own trumpet**. You might **sing someone's praises** but not your own. And you would only **bang the drum** if you were trying to arouse support for your cause from a somewhat resistant audience. Would you be happy to **play second fiddle** to someone? Probably not. And you definitely wouldn't want to **harp** on about it (see page 185).

The media is often preoccupied with questions of harmony or disharmony, and sometimes it takes on sexual overtones. Don't forget the former prime minister John Major urging his Cabinet ministers to **sing from the same hymn-sheet** and display unity at a time when their activities between the bed-sheets were arousing more interest than their policies. Music is a sensory experience. If you are **in tune** with someone, you aren't necessarily playing music together. And if something sounds **out of tune**, it may not be an instrument. **Playing by ear** usually means being able to play a piece of music without reading it off a score, but we also use this metaphor in a situation when we haven't planned in advance how to behave. In the same sense, we might say that we'll **busk**[7] it.

The word **music** has come to mean much more than mere notes. The phrase **music to my ears** – to hear good news – was used before 1586 by one of literature's greatest live–fast–die–young figures,

---

6 A word that, disappointingly, the *OED* gives as 'origin unknown'.
7 1851, Henry Mayhew *London Labour*: 'Busking is going into public houses and playing and singing and dancing.'

Sir Philip Sidney, in his prose romance the *Arcadia*. And at some time in the 1930s those crazy, sex-mad jazz[8] players started using expressions like **to make sweet music** and **to make beautiful music together** as euphemisms for having sex. The verbs **rock** and **roll** were used for the same covert purpose in American rhythm and blues of the early twentieth century, though it wasn't until 1951 that disc jockey Alan Freed united the two.

Ever since Freed's immortal coupling, **rock and roll** has been getting steadily louder and louder – and louder. But then, in about 1983, the rock star Nils Lofgren made a significant breakthrough. How about, instead of playing louder, playing… quieter? He achieved this by swapping his electric guitar for an acoustic guitar. *The Washington Post*, which was there to witness this moment, described the event by using the word **unplugged**, as if he had simply pulled the plug on his **axe** – the rock word for guitar since 1967[9] (*Melody Maker*). 'Unplugged' suggested a change in direction: a determination to explore a different side of one's musical personality. It was a back-to-the-land[10] statement.

It could also imply a certain daring. Here, at least, audiences could judge whether the artist really could play, once all that rock posturing had been shorn away. For jazz musicians, playing 'unplugged' never really came into it, since what decided their fate in the first place was how well they played their instruments.

A fair number of words have come into use from the instruments themselves. The word **horn** is cited as a wind instrument by the *OED* as early as *c*.825, but by *c*.1000 had the biological definition 'hard outgrowth' (*CED*), and was often pointed, so it is hardly surprising that by 1785 it had gained inclusion in Francis Grose's

---

8 Many suggestions have been offered for the origin of 'jazz', but none that have satisfied the *OED*.
9 Though prior to that, since 1955, it used to mean 'saxophone'.
10 First attested in *The Times* in 1894.

Classical Dictionary of the Vulgar Tongue (1785) as an erect penis or 'temporary priapism'. As James Joyce so concisely put it in *Ulysses*: 'Got the horn or what?' **Horny**, meaning 'lecherous', has been in use since at least 1889.

The piano has also contributed much to our vocabulary. **Putting the dampers** on a project implies toning down its full impact, since the damper is the piano pedal that can be used to make the sound softer. The organ, on the other hand, has given us an expression – **pull out the stops** – that means exactly the opposite. The 'stops' are the plugs that the organist gradually pulls out to make the sound louder. If they're out the whole way, the organ is playing at top volume.

Let's take the word **harp**. As a verb, it originally had the straightforward meaning of 'to play on a harp', but soon it began to imply the slightly irritating noise that someone makes when he or she plucks at the same string all day long. Shakespeare was among those who used the term metaphorically with such phrases as 'Still harping on my daughter?' (*Hamlet*, II.ii) which any wearied father might still use in the same way to this day. Who plays the **clarion** these days? Ever since the fourteenth century, it was a shrill-sounding trumpet, but now it's remembered only for its metaphorical call – rousing people to action.

In the sixteenth century a **drum** was merely something you beat to make a rhythmic noise. In the eighteenth century it became the instrument that was played as a soldier was formally expelled from the army – he was officially **drummed out**, an expression still used today, but in a much wider context. Ever wondered why someone should be as **fit as a fiddle**? That comes from medieval times, when the violin player was supposed to dance about gaily while he performed. He therefore had to be pretty fit. To be **on the fiddle**, incidentally, had absolutely nothing to do with the violin but was an unrelated nautical term. The most reliable explanation is that the specially designed trays from which sailors ate at sea were called 'square plates' (hence the expression a 'square meal'), and these plates had raised edges to prevent food sliding off in rough weather. These edges were called 'fiddles', and sailors who had done some sharp bargaining or a slightly shifty deal with the cook would pile their food up 'on the fiddle'. But, who knows, maybe the rolled edge of the tray actually resembled the body of a violin?

And what of composers? Wagner is one of the few composers whose name went into more general use during his own lifetime. **Wagnerian** first appeared as an adjective in 1873, with the perfectly straightforward definition 'pertaining to Wagner'. Since the great composer's music is almost always grand and solemn, the word soon came to refer to anything that was grand or epic. The word **unison** also demonstrated a shift in meaning from its straightforward origins. It was first used in 1574 as a purely technical description of notes of the same pitch. By 1730 it had come to mean several notes played together to make a harmonious sound. By 1780 the phrase 'in unison' had taken on the more metaphorical tone it has today.

Dance, too, made a contribution to our vocabulary. **Choreography**, from the Greek words *khoreia*, meaning 'dance', and *graphia*, meaning 'writing', originally applied purely to dance, but now almost anyone's behaviour can be choreographed for the press or the public. The verb **to sashay** is first noted by the *OED* in 1836. This American usage is a mispronounced form of the French dance-step *chasse* and, as the *OED* records, it went from that – sometimes as part of a square dance – to 'glide', then to 'move diagonally'. Today it is used, and sometimes over-used, to 'strut': some journalists never use 'move' if 'sashay' can be used instead.

Some people prefer to **waltz** than to sashay, from the German verb *walzen* (1780) which means 'to roll', and which came to mean the dance. Beginning in the Sixties, dance steps became less precise, from where the verb came to mean 'finding something very easy', such that one can these days be said to have 'waltzed' one's way through one's examinations, or into a job.

The expression 'a bit of a **knees-up**' comes from the 1938 song by Harris Weston and Bert Lee, at which dancers raised their knees high in accompaniment. The words – all together now: 'Knees up Mother Brown' – were so memorable that the phrase 'knees-up' took on a life of its own. *The Times* described the song as 'an injunction to apprehend nothing but jollity'. In *London Dossier* (1967), the guidebook to swinging London that had a secret agent theme, to cash in on the first four Harry Palmer novels, the novelist Len Deighton described one experience as being 'As indigenous to London as a Saturday-night knees-up in the boozer.'

In 1928, Louis Armstrong released a record called 'Don't Jive Me', with the sense of 'don't tease me'. The word **jive** was a short-hand expression on the streets of New York for Harlem slang. It is mysterious in its origins, but may be related to that other equally mysterious word, jazz. And, of course, we all know that **it takes two to tango**, referring to the dance that the print world noted in the last decade of the nineteenth century as having sprung from the gipsy or black communities. 'Takes Two To Tango', a song written by Al Hoffman and Dick Manning, was published in 1952. Pearl Bailey made it a hit, whereupon it became proverbial.

Stage and screen

In other fields of performance, theatre in particular has given rise
to much gradually extending vocabulary. What exactly is the
limelight, for example? Originally, it was a very bright light caused
by heating a piece of lime in an oxyhydrogen flame – perfect for
casting a particularly strong light on the stage. It had been in use
since at least 1826, until Wilfred Granville, in his 1952 *Dictionary of
Theatrical Terms*, defined **fond of the limelight** as 'greedy for notice'
or 'one who claims the centre of the stage'. And the biography of
T.E. Lawrence, aka Lawrence of Arabia (1888–1935), was entitled
Backing into the Limelight, rather appropriate for a man who could
steal the show while protesting to one and all that he was doing
nothing of the sort.

The plain meaning of to **steal someone's thunder**, according
to the *CCD*, is 'to lessen the effect of someone's idea or action by
anticipating it'. The *CED*, on the other hand, gives it as 'to make
use of someone's invention against him'. But the origin is a jewel
of theatrical legend, and, most amazing of all, historically accurate,
though the poet and dramatist John Dennis (1657–1734) must have
wished it were not so. Dennis's play *Appius and Virginia* was staged
at the Theatre Royal in London's Drury Lane in 1709. According
to the renowned theatrical historian and gossip Colley Cibber
(1671–1757), the play's dramatic intensity at one point required the
sound effect of thunder. To achieve this, Dennis had worked out that
bashing together large sheets of tin and then thumping them with
a drumstick would, fairly accurately, produce the sound required.
The inventiveness of the stage thunder was not, alas, matched by the
quality of the drama, and the play lasted only four nights. The next
production was *Macbeth*, by a certain W. Shakespeare, altogether a
more bankable number that also had a fair few storm scenes, and the

theatre manager saw no reason why he should not keep the thunder machine and use it for his next production. Dennis, smarting, went to the opening night, heard the thunder and – poor man – was heard to shout, 'Damn them! …They will not let my play run, but they steal my thunder.' Sad but true.

A phrase coined a hundred years later – **old chestnut** – stems from a play being performed in London in 1816. In his book *To Coin a Phrase: A Dictionary of Origins* (1981), author Edwin Radford quotes a character called Pablo in the play *The Broken Sword* by William Diamond. Pablo corrects a reference to a cork tree by saying: 'A chestnut! I have heard you tell the story twenty-seven times.' Whether the popularity of the expression stemmed instantly from the text of the play itself, or from the performers' propensity to use the phrase outside the theatre, is now shrouded in the mists of time, but it entered the language for ever.

Theatre has given us many more expressions that have passed into general currency. Politicians, in particular, are inclined to **play to the gallery**, first making sure that the **backdrop** is flattering. Boring colleagues or in-laws tend to deliver **monologues**, and many of us indulge in **dress-rehearsals** for the real thing, whatever that event might be. We all know people who get a bit melodramatic at moments of crisis, who can't **follow the script** or who need constant **prompting**. Others might simply **fluff** their lines. The word **protagonist** is Greek for 'an actor who plays the first part', and was introduced into English in the seventeenth century to describe the principal character in a play. By 1839 the word had acquired a less specific application, and had come to mean the leading personage in any contest. Of course, after the curtain comes down and the critics are out, the entire play may be **panned**. In 1839, this verb meant 'to wash gravel in a pan' and had been imported from America during the gold-rush of the late nineteenth century. When the gold-rush collapsed, so did the hopes of the settlers, and their dreams failed to **pan out** (1865). Shortly afterwards it took on a figurative sense when critics were accused of **panning** shows.

The TV and film industries in general have brought many technical words into mainstream English. Informed people are **in the loop**, while we regularly leave our mistakes **on the cutting room floor** – and instead give **edited highlights** in a presentation. Reports that are slightly confusing are often referred to as **unfocused**, while an employee may complain that he or she is playing merely a **bit part** or feels like an **extra** in the company.

Of course, the scripts for television and film are also plentiful sources of modern vocabulary, even managing by the alteration of one letter to make a taboo word acceptable during peak viewing hours. The euphemistic alteration of 'fuck' to **feck** was popularized by the novelist Roddy Doyle and the writers of the Channel Four sitcom about three Irish priests and their eccentric lifestyle, *Father Ted*. However, its use as a verb first came to the attention of the *OED* editors in Christopher Nolan's 1987 novel *Under the Eye of the Clock*, when 'fecked', as in 'I'll be rightly fecked if he's not here', was defined as 'to be put into a difficult or hopeless situation, to be in trouble'. But only three years later, when Doyle wrote in *The Snapper*, 'If he'd said it half an hour earlier even I'd've told him to feck off', it's pretty clear that the sense is a little different. And in *Father Ted* (1999), writers Graham Linehan and Arthur Matthews went one further in family entertainment and turned a taboo word into a buzzword:

> **Mrs Doyle**: Now Father, what do you say to a cup?
> **Jack**: Feck off, cup!

Linehan and Matthews have ten quotations cited in the new *OED*. The first four are to be found in the entries Feck (noun), Feck (verb), Fecker and Fecking.

In the UK, the **full monty** once referred either to the purchase of a complete three-piece suit or the popularity of Field Marshal Montgomery (1887–1976), depending on whom you asked. Over the years, and particularly since the film of the same name became such a hit in 1997, the 'full monty' has become an increasingly popular way of saying 'the full amount' or 'to go the whole way in any enterprise'.

TV programmes such as *Goodness Gracious Me* and *The Kumars at No. 42* have had a massive cultural influence on English, and dictionary compilers are now keeping a careful ear out for new programmes from the BBC Comedy Unit, perhaps in the hope of catching the latest Asian words to be brought into everyday use. That chicken tikka masala we're all so fond of may be inauthentic, but there is nothing artificial about the *chuddies* (Hindi for 'underpants') that the characters in these programmes challenge each other to kiss when they feel so moved.

Page-turners

In the nineteenth century, the arrival of greater literacy, combined with the availability of cheap literature, gave rise to the ascendancy of the genre novel. The publication of Horace Walpole's *The Castle of Otranto* in 1764 launched the genre which became known as the gothic novel and inspired Mary Shelley's *Frankenstein* (1818) and – as the century produced ever darker works amid ever more shadowy and collapsing surroundings – Bram Stoker's *Dracula* in 1897. The name **Frankenstein** has been much misunderstood, being taken to mean a man-made creation which gets out of control and threatens

to destroy its inventor. In fact, Frankenstein was the maverick
scientist who produced the beast.

Dracula was the King of the Vampires and the patron saint of
people with fangy side-teeth. The *OED* quotes the *Times Literary
Supplement* (1971), which had dug up the information that 'Prince
Vlad of Wallachia, who died in 1476, was also known as Dracula',
and that his surname was spelt in a variety of ways, but the word
vampire is of Slavonic origin and means some creature or person
that – given half a chance – would suck other people's blood for
nourishment. Subsequent biologists used the same 'vampire' word
to describe the behaviour of mosquitoes and bats. The word was
abbreviated, around 1911 according to the *OED*, to **vamp**, meaning
a woman (commonly a character in movies) who goes out to attract
men and then sucks them dry of their money.

In the eighteenth century, Samuel Richardson had written
the seminal novel *Clarissa*, which, in its own way, led gradually to the
rise of what became known, by 1980, as the **bodice-ripper**. This was
a literary name for an erotic novel, often set against a distanced but
historical backdrop. What had started as a moral treatise on the
importance of chastity had become an excuse for some gratuitous
sex scenes, lightly strung together with a vaguely plausible plot-line.
The 'bodice-ripper', as a term, is quintessentially British: the
Guardian has over 15,000 references to it on its website compared
to the *Washington Post's* twenty-three.

With very different ends in mind, Gerald Mills (1877–1928) and
Charles Boon (1877–1943) formed the publishing house Mills &
Boon in 1908 (they were born in the same year: it was meant to be).
Mills & Boon set out deliberately to create pure, romantic fiction,
and it was no wonder that the company became referred to rather
stuffily by authors who would never have dreamt of writing in that

style but who could have done with the cash that their leading authors earned. The poet Philip Larkin wrote to his friend Kingsley Amis about the title of his novel *A Girl in Winter* when it was published in 1947: 'though I believe I discarded it on the grounds of sounding **Mills & Boony** (if you know what I mean) [it] does conjure up a more precise image than the present one does'.

Whodunits (literally, 'Who done [i.e. did] it?') is another name for the detective novel and continued a long-standing fascination with crime, murder and the solving of them. The first *OED* reference, in a review in *News of Books*, to a 'satisfactory whodunit' is from 1930. Other 'whodunit' writers include Dorothy L. Sayers (her creation was the delightfully aristocratic detective Lord Peter Wimsey) and Ellery Queen (specializing in tough American cop tales), but the most famous proponent of the genre is Agatha Christie (who gave us Hercule Poirot and Miss Marple). Raymond Chandler, whose novels became classic *film noir* movies, is one of the few detective writers to have become an adjective, albeit one not yet recognized by the *OED*. For a novel to be 'Chandleresque', it has to be sharp, smart and as crisp as a well-starched shirt.

One of the finest exponents of comic fiction was P.G. Wodehouse (1881–1975), a man who was somehow able to invent an enormous amount of words for his chosen field of upper-class twittery (though the phrase 'upper-class twit' has not yet been recognized by the *OED*). Wodehouse personally introduced twenty-three brand-new words into the English language, from **cuppa**[11] to the excellent **lame-brain**,[12] and from **ritzy** (which means 'classy', like the hotel) to **to snooter** ('to harrass', 'to bedevil'[13]). He also experimented

---

11 'Come and have a cuppa coffee.' *Sam the Sodden* (1925).
12 'A girl with an aunt who knew all about Shakespeare and Bacon must of necessity live in a mental atmosphere into which a lame-brained bird like himself could scarcely hope to soar.' *Mr Mulliner Speaking* (1929).
13 'My Aunt Agatha … wouldn't be on hand to snooter me for at least another six weeks.' *The Inimitable Jeeves* (1923).

with the verb **to what-the-hell** (meaning 'to demand an explanation angrily'), and whereas the Victorian novelist Mrs Gaskell, in a letter written *c*.1855, referred to the normal word for 'drunk' as **squiffy**, Wodehouse coined his own – **whiffled** – in *Meet Mr Mulliner* (1927). He was also the first writer to use **zing** as an interjection in *Damsel in Distress* (1919).

The Washington Post noted in 1917 that **oojah** was a handy word to use in place of whichever word you had forgotten, a little like 'thingummy' or 'whatsisname'. Wodehouse crossed this with 'spiffing' in 1917 to produce the demonstrably silly **oojah-cum-spiff**, to mean either something that one can't remember, or something useful that one doesn't really want to name.

A different type of fiction, which entered the language in the 1970s, is the 'Aga saga'. An **Aga** is defined in the *OED* as the acronym formed from the initial letters of the Svenska Aktiebolag Gasaccumulator, the Swedish Gas Accumulator Company, which was the original manufacturer of the sort of home-heating and cooking system popular among well-off types with solid wood floors. 'Aga sagas' defined a genre of fiction writing set in the country, and described marital infidelity and rolling country hills. Joanna Trollope is the high priestess of the form, and we shall be eternally grateful to her for daring to insert the recently coined word **spoddy** – 'having the characteristics of a **spod**: a dull or socially inept person' (1989 is the *OED*'s earliest usage for the noun) into her 1993 novel *A Spanish Lover* with the immortal lines, 'Remember those French boys we had to have at school? They were utterly spoddy.' In 1993, *Newsday* magazine noted that the Female Literary Tradition had been renamed **chick lit** at Princeton University. One 'chick lit' heroine is Jackie Collins, author of such works as *Dangerous Kiss, Deadly Embrace, Hollywood Wives, Hollywood Divorces* and – when two-word titles just won't do – *Lucky*. Her sister Joan Collins, who starred as Alexis Carrington in ABC's 1981–89 high-life saga *Dynasty*, was described by *Adweek* magazine in 1985 as a **megabitch**. The novelist Jilly Cooper – who lies somewhere between writing 'bodice-rippers' and 'Aga sagas' – used the same combining form **mega–** in her 1991 novel *Polo* when she wrote, 'He finally located him in the Four Seasons in New York, closing a mega-deal with some Italians.'

Popular literature has succeeded by building an almost tangible link with the reader. The pop-culture era that feeds it is one of the most dynamic sources of new words, but also one of the most fickle. New words are constantly bubbling up and then down again, which can leave devotees of those words stranded in a vocabulary from which the world has moved on. Such creatures are easily spotted by their archaic language (and clothes), but they should be treated with respect. Many of the words that they still use have had their fifteen minutes of fame and would disappear altogether if some oldsters didn't keep using them. It isn't only literature that has a short attention span, though. The next chapter looks at some of the words produced by the other relentlessly innovative worlds of science, technology and warfare.

chapter eight

THE APPLIANCE OF SCIENCE

When DIANA ROSS can have a hit song called "CHAIN REACTION" (1985), you KNOW that we have, to some extent, become DESENSITIZED.

The Appliance of Science

If you were to take a stick, neither very long nor particularly sharp, and use it to divide all the words in the English language into two separate fields, how would you do it? For generations, society has corralled all our words into two extremely overpopulated and ill-fitting camps, namely, arts and science. It's obviously not an ideal arrangement, crammed as it is with exceptions and words that occupy a shadowy no man's land,[1] but the worlds of science, technology, computing and medicine have enriched the language in many ways, and from many sources. Of course, many of these terms are words that the non-scientific community will never meet, and the first editors of the *OED* had to make some hard decisions about which words to include and which to omit, because if nothing was left out – every pill, every brand name – the whole book would have been significantly larger than its eventual size (see Chapter 3, page 99).

In this chapter we will join the continuing debate, looking at the relationship between science, technology and the military, which has been crucial throughout history.

Technobabble

The Chinese invented solid-propellant **rockets** (from the French *roquet* or adapted from the Italian *rochetta*) in 1232 during the military siege of Kaifeng, the former capital of Henan Province. Where arrows could not penetrate, rockets set fire to tents and

---

1 No man's land – the earliest (*c.*1350) usage is defined as '(A piece of) waste or unowned land; an uninhabited or desolate area'; first military use 1864.

wickerwork fortifications. In Europe and North Africa during the fifteenth century, rockets were used mainly to set fire to the rigging of enemy ships in naval battles, but thereafter the technology was restricted to fireworks. It was several centuries later before William Congreve (1772–1828) resurrected them for use in the Napoleonic Wars.

The naming of things is integral to the process of invention, and whenever inventors have discovered a new thing, they have been careful to give it a name that, in part, is the manifesto of its qualities. When George Stephenson's steam locomotive Rocket won the Rainhill Trials in 1829, its inventor didn't just have the best steam engine: he had the best name for it too (see box). The other competing engines were called *The Novelty*, *The Nonpareil*, *The Cycloped* and *The Perseverance*. The *OED* has six different homonyms for the word 'rocket' – i.e. they're all separate, etymologically distinct words. Nowadays we might say that something 'goes like a rocket', but in the days when rockets were merely fireworks, designed to burst in the air and scatter a shower of sparks, the word didn't pack quite the same punch. The phrase 'like a rocket' only went into circulation when the political theorist Thomas Paine (1737–1809) included it in his seminal work *The Rights of Man*. In 1792 he said of his political rival Edmund Burke (1729–97) that 'he rose like a rocket, he fell like the stick', which became proverbial and was reused by other great writers, including James Joyce (1882–1941) and George Bernard Shaw (1856–1950).[2] Nowadays we talk about 'giving someone a rocket', a synonym for a telling-off. No one, to date, has attempted to coin any phrases that include the word 'cycloped'.

Just as scientific processes work with everyday objects (wood, coal, steam, etc.) to achieve out-of-the-ordinary results, so scientists

2 1922 James Joyce, *Ulysses*: 'My fireworks. Up like a rocket, down like a stick.' 1950 George Bernard Shaw, *Farfetched Fables*: '"Political adventurers and tin Jesuses" rose like rockets to dictatorships and fell to earth like sticks.'

sometimes take or invent names for their discoveries from the world around them. Louis Pasteur (1822–95) was a brilliant chemist and bacteriologist. Alongside his work with **fermentation** – a term originally from the Latin *fervere* (to boil) via *fermentare* – he went on to unravel the complex medical histories behind rabies, anthrax, chicken cholera and silkworm disease. He also became one of the best-known brands in science, giving his name to the process of **pasteurization**, and also to the Pasteur Institute, the Pasteur flask, the Pasteur treatment, the Pasteur pipette, the Pasteur reaction and the Pasteur effect.

In 1798, several years before any of Pasteur's breakthroughs, the Gloucester physician Edward Jenner (1749–1823) published his research on smallpox, noting that milkmaids who had contracted cowpox appeared to have immunity from the much more serious smallpox. He began to inoculate people with a preparation made from cowpox pustules, and this process became known as **vaccination**, from *vacca*, the Latin word for 'cow'. If Dr Jenner had lived in more modern times and had an agent, the process might have been called 'Jenneration'.

The invention of two Scottish engineers, Thomas Telford (1757–1834) and John Loudoun McAdam (1756–1836), could be described as groundbreaking in the literal sense of the word. Both devised methods of improving road-building, although one proved more enduring than the other. There is one reference in the *OED* to a 'telford road', made from broken stones (1896). McAdam, meanwhile, gave his name to the **macadamizing process**, which is the name given to his tightly packed and symmetrical arrangement of broken stones covered with smaller stones. So sturdy is this foundation that the process is still used in road construction today. The layer of tar laid over the stone surface (first cited 1903) became known as **Tarmac**. When spelt with a small 't' it denotes an airfield or runway, and to appear in the dictionary in both upper and lower cases is a sure sign of achievement

Science is not sentimental. We know nothing of the tireless experimenters who might have spent years of their lives trying to invent something only to to find that someone has beaten them to it. The world's first patent on a ballpoint pen was issued on 30 October 1888 to John J. Loud of Massachusetts, but though the design was on the right lines, the flow of ink was irregular. Eventually, two Hungarian brothers, László and Georg Biró got the ballpoint technique down to a T (or tee[3]) with a stainless steel ball. The brothers applied for a patent on the pen in 1938 and the world got its first **biro**. The pen was a hit with the Royal Air Force during the Second World War, as the ballpoint didn't leak despite the reduced air pressure at high altitudes. In 1949 a Frenchman, Baron Marcel Bich, introduced a new, improved ballpoint to Europe. The BiC Crystal is currently the world's most popular ballpoint, selling 14 million a day across the world. These days, we tend to write with a BiC but still call it a 'biro'.

---

3 T or tee, first cited 1693. The original sense of 'T' here is unclear. 'Suggestions that it was the tee at Curling, or at Golf, or a T square, appear on investigation to be untenable,' says the *OED*. Maybe it referred to the proper completion of a 't' by crossing it. The phrase 'to a tittle' (i.e. to a prick, dot, jot) with the same sense was in use nearly a century earlier.

Home comforts

There is a saying, 'Necessity is the mother of invention', and this was proved resoundingly true in 1907 when an Ohio department store janitor called James Murray Spangler came up with a device that he hoped would reduce the frequency of his asthma attacks. Suspecting that his carpet sweeper was throwing up too much dust, he devised a crude vacuum cleaner using a soap box, an electric motor, a broom handle and a pillow case. He gave one of the vacuums to a friend called Susan Hoover, who liked it and told her husband, a leather-goods manufacturer called W.H. 'Boss' **Hoover**. He bought the patent from Spangler in 1908, kept him as a partner and in 1926 started promoting his product with advertisements such as 'A hoovered room … is … free from dust'.[4] That wasn't the only time the name Hoover became a verb, but 'to hoover' certainly caught on more widely than 'hooverize', a word that H.B. Gross advanced in the *New York Tribune* in 1917 to describe saving food in the way being extolled by future president Herbert Hoover.

'Boss' Hoover and Spangler became wealthy: we could even say they hoovered up loads of cash, and even in these days of Dysons and other brands, the word 'hoover' – whether as noun or verb – got in first and is hard to shift. The novelist H.G. Wells (1866–1946) wrote in *All Aboard for Ararat* (1940), his parable of the coming world crisis, 'I shall feel like a man trying to sell Hoover cleaners to an Arab encampment in a dust storm'. And the magazine *Engineer* pointed out a growing anomaly in 1971: 'How many housewives hoover the carpet with an Electrolux?'

Some other domestic advances have also wormed their way into new contexts. Perhaps you've been in a meeting when a good idea is recognized and heard the boss say, 'Now we're cooking with gas.' Strange how some phrases don't catch on: 'We're really using the hot

4 From 1926 or 1927 in an advert quoted in the *OED* from the *Army & Navy Stores Catalogue*.

plate now' or 'Straight out of the microwave' or 'Let's put this on the Primus and see if it boils'. Not yet, it seems.

Inventions, discoveries, the patenting of formulas… all represent a decisive step forward, and the name of an invention can symbolize that process. You could be so proud of your new non-stick product that you might choose to stick forever to its proper scientific name – 'polytetrafluoroethylene'. But if, on the other hand, you give it a snappier name – **Teflon**, say – and the product works, it will have a far longer life. About forty years after it was registered in 1945, when the likes of President Ronald Reagan seemed incapable of getting anything right but always escaped censure, it provided the media with the perfect, pithy description for him: 'the Teflon president'. So maybe it was just as well that the coating's inventor, Dr Roy J. Plunkett, didn't go for immortality on a personal level.

Taking care

Teflon gave us safe cooking: the **condom** gave us safe sex. Is the rise of the condom a testament to the life's work of a Dr Condom (aka Quondam, Condon and Conton), a supposed pox-doctor? The *OED* is in no doubt on the matter. 'Origin unknown,' it says. 'No seventeenth-century physician named Condom or Conton has been traced, though a doctor so named is often said to be the inventor of the sheath.' So poor Dr Condom, if he ever existed, is lost to history, unlike the very real Thomas Crapper, by whose name hangs a different tale.

The Dutch word *krappen* means 'to pluck' or 'cut off'. Mix that with the Old French *crappe* (siftings) and the Anglo-Latin *crappa* (chaff), and you end up with the Late Middle English, fifteenth-century word **crap**, meaning 'the husk of grain'. Even then, though, 'crap' led something of a double life, since it was also a plural word for 'the residue formed in boiling, melting, or rendering fat; crackling'. Within a few centuries, the word had come to mean, by 1879, 'the dregs of beer, etc.', so it is hardly a surprise that by 1898 the *OED* defines 'crap' as 'excrement; defecation', and in the same year as 'rubbish, nonsense; something … worthless…' But sorry, Thomas Crapper fans. He wasn't born until 1836, and he didn't invent the flush toilet, so any confusion with his name is entirely accidental.[5]

The truth can hurt, which is why medicine sometimes helps us by wrapping our symptoms in a protective, condom-like sheath of scientific terminology. You may feel that you have a shocking hangover, for example, but would you hurt any less if you were told that you were suffering from **crapulence**? It has nothing to do with 'crap', being derived from the ancient Greek word *kraipalē* , meaning 'a drunken headache'.

Greek bestows the same aura of respectability on various professions. For example, would you rather talk to a mind doctor or a **psychiatrist**? Whom would you trust more? When you know that *psuchē* means 'breath, life or spirit', and *iatros* is Greek for 'doctor', there's not much to choose between them, yet the word derived from Greek has far greater gravitas. Imagine you go to see your doctor with chest pain and he or she tells you that it's **angina**, a 400-year-old word (first attested from 1590) that means, essentially, 'severe pain'. This technical term makes you feel better, though it might be less reassuring if you know that 'angina' comes from the Latin *angere* (to choke, strangle) and the Greek *ankhonē*, which also means 'strangling'.

Another good example of a word that impresses was used in British Telecom's TV advert from the 1980s featuring Maureen Lipman as 'Beattie', who consoles her grandson over his mediocre examination results. 'An ology. He gets an ology and he says he's

---

5 Thomas Crapper was, though, a sanitary engineer and successful businessman who went on to invent and patent various improvements to the flush toilet, so you do sometimes find old toilet fittings with his name on them. Was this a case of a man's surname deciding his fate?

failed. You get an ology, you're a scientist!' The word **ology**, from the Greek *logos*, meaning 'word' or 'reason', actually has a more respectable history than its use in the TV adverts implied. Charles Dickens in *Hard Times* (1854) wrote, 'Ologies of all kinds, from morning to night. If there is any Ology left ... that has not been worn to rags in this house ... I hope I shall never hear its name.' The word was, in fact, first used in 1811 for the same effect by writer Edward Nares: 'She ... was therefore supposed to understand Chemistry, Geology, Philology, and a hundred other ologies.'

When scientific terms get clinical, sometimes it's more palatable to abbreviate them or turn them into acronyms. Shortenings can soften the stark reality of hospital terms: AKA (for 'above the knee amputation') is a veiled reminder for where an incision should be made or a dressing applied. And if an acronym spells out a new word, such as **radar** (radio detection and ranging, 1941) or **laser** (light amplification by the stimulated emission of radiation, 1960), it can slip into the language very easily. When established, these words can be played with too: having a **gaydar** (1982), for instance, means you can spot someone who's gay a mile off.

Spreading the word

The rise of personal computing has seen the creation of a whole language that was only in its infancy twenty years ago, though the word **geek** is perhaps, says the *OED*, a variant of **geck** – Shakespeare spells it 'geeke' in *Cymbeline* (V.iv) (1623): 'And to become the geeke and scorne o'th'others vilany.'

The language of computers has repossessed certain words that, like 'geek' are probably more familiar to many of us in their new context than in their old. These include: 'virus', 'cookie', 'surfing', 'net', 'web', 'disk', 'memory', 'menu', 'mouse', 'save' and 'mobile'. Let's look at **scroll**. In 1606 it meant 'to write on a scroll of parchment'. In 1730 it meant 'to draft or make a rough copy', and in 1868 'scrolled' meant 'rolled or curled up', and is still used in that way by those writing in an art context: 'The body of the piece is richly encrusted with scrolling ormolu' (*The Times*, 1979). The data on computer screens was being scrolled up or down as far back as 1971, long before the machines were available to the mass market. When we **paste** (first attested 1975) these days, little glue is involved, and the word contains nothing of its original sense (*c.*1425) of pounding or grinding something into a paste. The language is moving on the whole time: invention dictates the need for new language.

Around the year 1200, **cable** was 'a strong thick rope made of hemp'. A variant reading of a familiar phrase in the Gospels of Matthew, Mark and Luke is that 'it is easier for a cable [not a camel] to go through the eye of a needle than for a rich man to enter into the kingdom of God'. One day people may be saying that it is easier for a camel to go through the eye of a needle than it is to get your broadband connection in the same week that you order it.

When we talk about the **web** these days, most of us are not talking about a spider's 'web', first attested around 1220 in the *OED*. The word **text**, a late medieval word from the Old Norman French *texte*, came from the Latin *textus*, which was derived from the verb *texere* (to weave), hence 'textile'. If ever a word has been disconnected from its roots, here is one. And yet technology has also achieved an incredible renaissance for a nineteenth-century word that was virtually dead and buried ten years or more ago. **Wireless** – the name given to early radio, even though the wires were only too evident – was all the rage during the 1890s. 'Wireless' technology might have seemed antiquated a few years ago, when the *OED* noted: 'Now chiefly historical, having been superseded by radio'. And yet wireless is back, and this time it really is wire-less. Way to go.

The **telegraph** was originally 'an apparatus for transmitting messages to a distance, usually by signs of some kind'. Its inventor, Claude Chappe (1763–1805), wanted to call it a **tachygraph**, from the Greek words for 'quick' and 'write', but his friend Miot de Mélito told him it was a bad name, and persuaded him to change it to *télégraphe* (from the Greek words *telos* 'far off' and *graphein* 'to write'), which he did, in 1792. The contraption first consisted of 'an upright post with movable arms', says the *OED*, and the signals were made 'by various positions of the arms according to a pre-arranged code'. Subsequent innovations included 'movable disks, shutters, flashes of light, movements in a column of liquid, sounds of bells, horns, etc., or other means'.

Another Frenchman, Jean-François Sudré (1787–1864), devised a system of telegraphic signalling using musical notes in 1828. (He also came up with a language called Solresol, but that's another story.) He then introduced a sort of foghorn, which was used to send signals to ships and trains by making loud sounds or notes. This device, which he called the **telephone** (first attested in 1835), took its name from the Greek words *telos* and *phōnē* 'sound'. Of course, everyone said it would never catch on.

The grapevine

No one ever heard something 'on the grapevine' until the American Civil War (1861–5), and the phrase is first attested by the *OED* in 1864. The 'grapevine' was the electric telegraph, the wires of which, like vine tendrils, had been spreading across America since Samuel Morse inaugurated the first line (from Washington to Baltimore) on 24 May 1844. The telegraph was a huge success and made a massive impact on how people lived, accelerating communications between communities.

Communications have come a long way since the telegraph. When, in 1611, the German astronomer Johannes Kepler used the term **satellite**, from the Latin *satelles* (attendant, member of a bodyguard), to describe a small planet that revolves around a larger one, he was adapting a word that had been in use from around 1548 to describe a 'royal lackey or flunkey'. The *OED* defines a satellite as 'an attendant upon a person of importance, forming part of his retinue and employed to execute his orders. Often with reproachful connotation, implying subserviency or unscrupulousness in the service.' This is certainly the sense in which the US writer Washington Irving (1783–1859) used it in his 1850 biography of the Irish dramatist Oliver Goldsmith (*c.*1730–74), when he referred to James Boswell being 'made happy by an introduction to Johnson, of whom he became the obsequious satellite'. Nowadays satellite technology has brought remarkable advances in communications, and we receive signals via a **dish**, an Old English word from the Latin *discus* (disc).

Fighting talk

One of the great sources of linguistic innovation has been warfare. Whether we like it or not, fighting is one thing that human beings do particularly well, and it can take something as apparently superficial as a domestic tiff or a boardroom squabble to put our language on a war footing. Whether we end up **digging for victory** and **spearheading** a charge, or closing ranks and waving the **white flag,**[6] it doesn't take much provocation for our thoughts and words to be peppered with the language of warfare. War has its own logic, and it certainly does not lack for drama. This has been well chronicled by, among others, the sixth- or fifth-century-BC Chinese military

---

6 Waving a white flag in seventeenth-century France did not mean you were surrendering: it was simply a demonstration of support for the Bourbons.

strategist Sun-tzu in *The Art of War*, and Niccolò Machiavelli (1469–1527) in his own *Art of War* (1521).

The phrase **theatre of war** seems to have been wheeled out for the first time by the First World War poet Edmund Blunden in his 1928 book *Undertones of War*. This did not seek to suggest that war was anything so vulgar as a box-office smash. On the contrary; after the initial rush, there was certainly no appetite to book front-row seats. But when political correspondents look around for an image these days, they don't have too much time to spend checking the historical accuracy of their references. To some, the mere hint of raised voices in the maze of Whitehall corridors is enough to substantiate an expression such as **trench warfare**, which became a characteristic of the 1914–18 conflict.

For a long time, the source of names for weaponry was the natural world. **Grenades**, named after their resemblance to the pomegranate (*granada* in Spanish), must have been tossed in anger well before they were first attested by the *OED* in 1591 but fell out of military fashion in the eighteenth century. During the sixteenth century a **torpedo** was a ray-like flat fish that emits an electric discharge, but in 1776 an American called David Bushnell[7] turned it into a sea-going **mine** that could be clamped to an enemy ship.

In more modern times, the prettily named **daisy-cutter** – 'a horse that in trotting lifts its feet only very slightly from the ground' (1791) – lent its name to something much uglier: one of the world's largest bombs, first used in 1970 in Vietnam to clear undergrowth, which has to be parachuted to its target from a cargo plane. It should not be confused with a cricketing 'daisy-cutter', which is a devilishly low ball, bowled under-arm.

---

7 David Bushnell (1742–1824) from Saybrook, Connecticut, was an inventor during the American Revolutionary War. He created the first submarine – called *The Turtle* – to be used in combat, in 1775. He proved that gunpowder could be exploded under water and he invented the first time bomb, which, using a clockwork fuse, could be exploded remotely.

Another deadly weapon with a deceptively gentle name was the **cruise** missile, which came from the Dutch word *kruisen* (to cross), and was an American development of German V2[8] technology. The original (1698) meaning of 'cruise' was 'to sail to and fro over some part of the sea without making for a particular port or landing-place, on the lookout for ships, for the protection of commerce in time of war, for plunder, or (in modern times) for pleasure'. 'Cruising' has also been known to imply walking or driving around in search of (usually gay) sex since at least 1904.

Any navy that can call on the services of cruise missile technology has to be said to have a head-start in any looming battle. And if it has enormous big ships with an aversion to sinking, so much the better. The British navy launched the first battleship in the world on 18 February 1906. It was called the *Dreadnought*, which until then had meant 'A thick coat or outer garment worn in very inclement weather'. The word is cited in Archibald Duncan's 1806 *Life of Lord Nelson*: '"I am lord Nelson," replied the hero ... throwing aside his green dreadnought.' Captain Cook, on his voyage towards the South Pole, describes a jacket made from a thick woollen cloth called a 'Fearnought' (1790).

Both dreaded and feared in wartime was the simply named **shell**, with its military meaning first cited in the *OED* at the twenty-first definition – after crustaceans, pearls, tiles, eggs, coconuts, seeds, tortoises, a racing boat, an armadillo and 'the bottom part of a turnip remaining after the root has been scooped out by sheep' have been dispatched. Then we find 'a case of metal, etc. in which powder and shot is made up, especially for use as a hand-grenade' (1644), followed by 'explosive projectile or bomb for use in a cannon or

---

8 The V2 was a much-feared German rocket bomb, designed by a team led by the rocket scientist Wernher von Braun, which followed the V1 or 'doodlebug' (1944–5). The V2 was used mostly against British and Belgian targets towards the end of the war.

mortar' in the 1940s. A particular type of shell – 'a hollow projectile containing bullets and a small bursting charge, which, when fired by the time fuse, bursts the shell and scatters the bullets in a shower' – was invented during the Peninsular Wars of 1808–14 by Major General Henry **Shrapnel** (1761–1842). During the Blitz,[9] the period of intensive German attacks on British cities, particularly London, in 1940, the contemporary historical record *Notes & Queries* commented with admirable sangfroid that 'the shell fragments which are at present descending upon its devoted head are unhesitatingly referred to by the public as "shrapnel" and the correct expression, "shell fragments", has begun to verge on pedantry'.

Shell shock, that condition of extreme psychological trauma that the First World War bombardments produced, was first cited around 1915. Ewart Alan Mackintosh in *War, the Liberator* (1918) described how 'The Corporal … collapsed suddenly with twitching hands and staring, frightened eyes, proclaiming the shell-shock he had held off while the work was to be done'. The phrase has since been cleansed, rubbed down and sent to fight again, though this time in mufti (see Chapter 6, pages 153–4). When Graham Lee won the 2004 Grand National on Amberleigh House, he was said to be 'shell shocked', but in a good way.

Paul Fussell in *The Great War and Modern Memory*, his cultural study of the years 1914–18, points out how our language has been militarized since that conflict, which was the first time for centuries that warfare had seemed close to home. Much **sabre-rattling** had preceded it, although that term was not attested in the *OED* until 1922. It means 'to threaten military action without actually committing troops', and it isn't only generals who practise it. Anyone who indulges in this with more seriousness of purpose might find

---

9 'Blitz' is a shortened form of the German word *Blitzkrieg* (lightning war).
On 9 September 1940 the *Daily Express* reported: 'Blitz bombing of London goes on all night.'

himself described as a **warmonger**, which the *OED* defines as 'One who traffics in (or) seeks to bring about war'. Since early Old English times (*c*.598), the word **monger** has lived a dangerous double life, both as a 'person engaged in a petty or disreputable trade or traffic' (scandalmonger, whoremonger) and as an otherwise respectable 'dealer, trader, or trafficker in a particular commodity', such as fishmonger and ironmonger. They may be a bit noisy at times, but that's no reason to stigmatize them.

Still, it could be that it's just too late to rehabilitate the monger's stained reputation; it would be like mounting a **rearguard action** – 'defensive stand by the rear-guard of a retreating army' – which, as the *Westminster Gazette* first pointed out in 1898, is 'the worst of all battles to fight'. Since then, many others have tried. In 2005 it was deployed by the *Daily Telegraph*'s film critic to describe George Lucas's latest *Star Wars* film: 'a two-hour rearguard action against encroaching tedium'. These days it means an ultimately futile effort, but one that is worth it nonetheless. A similar tactic, perhaps more wily, could be called a **Parthian shot**. Parthia was a region of the Achaemenian Empire and later a kingdom in what is now the Khorasan region of Iran. Parthian horsemen had a fascinating, possibly mythical way of fighting, which those people reluctant to use a classical allusion – or unfamiliar with its classical origins – also call a **parting shot**, which sounds similar, but misses some of the point. The Parthians used to confuse the enemy by continuing to shoot arrows while appearing to run away. This must have baffled their foes, who assumed the battle won, only to see that the retreat was tactical and the danger was still very much alive. For a modern equivalent, imagine your partner has just chucked you and you let yourself back into the flat to cut holes in his or her clothes. That's a form of Parthian shot. It's not recommended, but it has been known to happen.

There are levels of defeat in warfare, and certainly there are levels of victory too. A **pyrrhic victory** is named after Pyrrhus of Epirus (319–272 BC). Pyrrhus was a Greek king, famed for taking on the Romans. In 281 BC he took a commission to do so from the people of Tarentum. He fought and beat the Romans, with the help of elephants, first at Heraclea and again (in 279 BC) at Asculeum, but his casualties were massive. When someone congratulated him on his victory he is said to have replied – in one of the great satirical utterances of classical civilization – 'One more victory like this will be the end of me.' Ever since the remark came into circulation, a 'pyrrhic victory' has meant just that; a victory in which the price paid is so high that it's debatable as to whether the 'winning' side has achieved anything useful.

War is hell, however **battle-hardened** you are – whether you've been **manning the barricades** with **all guns blazing**, or **battening down the hatches** so as to sit it out, or facing troubles in true **Dunkirk spirit**.[10] Sometimes, though, there is an alternative to fighting. These days, if you said you had **spiked somebody's guns** or **seen them off at the pass**, you would be indicating that you had anticipated and thereby nullified the harm you were expecting them to do you. Had you attempted the same manoeuvre in the seventeenth century, you would have had to drive nails into the touch-hole of the enemy's gun so that it could not be fired. In this way the enemy would be **disarmed**, a word that William Caxton, the first English printer, used in this sense in 1481, when it also meant 'to dismantle a ship' and 'to strip an animal of its horns, claws or teeth'. Chaucer used it even earlier, around 1374, to mean 'deprive of power,

---

10 Dunkirk: 'French Channel port, scene of the evacuation of the British Expeditionary Force in 1940 … [by] a host of small boats while under constant attack from the air.' In 1961 a writer in *The Listener* magazine observed that 'The Dunkirk spirit of only starting to try hard when it becomes really necessary is deeply ingrained in the British character.'

to injure or terrify', until Thomas Beale, in *The Natural History of the Sperm Whale* (1839) described how someone (not the whale) 'Beckoned us to approach with winning and **disarming** smiles'.

Equally disarming was the late Lord Scarman's visit to Brixton after the race riots of 1981, when he earned respect among the black population by referring to them as 'living on the **front line**' – a phrase dating back at least to the First World War. He might also have described the events as **snafu**, a Second World War acronym used by American troops, which stood for 'situation normal: all fouled (or fucked) up' (1941).

If you have ever been sent on a **hopeless mission**, you might like to recall the **kamikaze** ('divine wind') that supposedly destroyed the ships (and 100,000 men) of the invading Mongols at Inari Bay in August 1281, and then passed into Japanese folklore as a miraculous victory. The word 'kamikaze' (*kami* means 'divinity' and *kaze* means 'wind') took on a horrific significance in the Second World War when Japanese pilots crashed their own planes on to the decks of US and Australian ships in the sea around the Philippines, a tactic first used in 1944 but not recorded in print until 1945.

The word 'kamikaze' was obviously much in evidence after the attacks on the World Trade Center and the Pentagon building on 11 September 2001, but it can also be used on altogether more flippant occasions, as when it was used to describe the Sri Lankan cricket team's disastrous running between the wickets against the West Indies in 2003. 'Kamikaze' is, of course, a euphemism: the more violent the attack, the more deceptively civilized the language. **Carpet bombing** sounds like 'carpet slippers', but has a much harsher reality: it was coined in 1945 to describe laying waste to a large area of land. And the term **collateral damage** – meaning 'Whoops, looks like we hit some civilians' – was used first by the Pentagon/CIA in August

1988, after an air attack on the Al Shifa bomb-making plant in Sudan. Nowadays, it's not uncommon to hear it used to refer to any unintended victims, such as children in a divorce case.

If that is one case of military hardware **impacting**, as they say, on flesh and blood, we should not forget the mother and father of all civilian air-raids: on Hiroshima and Nagasaki. The first **atom bomb**, called 'Little Boy', exploded over Hiroshima on 6 August 1945, killing over 60,000 people. The second bomb, called 'Fat Man', exploded above Nagasaki on 9 August, killing about 42,000 people. The Americans claim that using the atom bomb was the least worst option, and they could be right, but a new word, **fallout**, entered the language. This refers to the contaminated particles thrown up by the explosion that then fall back down to earth. That word, so shocking in its true meaning, is now used simply to mean 'consequences' in far less serious situations, as in 'Net weathers WorldCom fallout'. Similarly, you might read that Thierry Henry remains Arsène Wenger's **nuclear option** at Highbury. And when a pop diva such as Diana Ross can have a hit with a song called 'Chain Reaction' (1985), you know that we have, to some extent, become desensitized to the horrific images that used to accompany these words.

Language can protect us from many horrors, but it can also expose us to many more. It's in our nature that we want to take a look: that is the appeal of **taboo** (see Introduction, page 29). Soldiers on active service traditionally find out more about the seamy side of life than they would have done on **civvy street** (in civilian life). For them, it's a process of discovery equivalent to the greatest efforts of scientists and surgeons. Science flourishes in times of danger, soldiers behave like superheroes in battle conditions, and language is rarely so inventive as when it is under constraints of one kind or another. Some colourful examples of language under stress are contained in the next chapter.

chapter nine

MIND YOUR LANGUAGE

The French refer to us
– when they can bear to –
as 'LES FUCKINGS'
BECAUSE THATS <u>THE</u> WORD
they keep hearing us use
when we're <u>EN VACANCES</u>.

Mind Your Language

Swearing is a strange thing: it often expresses two contradictory conditions simultaneously. We swear to show fear, and also to show that we're not afraid. We take the name of God in vain at precisely the moment when we should be most circumspect ('Jesus, sorry I didn't recognize you, Vicar'). Swearing can help to release tension. We swear when we are angry, or to emphasize a point, or when we feel that we've lost control of a situation. We swear in order to shock, to impress or to flirt. We swear to show that we care, and to show that we couldn't give a **toss**.[1] Bad language is called 'transgressive'[2] because it goes beyond or steps over a line of general acceptability.

But the use of language as a weapon need not just be about four-letter words. As we shall see, many communities have been marginalized or discriminated against on account of their race, gender or sexuality by mainstream society, which uses language to keep them in an inferior position. When these groups seize back the initiative, it is often language that helps them to recover lost ground and status within society.

**** words

Courtesy was introduced into Britain by the Norman invaders, who came over with William the Conqueror in 1066. Discourtesy had existed for centuries before, though not under that name. The idea of courtly behaviour overrode the much coarser ways and language

---

1 Toss: 'In negative contexts: a jot, a whit, a very small amount.' The first written use comes, amazingly, in George Eliot's *Daniel Deronda* (1876): 'I don't care a toss where you are.'
2 Transgressive – from the French *transgresser*, ultimately from the Latin *trans* ('across') and *gradi* ('go').

that had held sway until then, which is why the vast majority of swear-words are Old English or Anglo-Saxon. There might not even have been a corresponding term in the French spoken by the barons; and Latin, which they introduced to this country (see Chapter 1), was likely to have been considerably more genteel. **Wank**, for example, is Old English, while the more upmarket 'masturbate' is Latin. 'Fuck' is Old English; 'coitus' and 'intercourse' are Latin. 'Fornication' has splendidly classical roots, arising from the Latin word *fornix*, meaning 'arch, vaulted chamber' but also 'brothel'.

Swearing can be shocking, but it has always been central to our behaviour as human beings. Even the Greeks and Romans let rip now and again. Essentially, swearing takes three forms:

- ❊ Words to do with excretion
- ❊ Sexual language or imagery
- ❊ Religious or blasphemous[3] vocabulary

Excretion-related swearing starts early because small children are naturally curious about it. They quickly learn the taboo nature of certain bodily functions, and they continue to experiment with that knowledge in conversation. In the case of sexual imagery, it is hardly surprising that our thoughts turn to swearing when hormones start us raging towards puberty. And we invoke the name of the divine either to call upon or challenge them: either to call upon their strength for our aid or, more commonly these days, to disdain their perceived omnipotence.

Who swears? Pretty much everyone, it seems, if the circumstances are appropriate. Each society has its own sign language for obscenity, such as the V-sign, the single finger, the finger inside the circled fingers, but this is extremely limited in comparison with the spoken language, which offers a vast number of options. We swear in public, in private, on our own, with friends, at work, and sometimes in front

---

3 Blasphemous – from the Greek *blasphēmos*, meaning 'evil speaking'.

of our own family. But swearing is status-dependent. You would be more likely to swear at a fellow worker than at your employer, and you might not want to swear in front of an employee because swearing implies a sort of intimacy, and that exists only at certain social levels. You do it when you know you can get away with it. But how have attitudes to bad language changed over the centuries, and why have certain languages, such as English, developed such a multiplicity of ways in which to keep an uncivil tongue?

Historical swearing

When people give evidence in court these days, they have the option of swearing on the Bible that the evidence they are about to give is the truth, 'so help me God'. This is the oldest sense of the verb **to swear**, to which we find references in the laws of King Alfred (*c.*900) and the Lindisfarne Gospels (*c.*950), as the *OED* defines it, 'To make a solemn declaration of statement with an appeal to God or a superhuman being, or to some sacred object, in confirmation of what is said; to take an oath'. The sense of 'to swear at', as in 'to imprecate evil up by an oath; to address with profane imprecation' dates from the seventeenth century. The implication is that one would never commit perjury if the result was a lifelong sentence of eternal damnation.

Among the earliest blasphemies on record are Middle English ones that refer to parts of God's body, such as **'slids** (God's eyelids), **'sfoot** (God's foot), **'steeth** (God's teeth) and **zounds** (God's wounds). Referring to His bones, people were likely to exclaim **God's bodskins**, **odsbodikins** or **gadsbudlikins**. Another exclamation was **gadzooks** (God's hooks), which might refer to the nails that pierced Christ's flesh. As swearing has evolved, the body parts have remained, as in '**My arse!**' In these days of secularization, with fewer and fewer people attending conventional church services, expressions invoking the Godhead (Jesus, God, Christ) have lost some of their power to shock, but practising Christians are still likely to find them offensive.

The Church was all-powerful during the Middle Ages, but after the Reformation[4] its authority began to diminish. As people emerged from under its shadow, **devil** began to be used more as a term of abuse – proof that the very mention of Satan's name was no longer guaranteed to make everyone turn to stone. And as words such as **damn** and **hell** slowly lost their power to shock, there were always other words you could use if you had hit your thumb with a hammer, from **shit** to a handy new word that began with 'f'.

It was the Carmelite friars of Cambridge who were the first targets of bad language in writing. In a document written some time before the fifteenth century we find a line in cod Latin that reads, *Non sunt in coeli, quia gxddbov xxkxzt pg ifmk*. The first five words mean 'They are not in heaven because…' The next four words are written in a simple code: step back one letter in each case and you get *fvccant vvivys of heli*. The 'v' is pronounced 'u': take off the –ant third person plural ending and you are left staring at the word *fucc*, or **fuck** in modern parlance. The rest of this sentence is more or less English: 'they fuck the wives of Ely'. It's the sort of sentiment that you might expect to see scratched on a toilet door, and yet this disgraceful slur was made about the friars of Cambridge and the womenfolk of Ely.

The word 'fuck' is an ancient Germanic word. The Middle Dutch *fokken*, the Norwegian *fukka* and the Swedish *focka* mean roughly the same thing. However, it did not always occupy the hottest seat in the history of copulation. The apparently blameless noun 'swivel', which today is guilty of little more than helping an office chair to rotate, has something of a shady past, unconnected to its meaning as 'a simple fastening or coupling device made so that the object fastened to it can

---

4 The Reformation – a Protestant movement that, emerging in the sixteenth century, attempted to reform the all-powerful Roman Catholic Church.

turn freely upon it'. 'Swivel' was derived from the Old English 'swifan', which also gave us **swive**, a word that, from our earliest (fourteenth-century) records onwards, meant 'to copulate'. The impolite associations were certainly not lost on English speakers around 800 years ago, and Geoffrey Chaucer, for one, never missed a chance to insert a 'swive' when the situation arose: 'Thus swived was this carpenter's wife' is one example from 'The Miller's Tale'. The word continued to perform indelicately for centuries, although with more appetite north of the border, until it dropped pretty much out of sight in the eighteenth century. The *OED*'s last sighting of it is from a publication called *Secreta Secret* (1898): 'Don't bathe on a full stomach: nor swive.'

X-rated words

The shock value of 'fuck' has lessened a great deal over the years. If you still doubt it, ask a twelve-year-old wearing a French Connection UK T-shirt. Maybe this is because the British have found the word so fucking useful – excuse my French[5] – in normal conversation. Indeed, it has peppered so much of our speech that the French refer to us – when they can bear to – as 'Les Fuckings' because that's the word they keep hearing us use when we're *en vacances*.

'Fuck' is an incredibly hard-working word, with multiple grammatical uses. It is a noun: 'Frankly, my dear, I don't give a fuck.' A verb: 'Fuck me, I'm knackered' or 'I'm fucking off home now, OK?' An adjective, or a verbal adjective: 'It was just a fucking joke, right?' An adverb: 'That was fucking hard work.' A past participle: 'Fucked if I know.' And, of course, an interjection: 'Fuck off!' It's a strange thing to urge someone to do, since it's probably a fate that most people would gladly accept, but terms of abuse don't always obey the laws of logic. This taboo word may have lost some of its potency, but

---

5 *Harper's Magazine* 1895: 'Palaces be durned! Excuse my French.' Used as a euphemism for bad language ever since.

there is another four-letter word that still has the power to shock.

Language scholars have been speculating for years about the etymological history of the 'c-word' – or 'the female external genital organs', to quote the *OED*. Francis Grose in his 1788 *Dictionary of the Vulgar Tongue* defined 'c**t' [*sic*] as 'a nasty name for a nasty thing'. Eric Partridge (1894–1979), the famous linguist and author of *The Dictionary of Slang*, found something of 'quintessential femineity' (i.e. femininity) in the opening two letters of the word **cunt**.

Some writers who have traced the word's classical routes may be following their hopes, or a political agenda, or a pure coincidence, more than strict linguistic practice, since it's much more likely to be Germanic than from Greek or Latin. But just to see where this curious trail leads, certain academics have taken the Latin *cognosco* (I know) and derived from it words such as 'connote', 'canny' and 'cunning'. Then they take a noun such as *cuneus*, which means 'a wedge', and the related *cunnus*, which does (finally) mean the 'female pudenda' or, in Horace's words, an 'unchaste woman'. A little bit of *cognosco* and a lot of *cunnus* imply, they say, that **cunt** combines quintessential femininity and some Earth Mother-know-it-all wisdom. These examples might help explain why Geoffrey Chaucer sidesteps the obvious in 'The Wife of Bath's Tale':

> *For certeyn, olde dotard, by youre leve,*
> *Ye shul have queynte right y-nough at eve.*

The word 'queynte' was a familiar euphemism for 'cunt', though later on the bawdy wench alludes to her sexual prowess more fulsomely when she says:

> *And trewely, as myne housbondes tolde me,*
> *I had the beste quoniam mighte be.*

'Quoniam' is the Latin word for 'whereas', so the euphemism here is 'whatever' or 'whatsit' or, as some might say, 'thingy'. There have been other variations right up to the modern day, from the nineteenth-century 'hootchie-cootchie' to a suggestion of sexual gratification in the Small Faces' psychedelia-soaked hit 'Itchycoo Park' (1967). Elsewhere, cunts have featured on the British landscape as far back as the year 1230, usually based near red-light areas. There was a Gropecuntelane in London and in Oxford (where it was later renamed Magpie Lane), a Grapcunt Lane in York (which became Grape Lane), a Cunte Street in Bristol (later renamed Host Street), and a *Rue Grattecon* (scratchcunt street) in Paris. London's Gropecuntelane was later shortened to Grope Lane, then Grub Street in the eighteenth century, then Milton Street in 1830. All this street renaming is probably just as well in purely commercial terms: it wouldn't look too good on a business card to have your office based in Gropecunt Lane.

The language used by the characters in Geoffrey Chaucer's *Canterbury Tales* was among the fruitiest[6] in early English literature, but elsewhere bad language was not necessarily bad. 'Svmmer is icumen in' was written in approximately 1240. It was a Middle English chart-topper, and it runs as follows:

Svmer is icumen in	Summer is a-coming in
Lhude sing cuccu!	Loudly sing cuckoo
Groweth sed and bloweth med	Groweth seed and bloweth mead
And springth the wude nu.	And springs the wood anew
Sing cuccu!	Sing cuckoo!
Awe bleteth after lomb,	Ewe bleateth after lamb,
lhouth after calue cu,	Calf loweth after cow,
Bulluc sterteth, bucke uerteth.	Bullock starteth, buck farteth,
Murie sing cuccu!	Merry sing cuckoo!

---

6 Fruity, 1. mid-seventeenth-century adjective, Of or pertaining to or resembling fruit. 2. 1844. Of wine: having the taste of the grape. 3. *colloq.* Full of rich or strong quality; highly interesting, attractive, or suggestive.

Bullocks start and bucks fart, and nobody seems to care. It wasn't obscene, of course: barely even bawdy. It was merely a frank expression of rustic life, close to the earth, the animals, the elements. If the Victorians objected to the odd word, that was in part because of the genteel horror of bodily parts – or farts – which was a reaction to the loucheness of the eighteenth century. Queen Victoria's prudery was not intrinsically religious, but muscular Christianity had never been as strong as in the nineteenth century. And of course, there are no rude words in the Bible, are there?

Biblical bad language

The Bible, which has had so much effect on our turns of speech (see Chapter 4), also contains strong words and (as TV announcements occasionally warn us) scenes of a sexual nature. Take the cities of Sodom and Gomorrah: their destruction in approximately 2000 BC, graphically delineated in Genesis 18–19, was linked to their reputation for 'immorality'. 'Sodomy' has been a byword for homosexual sex since records began – 'vile sunne of sodomye' (according to Robert of Gloucester's *Metrical Chronicle* (1297), cited in the *OED*). Gomorrah, on the other hand, seems to have got off lightly. (Gonorrhoea? No, different story: that means 'flow of seed' in Greek.) A similar flow of seed connected the brothers Er and Onan (Genesis 38:9). Er was the first-born son of Judah, and when he died childless, Judah ordered Er's brother Onan to marry the widow Tamar. Onan, though, seems not to have fancied marriage to Tamar, so he 'spilled [his seed] on the ground'. He tossed himself off, in other words. This, we are told, 'displeased the Lord: wherefore he slew him also'. It was a German writer who first coined the term 'onanism' in 1649. Since then, the term, sometimes translated as 'self-pollution', has spread around the world, and Onan's name, if not his seed, lived on long after him.

Within the books of the Bible there is prostitution (Ezekiel 23:8, Hosea 1:2), rape (Genesis 39:7–23, 2 Samuel 13:1–14), incest (Genesis 19:30–38), testicle-squeezing (Genesis 24:2–9, 47:29), as well as flashing (by David, 2 Samuel 6:14 and 16:20–23) and mass foreskin-slashing (David again, Samuel 18:27). In the second book of Kings (18:27) and Isaiah (36:12) the Assyrian Rab-Shakeh asks if his men are expected to 'eat their own dung and drink their own piss'. A phrase uttered in wrath and that (politely) translates as 'every man-child' but actually means 'he that pisses', is sprayed across six places in the first book of Samuel (25:22, 25:34), the first book of Kings (14:10, 16:10–11, 21:21) and 2 Kings (9:8).

After the Reformation, literary censorship was undertaken by the Privy Council,[7] and theatrical censorship by the Master of the King's Revels. Writers such as William Shakespeare had to find subtle ways of inserting earthy words. An example of how he did this appears in *Measure for Measure*, when he used 'counsellors' as a pun on 'cunt-sellers': 'Good counsellors lack no clients' (I.ii). In *Twelfth Night* Malvolio spells it out: 'By my life, this is my lady's hand! These be her very C's, her U's, and her T's' (II.v). If the 'and' were pronounced distinctly enough as 'en' (N), the audience would have been left in no doubt as to the reference. The most famous Shakespeare 'cunt' pun is when Hamlet asks Ophelia: 'Do you think I meant country matters?' (III.iii), emphasizing the first syllable of 'country' in case the matter is at all ambivalent. He had tried this before, in *The Comedy of Errors* (1590): 'she is spherical, like a globe; I could find out countries in her' (III.ii), and in *Henry IV Part Two* (1597): 'The rest of thy low-countries have made a shift to eat up thy Holland' (II.ii).

---

7 Formerly the inner cabal of the sovereign consisting of princes, archbishops and specially chosen ministers, past and present.

The punning reference is to Holland, one of the Low Countries, and also to the position of the vagina, low down the body.

Despite the word's ubiquity in the past, 'cunt' is still the ultimate taboo utterance. When a Tony Harrison poem containing it was broadcast on Channel 4 in 1985, the *Daily Mail* splashed its front page with the banner headline 'FOUR-LETTER TV POEM FURY'. And two years later, amid the sometimes unendurable tension of one of the worst-tempered Test series in cricket history, Pakistani umpire Shakoor Rana went several steps further than lifting one finger in the air when he called Mike Gatting a 'fucking, cheating cunt'. The *Independent* was the only newspaper that printed his tirade uncensored.

'People who swear,' say disapproving parents, 'are just displaying their lack of vocabulary.' In fact, there is an absolute wealth of swearing vocabulary to choose from, some of it 'disguised' to conceal its roots. Few maiden aunts would be thrown into a flutter at the sound of the word **berk,** for example, surely an innocuous word for a 'fool'. In fact, it came into the language during the 1930s (first attestation 1936), and is cockney rhyming slang: 'Berkshire (or Berkeley) hunt' – 'cunt'.

Thomas Bowdler and the Victorians

The Obscene Publications Act became law in 1857, in a bid to keep us all safe from unprotected (i.e. uncensored) literature. Someone who would have been among its most enthusiastic proponents, had he not died before it was passed, was the Edinburgh doctor Thomas Bowdler (1754–1825). Bowdler made it clear that he loved Shakespeare, but nevertheless believed that nothing 'can afford an excuse for profaneness or obscenity; and if these could be obliterated, the transcendant [*sic*] genius of the poet would undoubtedly shine with more unclouded lustre'. He proved so zealous at expurgating texts that 'to bowdlerize' means just that. His ten-volume *Family Shakespeare*, 'in which nothing is added to the original text; but those words and expressions are omitted which cannot with propriety be read aloud in a family', went on sale in December 1818. Every reference to 'God' is replaced by 'Heaven'. Bowdler's main tool, however, was a pair of scissors – not the most agile editing device – so many speeches were simply hacked and ended up resembling a hedge that has been ruined by an incompetent gardener.

Having struggled with many of Shakespeare's passages, as it were, he gave up altogether on *Othello*, advising that as it was 'unfortunately little suited to family reading', it should be transferred 'from the parlour to the cabinet'. Bowdler's work was successful during his own lifetime, and went through five editions by the 1860s. He even attempted to work a similar magic with Edward Gibbon's *The History of the Decline and Fall of the Roman Empire* (1776–88). Luckily, he never got his hands on John Cleland's *Fanny Hill*, or *Memoirs of a Woman of Pleasure*, which came out, to titillate literate adults, between 1748 and 1749.

As society grew ever more genteel during the nineteenth century, more and more effort went into ensuring social delicacy. This purification process lasted for some time, as indicated by a 1959 edition of Chambers's *Twentieth Century English Dictionary*. Its editor, William Geddie, MA, B.Sc., described his aim as 'to include all words in general use in literary and conversational English', but he acknowledged that he had cut out 'some dead slang'. The chances are, therefore, that Dr Geddie did not use the words 'fuck', 'cunt' or 'wank' in his conversational English, since they certainly appear nowhere in his dictionary. Nor do we find any mention of the lesser horrors **shit, crap** or **bollock**. One of the chinks in his lexicon is the noun **twat**, which he had to admit came from a line of verse by Robert Browning in which it referred to nuns' head-gear. (The great poet seems to have misunderstood the 1660 poem *Vanity of the Vanities* by Sir Henry Vane the Younger: 'They talked of his having a Cardinall's hat, They'd send him as soon an Old Nun's Twat.') The coy entry in Chambers for 'twat' reads 'pudendum muliebre: (*Browning*, blunderingly) part of a nun's dress'. The Latin words mean 'female organ'. Browning's poem, *Pippa Passes* (1848): 'Then owls and bats / Cowls and twats / Monks and nuns in a cloister's moods / Adjourn to the oak-stump pantry.'

Translators and editors went to great lengths to avoid causing offence to readers, some of whom might be ladies, and who would be genuinely scandalized by ripe language or indelicate scenes. Half of the nineteenth-century editions of Jonathan Swift's *Gulliver's Travels* (1726) were bowdlerized, writes Noel Perrin in his book on Thomas Bowdler (see Further Reading, page 294). Swift writes of the younger members of the tiny Lilliputian army looking up, as they marched through his legs, to catch a glimpse of his genitals – but not in the Victorian classroom editions. When the tables are turned and Gulliver is a homunculus amid the giants of Brobdingnag, Swift recounts visiting the boudoir of a lady, one of whose breasts 'stood prominent six Foot, and could not be less than sixteen in Circumference. The Nipple was about half the Bigness of my Head, and the Hew both of that and the Dug so varified with Spots, Pimples, and Freckles, that nothing could appear more nauseous.' Again, the description rarely remained to trouble Queen Victoria's schoolchildren.

These days, the Lord Chamberlain's Office (LCO) attends to such matters as state visits, investitures, garden parties, royal weddings and funerals. But the LCO used to be the official censor for all theatres in Britain. So long as theatre companies produced licensed plays, no problem arose. But increasingly during the 1960s, independently minded writers and directors were looking to put on more controversial work. It is not uncommon when looking at manuscripts of plays presented during that period to see the Lord Chamberlain's blue pencil striking out lines that were considered unsuitable. The Royal Court Theatre in London often fell foul of the LCO, one notable occasion being when it wanted to stage *Saved*, Edward Bond's 1965 play about urban violence, in which a baby is stoned in a pram. The theatre frequently resorted to declaring itself a private club so that it could perform works without fear of prosecution.

Curiously, it wasn't just groundbreaking new theatre to which the Lord Chamberlain objected. Classical works, such as *Lysistrata* by Aristophanes, *Mrs Warren's Profession* by George Bernard Shaw, and *Hedda Gabler* by Henrik Ibsen all fell foul of the LCO, until the institution was abolished under the Theatres Act of 1968. The fact that the Lord Chamberlain's Office was once considered necessary, however, is further evidence of the power of language.

What a load of bollocks

Has any other part of the body acquired so many alternative names? Here are just a few:

Apricots; Balls; Bollocks; Cobblers (Cobbler's Awls); Cods; Cojones; Conkers; Family jewels; Goolies (see Chapter 7, page 181); Henry Halls; Knackers; Love-apples; Lunchbox; Maracas (knackers); Meat and two veg; Nadgers; Nads; Niagaras (Niagara Falls); Orchestras (Orchestra Stalls); Nuts; Packet; Plums; Privates; Pills; Rocks; Stones; Taters; Town Halls; Unmentionables.

Rude words and euphemisms

As well as hard-core, X-rated[8] words, there has never been a shortage of boorish[9] words with which to abuse others or oneself. The Middle English word 'pillicock' meant 'penis' around 1300–25. By 1598 it meant 'young boy'. The *OED* cites a sixteenth-century use of **pillock** in the sense of 'the penis', spelt 'pillok'. The 'pillock' spelling dates from the 1970. The child's term **willie** also appeared in the early twentieth century, but that was long preceded by **dick**, the shortened version of Richard, which began to appear in the mid-sixteenth century, and had hardened into a familiar term for the male private parts by the late eighteenth century.

The *OED* lists eight separate nouns all called **cock**, as well as one, almost certainly a mistake, in Dr Johnson's *Dictionary*, meaning 'the notch of an arrow'. But there is really only one which concerns us: the first. Its twenty-three definitions begin with King Alfred referring to the domestic fowl, around AD 897. Definition number twenty, in language redolent of the *OED*'s first edition, reads 'Penis', followed by: 'The current name among the people, but, *pudoris causa* [i.e. to spare our blushes] not admissible in polite speech or literature; in scientific language the Latin is used.' The first citation is from *Amends for Ladies* by Nathaniel Field (1597–1619): 'Oh man what art thou? When thy cock is up?' The most recent citation is from *Landfall* (1969) by A.S. Byatt: 'She had her hand on his cock.' 'There's no need to be crude.' **Cocksucker** is attested from 1891. The same work, a scrap book by one Edward Farmer, defines 'cock-teaser' or 'cockchafer' as 'a girl in the habit of permitting all familiarities but the last'.

---

8 A government committee reported in 1950: 'We recommend that a new category of films be established (which might be called "X") from which children under 16 should be entirely excluded.'

9 Boor, c.1430: 'Husband, peasant, countryman, a clown.' 1598: 'A peasant, a rustic, with lack of refinement implied; a country clown … Any rude, ill-bred fellow.'

And then there's **prick**, which has only one entry for the noun. Around AD 1000 it meant 'an impression in a surface or body made by pricking or piercing; a puncture.' The fifth sub-heading, and by far the fullest, concerns 'Anything that pricks or pierces; an instrument or organ having a sharp point.' (We're getting closer.) There are five further definitions within this but the seventeenth definition, in the 1989 second edition of the *OED*, is more up-front: 'The penis. *coarse slang*,' it says simply. The first citation is from 1592: 'The pissing Boye lift up his pricke.' The late Ed McBain (1926–2005) gets the last citation, from his 1976 novel *Guns*: 'Jocko had … a very small pecker … Blood on the bulging pectorals, tiny contradictory prick.' The word 'prick' as 'vulgar term of abuse for a man' is wholly twentieth-century. Eric Partridge noted 'prick-teaser', akin to 'cock-teaser', in the supplement to his *Dictionary of Slang* (1961).

It is a curious fact that the rudest letter in the alphabet, measured in sheer numbers, may well be B. The word **bastard** entered the language via Old French from the medieval Latin *bastardus*, though, appropriately perhaps, we are not quite sure of that word's parentage. The Old French *fils de bast* meant 'packsaddler's son', and was used, incredibly, to describe 'the offspring of an amorous itinerant mule driver', who stopped for long enough to use a packsaddle for a pillow but was gone again by sunrise. Extraordinary if true.

There is also **bloody**, of course, which these days hardly raises an eyebrow, but was once considered ruder than 'fuck'. It has been used to add emphasis since the mid-seventeenth century, and may have some sort of aristocratic connection, given the 'bloods' (a word for aristocratic rowdies) and their inability to hold their drink without serious consequences for lawns, windows, chambermaids and so on. **Bloody drunk** was another way of saying 'as drunk as a lord'. 'Bloody' was held in high esteem as a swear-word, and frequently went unspelt when quoted until quite recently. Perhaps people believed that the blood in question was that of Christ; some thought the word was a truncated version of 'by Our Lady'.

A different type of b-word, **bugger**, was used originally to refer to heretics, especially the Albigensians, a small sect who flourished around southern France in the twelfth and thirteenth centuries and who followed the ancient religion of Manichaeanism, a creed which held that everything sprang from the two principles of light and darkness, or good (God) and evil (Satan). The Old French word for 'heretic' is *bougre*, via Dutch. This seems to have piggybacked upon the medieval Latin word *bulgarus*, meaning 'a Bulgarian'. At that time Bulgarians belonged to the Orthodox Church, which held views regarded as heretical by the Roman Church. During the sixteenth century, the term came to be equated with sodomy, on the grounds that forbidden sex was synonymous with heresy, and from the early eighteenth century onwards the word 'bugger' became a term of abuse directed at homosexuals. Casually, or 'In low language', says the *OED*, 'bugger' has since 1719 also been a term of affection: 'silly bugger', 'clever bugger', etc. **Bugger all**, first cited in 1937, means 'nothing'. The twentieth century transferred the meaning of the verb from sex to, simply, 'to mess up or spoil', or 'to be tired out'.

Those wanting to refer to sex in a vernacular way, but who dislike the words offered so far, have several less offensive terms at their disposal. **Bonk** is what people say when they can't bring themselves to say 'fuck'. A listlessly upper-class word, first attested in 1975, it probably comes from the sound made when two SUV vehicles have a minor collision in a Fulham side-street. 'Oh, sorry, did I bonk you?' says one driver, who then realizes, as the colour drains from his cheeks, that the comment could have been misinterpreted.

Earthier by far is the eighteenth-century use of the verb **to shag**.

Even if you weren't aware of its origins, this reeks of the farmyard: you can really imagine two shaggy-haired dogs getting down and having a good rut. Perhaps, for that reason, it wasn't the most romantic description ever coined for the act of union, though it may be why we forgive Mike Myers for naming his 'love interest' Heather Graham 'Felicity Shagwell' in the second Austin Powers film, *The Spy Who Shagged Me* (1999). 'Shag' is a word that demands not to be taken too seriously. In fact, it was hijacked for sexual purposes in the late eighteenth century: prior to that, the *OED* compared it to the Scots and Late Middle English 'shog', meaning 'to shake or roll from side to side'. **Screw** is another word that, since the early eighteenth century, has meant 'to have sex'. It also shares with 'fuck' the sub-meaning of implied clumsiness, as in 'I really fucked/screwed that up.' However, 'screw' turns in two directions at once, as it can also be used in approbatory expressions, such as 'He's got his head screwed on right, that boy.'

One other erotic 'b' is the everyday word for 'fellatio': the **blow-job**. Back in the 1970s, about the only place you could find language like that was in the controversial magazine *Oz*, which had started in Australia in 1963. 'Blow-job' is first noted in 1961 as the Anglo-Saxon term for 'fellatio' (from the Latin *fellāre*, 'to suck'). So where does blowing come into it, and why isn't it called a 'suck-job'? Does 'suck-job' just sound wrong? The explanation is unclear, especially since the *OED* has not, so far, stepped into this particular fray. But given that slang terms for sexual activities can be highly figurative (compare the verb 'to eat' as US slang for 'to practice fellatio or cunnilingus…', cited first in 1927), if we look at some of the other meanings of the verb 'to blow', some ideas emerge. One is that the action of blowing is like the water and air ejected through a whale's blow-hole, to which ejaculation is compared. The action of blowing bellows or the coals of a fire (both 1596) is figurative for stirring up passion or anger, which could be of a sexual nature. When something 'blows up' into an argument, it's clear that feelings are running high. When a soldier turns his 'blow-lamp' on to something, the object becomes extremely hot. Jazz musicians blow their horn, and the action of putting an instrument in the mouth could provoke comparisons. According to *Cassell's Dictionary of Slang*, 'blow-job' arrived from 'basket-job', which was a gay term in the 1940s, 'basket' being a slang word for the male genitals.

The journey of **come** towards sexual fulfilment has been eventful. The *OED* doesn't get round to it until the seventeenth definition, dating it as mid-seventeenth-century, by which time we have already met usages such as 'come to pass', 'come about' and 'come into being'. Be warned: the rules are different in other languages. If you're at the end of a meeting in Spain and you try to say, in Spanish, '*tengo que correr*', hoping it means 'I've got to run', you could be announcing that you're about to have an orgasm, or that you're, in hippy-speak, 'turned on', which would be unfortunate, whether you are or not.

Such simple words denote such energetic activities. 'Get', for example, had to wait until the twentieth century before to **get off with** meant 'to have sex with'. In *Iolanthe*, Gilbert and Sullivan wrote: 'I heard the minx remark / She'd meet him after dark / inside St James's Park / And **give him one**!' What was it that she was going to give him? We in the twenty-first century know, but did they? The draft material from the revision process for *OED3*, published June 2004, says that '…the mention of St James's Park (which at the time had a reputation for being frequented by prostitutes) may glancingly suggest the later sexual sense.' And as for the adjective 'hard', given its meaning, what chance did it stand, whether transmuted into a **hard-on** or **hard porn**? Perhaps we should leave it there and move on.

The language of hate

Racist words can still send a shiver down the spine. At the beginning of the nineteenth century in America, there was a little-used word that meant 'to divide logs into sections by burning them'. The word in question was **nigger,** whereas the word 'coloured' was not considered to be offensive to black people until the late twentieth century. By the middle of the nineteenth century, 'niggerdom' was in wide circulation (though it is marked by the *OED* as 'offensive'), and the word 'niggerize' could be used to mean 'to oppress or treat with contempt in a manner reminiscent of the oppression of black people'. A little later – either as a compliment or an insult – it meant 'to subject to the influence of black people; to assimilate to black culture'. When the respected black academic Cornel West said that the USA had been 'niggerized' after the attacks of 9/11, he was comparing its new national trauma with African-Americans' long history of coping with terror and death. In 1894 'niggering' seemed to have become an alternative for the term 'busking' (see Chapter 7, page 183), as performed by black and white minstrels. In the second half of the nineteenth century we find examples of the word meaning 'to behave or live supposedly in the manner of a black slave; to work very hard, do menial work'. And all this from a process which goes back, via the 1568 French word *neger*, to the humble Latin adjective *niger* (black).

Between 1574 and 1833 the word 'niger' (or 'nigre' or 'nigor'[10]) is used frequently to refer to black people, 'possibly with no specifically hostile overtones', says the *OED* cagily. In 1932 the Harlem intelligentsia were known as the 'niggerati',[11] and 'nigger' went through many other derogatory changes of clothing, so it is with something approaching relief that, after a period in the 1980s when it was customarily referred to (from 1985) as the 'n-word', we find the rap and hip-hop community reinstating 'nigger' on its own terms as a political gesture. They appropriated the spelling too, so that it comes out as 'nigga' or 'nigguh', as in bands such as Niggaz with Attitude and the rap song 'Mnniiggaah'. In this, it resembles the soul/rap community's adoption of the word – and the spelling of – 'gangsta', 'sista', 'brutha' or 'mutha'. As the *OED* notes: 'The resurgence of the form *nigga* (plural often *niggaz*) and other forms without final –*r* in late 20th-century use (especially in representations of urban African-American speech) is probably due to its deliberate adoption by some speakers as a distinct word, associated with neutral or positive senses.'

Another racial group that has been the target of a large amount of denigratory[12] language is the Jews. European Jews have been speaking Yiddish since at least the thirteenth century – two-thirds of its vocabulary is German – as well as referring to themselves as

---

10 The range of spellings recorded by early explorers and other curious observers is awesome. A quick scan finds 'Neigers' (1568), 'neegers' (1587), 'Neagers' (1599), 'Negars' (1624), 'neger' (1686), 'Niegors' (1776), 'neegger' (1827), 'negre' (1866), 'naygars' (1913) and 'neegur' (1961).
11 The coinage of the term is usually attributed to Zora Neale Hurston, a member of the group.
12 Denigrate: 'To blacken (especially a reputation)' (*CED*). The word is derived, again, from the Latin *niger*.

'Yidden' in the plural, or a singular **Yid**. But among those hostile to the Jews – and there have been one or two over the years – variations on the word 'Yid' became a term of abuse in whichever European country they congregated. In Britain, large numbers of Jews entered the country in the late nineteenth century, and it wasn't long before 'Yid' became widely used, though not always with abusive intent. But, in a triumphant turnaround, modern, secular Jews have reappropriated the word, most notably in the case of the fans of Tottenham Hotspur Football Club, who have been referring to themselves proudly as the 'Yid Army' since the 1970s. It's now almost synonymous with 'Spurs fans' – certainly among rival supporters – even though Jews are not demographically dominant on the terraces.

Pride and prejudice

When Oscar Wilde's *The Importance of Being Earnest* opened in London on Valentine's Day, 1895, he was a national treasure. And yet within 100 days, Wilde, aged forty, was ruined and facing a court case. The reason was that for the previous two years Wilde had been having an affair with Lord Alfred 'Bosie' Douglas. When Bosie's father, the Marquess of Queensbury (originator of the rules of boxing), found out, he was apoplectic, and left a calling card at the Cadogan Club with the words: 'To Oscar Wilde, posing as a Somdomite' [*sic*]. Although he misspelt it, perhaps owing to his heightened emotions that day, we know what he meant.

Sodom, as discussed earlier (see page 226), was a man's town that loved to party. But homosexuals have had almost every term of abuse thrown at them over the years. The word **poof**[13] was just starting to be used in Oscar Wilde's time, and **faggot** came into widespread use in the USA after the First World War. In 1966 the *New Statesman*

---

13 Probably a corruption of 'puff': 'An effeminate man; a male homosexual.'

wrote that 'The American word "faggot" is making advances here over our own more humane "**queer**".'

Several others are used in Frederic Raphael's 1960 novel *The Limits of Love*: 'Great thing about **gay** people…' 'Gay?' Tessa said. 'Bent, queer, you know. Homosexual.' The word 'gay' was obviously unfamiliar at the time, but had been prison slang for 'homosexual' since the 1930s. Christopher Isherwood (1904–86) used 'queer' in his classic 1939 novel *Goodbye to Berlin*: 'Men dressed as women? … Do you mean they're queer?'

The first person to try to return control to the hands of the host community may have been the radical writer Paul Goodman with his 1969 essay 'The Politics of Being Queer'. Lesbians, meanwhile, were reassessing terms such as **dyke**, and these days that word can be a term of abuse or a simple declaration of identity, depending on the motivation of the speaker. After the shock of Aids, a greater sense of solidarity entered the gay community, and cheaply derisory terms, such as **carpet-muncher** and **pillow-chewer**, began to lose their capacity to hurt.

'Queer' has come into its own as Channel 4 proved with its screening of *Queer as Folk* (2002) and the US series *Queer Eye for the Straight Guy* (2004). At the time of writing the Amazon website has fifty-four books with 'queer' and 'politics' in the title. Not so **bent**.[14] **Coming out** used to describe the ritual of a young woman being launched into society and thus on to the marriage market. 'Miss Price had not been brought up to the trade of coming out,' wrote Jane Austen in *Mansfield Park* (1814). Towards the end of the 1960s, 'coming out' began to mean 'stating publicly' that one was homosexual.

In 1990 the *Los Angeles Times* and the *Guardian* newspapers were reporting that some gay activists in both the USA and the UK had instigated a campaign of outing prominent homosexuals who might

---

14 First cited in the *OED* in c.1374, by Geoffrey Chaucer. With homosexual meaning in 1959.

not want their sexual preferences to be made public. But a year later, 'outing' had spread to, for example, the Bald Urban Liberation Brigade of New York City, whose shock tactics (posting flyers) threatened to expose celebrities with toupées that they refused to acknowledge. Marketing and advertising companies are keen to catch some of the pink pound, a term first used in connection with the economic clout of the gay community in 1984.

Sticks and stones...

The words in this chapter represent language at its sharpest. Even typing some of them feels strange. Many have been created deliberately to cause maximum offence. And yet, as the last section shows, words, unlike missiles, can be sent back to their place of origin with their meaning completely rewritten. This represents the final act of revenge by the supposedly injured party, and it happens when the word is embraced and defused by the whole community. The world of abuse is one of the most dynamic and changeable in linguistics: new formations are coming and going with amazing speed because they depend on novelty to achieve their effect. Once we have got used to them, they lose their sting.

We haven't dealt at length with the cadre of words that has been turned on society's handicapped people, but one example is **spaz**, a shortened form of 'spastic', which was hurled at unfortunate victims, able-bodied or not. The word has, of course, been reappropriated by disabled people. A few years ago, society decided that the word 'spastic' was too hurtful, though, and we were encouraged to use alternatives, such as 'differently skilled' and 'mentally or physically challenged'. At the same time, the British Spastics Society lent its authority to the campaign by changing its name to Scope. It was a brave effort, but it didn't take some playground wag long to come up with a new term of abuse: **scope**.

Some of our favourite terms of abuse have a more matey lyricism about them that reduces the force of their invective. Take the word **wazzock**. No one is going to take someone to court for calling them a 'wazzock': it's not a high-octane term of abuse. It just means someone who is a little bit silly or annoying, or both. Its northern bluntness is appealing, and it achieves its effect through its combination of familiar sounds. The 'wazz' contrasts ironically with the swiftness of 'whizz', and the ending '–ock' reminds us of other words like **pillock**. You might think they were equally ancient terms of abuse, but whereas 'pillock', as we have seen, is first attested from 1535, 'wazzock' is first attributed to the comedian Mike Harding ('you cloth-eared wazzock') in his 1984 book *When the Martians Land in Huddersfield*.

Subsequently, the word has spawned the verb **to wazz**, rhyming with 'has', i.e. 'to piss'. The *OED* writes 'Origin unknown' against 'wazzock', but this author's private theory is that if you scrunched up the word **wiseacre** – first noted in 1595, meaning, among other things, 'a foolish person with an air or affectation of wisdom' – and then straightened it out again, it might make a sound very like 'wazzock'.

'Wazzock' is one of those words whose sound defines - or limits - itself. It's a silly-sounding word (you wouldn't want your plane flown by a wazzock, even if you didn't know exactly what it was). F-words and C-words sound shocking: that's their job. Daft words *sound* silly. Occasionally one gets away, such as **wrangler**, which might not immediately suggest its eighteenth-century meaning of an undergraduate with a first-class honours degree in Mathematics from Cambridge University, but that's one of the exceptions. Most words do a pretty good job of meaning exactly what they sound like. The next chapter tests that statement, to an even more extreme degree.

chapter ten

TO ER IS HUMAN
IS HUMAN

OH (pre 1925) could indicate,
among other things,
"SURPRISE, FRUSTRATION,
DISCOMFORT, <u>LONGING</u>,
DISAPPOINTMENT, SORROW,
RELIEF, hesitation."

To Er... is Human

Some dogs look like their owners. Some words sound like their meanings. When you make a twig **snap**, or hear leaves **rustling**, the verbs that describe those activities have an uncanny knack of copying the activity that is taking place. Snaps have been around for just over 500 years: rustles for a hundred years longer. Both fall into a vaguely slapstick category of English language words. Not content with meaning whatever they mean, they have to go and act the word out for you with their very sound. There is, mercifully, one word that embraces all this strenuous activity rather more efficiently than I have been able to express so far, and it would be the literal truth to say that the Greeks have a word for it: in fact they have two words. The noun *onoma* means 'name', and the verb *poiein* means 'to do'. Put them together (in ancient Latin) and filter them through a little mediaeval French and you come up, in around 1553, with the word **onomatopoeia**. It's a word that gets out there and explains itself. We shall be exploring many such words in this chapter.

Sounds like

Onomatopoeic words are the most touchy-feely class of words in the language. They get out on the campaign trail and work for their usage, which is why so many of them are firm favourites among young and old. But there are many different elements of a word that make us like it. In some cases our response to a word may be purely emotional (mama), perhaps cultural (Picasso), or even professional (client contact). In other cases, it's just the sound that appeals to us, and onomatopoeic words are particularly pleasing in this respect. These are words such as **squelch** and **thud,** which, according to the *CCD*, are 'imitative of the sound of the noise or action designated'. Perhaps onomatopoeic words are the ones they give to L-plate lexicographers, since their etymology takes them on a stroll through the alphabet, from **boohoo** (*c.*1525) to **pop** (*c.*1386) and **whizz** (pre-1547). It's also nice to see so childish a word as 'boohoo' (spelt 'bo ho, bo ho!') admitted to the language via the works of an early poet laureate, John Skelton (*c.*1460–1529).

Cat lovers might be interested to know that **miaow** has twenty-one alternative spellings, and that the sound cats make is roughly the same everywhere in the world. If only other animals were so consistent. Pigs go **oink** in Britain, but *groin groin* in France, *knor* in the Netherlands, *xrju-xrju* in Russia, *chrum chrum kwik* in Poland, *röf-röf* in Hungary and *būbū* in Japan.

Did onomatopoeia help us to speak? This is the 'ding-dong' theory favoured by some linguistics experts, which claims that we make sounds that mimic those of the natural world around us. We hear the rain and say **pitter-patter**; we hear birds and say **tweet-tweet**; we hear a snake and say **hiss**. It must apply the other way round too. A dog's world is also onomatopoeic, or – as it's shorter – echoic. Dog wants to go for a walk: **woof woof.** Master not interested: **shhhh.** Master gives in: **sighs,** gets up, opens door (**creak**), closes door (**slam**), feet and paws **crunch** on the gravel, dog does a pee (**tinkle-tinkle**). A car **zooms** towards them. Dog sees cat (**yelp/yowl**), gives chase and – **beep** – **screech** – very nearly ends up as a nasty **squidge** in the road.

It sounds like something out of a children's comic, and if you look at one, it's patently true that the writers can't get enough of strange sounds. The *Dandy*, *Beano* and many other well-known comics have produced some of the finest interjections ever written. The great 'Desperate Dan', for example, experiences or gives voice to a broad range of exclamations, including **niff**, **sploosh**, **whoosh** and **yarf**. Whenever he produces or provokes these sounds, however interchangeable they might seem, they perfectly complement the illustration that they accompany. In reality, few will end up in a dictionary. They're one-offs that light up the page for a moment before sinking and dying. Perhaps the writers have a library of exclamatory sounds that they can turn to, but making them up is probably half the fun of the job. In fact, it's also fun to imagine how they came up with such gems as **krung**, **foosh**, **phft** and **mumph**.

We don't know how many of these letter-sounds are coined each year, but there are many, and some have actually made it into dictionaries. The provenance of 'niff', for example, meaning 'to emit an unpleasant odour'), is discussed at some length in the *OED*. Is it formed by removing the first letter of **sniff**? But 'sniff' doesn't have the same meaning as 'niff'. Perhaps, then, it's from **whiff**? We can't be sure, though the *OED* adds: 'It is also remarkable that *niff*, as a verb, is first recorded from a school in Derby, but as a noun, is attributed by Joseph Wright's *English Dialect Dictionary* to Sussex. This perhaps points to wider, undocumented distribution in regional English.' The source in which the word was found is John S. Farmer's *Public–School Word Book* (1900), which lists it as '*Niff*, verb (Derby), to smell'.

The British public schools[1] have contributed their own very special stock of favourite words to the English language. The following series of exclamations appeared in the *Magnet* comic for

---

[1] More often called 'independent schools' these days, most of them date back to the eighteenth and particularly the nineteenth centuries. They were called 'public' to distinguish them from 'private' education, which was done either with home tutors or through the church.

boys in November 1909: 'Oh!' roared Bunter, as Bulstrode's heavy boot biffed on him. 'Ow! Yah! Yarooh!' The *OED* decided that the word **yarooh** was 'A humorous stylized representation of a cry of pain', and they correctly identified it as being pretty much the unique property of the 'Fat Owl of the Remove', aka Billy Bunter. For less expensively educated children, a simple **ouch**, dating from no earlier than 1838, would have to do.

Linguistics experts are still trying to understand why some groups of letters affect us in different ways. Slip, slide, slither, slouch, slant, slash and others sound as if they are being dragged downhill by their own weight. Snag, snarl, sneak, sneer, snide, sniff (that word again), snigger and snivel all sound a bit dodgy. Swagger, sway, sweep, swing and swoop sound as if they can't stop shifting from side to side. And glamour, glare, glaze, gleam, glimmer, glint, glisten, glitter, glossy and glow are all a bit shiny: the Essex words of the language.

Feels like

It's amazing what difference a letter can make. Take three vowels: A, E and O and add an H to each of them. **Eh**, 'An ejaculation of sorrow', was first noted in 1567, but it is ante-dated by **Oh** (pre-1525), which could indicate, among other things, 'surprise, frustration, discomfort, longing, disappointment, sorrow, relief, hesitation'. The *OED* even goes to the trouble of speculating that the word **Ah**[2] may be derived from the French *A* or *Ah*.

If we wrote down an accurate typescript of our daily speech, 'eh', 'oh' and 'ah' would be among our most common expressions. They

---

2 'An exclamation expressing, according to the intonation, various emotions, as (1) Sorrow, lamentation, regret, passing into the regretful expression of a vain wish (2) Surprise, wonder, admiration (3) Entreaty, appeal, remonstrance… (4) Dislike, aversion… (5) Opposition, objection… (6) Realization, discovery, inspiration.'

are the true favourites of our working minds. But how would you define **mm** in a context such as, 'Mm! What's that smell?' 'Expressing satisfaction, approval, or assent' opines the *OED*. And how about 'You really want this job, mm?' The *OED* would classify that as 'expressing hesitation, reflection, or inarticulate interrogation'.

Nonsense words

The sounds of the world are reliable: they're our stabilizers. Perhaps they remind us of a time when, as babies, we knew what things looked like and what sound they made, but not their names: clocks still go tick, even with a quartz crystal inside. Spike Milligan's nonsense poem 'On the Ning Nang Nong' was funny and unsettling because straight from the first line – 'In the Ning Nang Nong where the cows go **bong**' – we knew that we were in a strange world where things didn't make the sounds we expected them to make. No doubt that was partly due to Milligan's harrowing experiences during the Second World War, when he and his fellow soldiers never knew what they were going to hear next. When peace came, he incorporated some of those wartime sounds – **wheeeh, boom, owwww** and others – into *The Goon Show* (1951–1960), a radio programme that was a sort of adult aural comic.

Some silly noises have been put to use in the commercial world, with highly successful results. Think of Rice Krispies going **snap, crackle** and **pop** and Alka-Seltzer going **plink plink fizzzz**. In these contexts the words are amusing, but they must be chosen with care. 'Snap' is funny in a breakfast cereal: not so funny with a broken wrist.

Many English Victorian eccentrics had a language of their own too, though none so well developed as that of the Oxford mathematician Charles Lutwidge Dodgson, better known as Lewis Carroll. In fact, the nearest to an everyday word we have inherited from his made-up lexicon is the verb **to chortle**, which is probably a blend of 'chuckle' and 'snort', from the poem 'Jabberwocky'.[3] He did the same with 'slithy' (lithe and slimy) and 'mimsy' (flimsy and miserable), acknowledging in the text that these were 'portmanteau words', i.e. two meanings packed up into one word.

The first stanza of 'Jabberwocky' is as follows:

> 'Twas brillig, and the slithy toves
> Did gyre and gimble in the wabe:
> All mimsy were the borogoves,
> And the mome raths outgrabe.

Carroll's nonsense verse is pure, inspired poetry. It also goes to the heart of the nature of lexicography. How, after all, can anyone properly translate the verses if none of the essential words has any literary precedent?

Compared to the Jabberwocky, the adventures of Bilbo Baggins, Gandalf and company, first in *The Hobbit* (1937) and then *The Lord of the Rings* (1954–5), were very serious indeed: the fate of the world was at stake. J.R.R. Tolkien's experience in the First World War, and his in-depth knowledge of the vocabulary of Middle English, which had been put to such good use during the preparation of the first edition of The *OED* (he worked as a staff member from 1917–20), must have helped him ensure that the word-frame of his two most famous works felt so authentic. His language is a mixture of studied elaboration and pure invention. For example, when he writes that the Great Ring was 'hot when I first took it, as hot as a **glede**', he is spot on, since 'glede', also spelt 'gleed', is an archaic word for a 'live coal or ember', which had fallen from use by the nineteenth century,

---

but was first seen in the Lindisfarne Gospels from around the year AD 950. But does the word, as used by Tolkien, have a life outside the books, or will it merely fade away, like the **kerplatz** and **yubyubyub** of Desperate Dan's victims? That is the question facing most dictionary compilers, and they resolve it simply by waiting – usually five years, maybe a bit less these days, to see what's left when all the noise has died down. A word has to bed itself into the language. Usage is what counts.

Words, like cats, go missing. They fall from grace and drop out of sight. We miss them, of course, but only the most hardened lexicographer would think of sticking a note to a tree with the message 'MISSING, in print, since 1827. Answers to the name **Humdudgeon**. Means "an imaginary illness". If found, please return.' Humdudgeon has dropped from sight and is unlikely to return, because words are lubricated by usage. Like humans, they need proper exercise to keep fit. Sometimes, too, another word comes along that seems to do the job better. Maybe this explains the more recent success of **Munchausen Syndrome**, named after Karl Friedrich Hieronymus, Baron von Münchhausen (1720–97), the original inventor of extravagant stories. His talent for fabrication is recorded as far back as 1823 in *Harper's Magazine* ('What a Munchausen tale!..') But it received official medical backing – 'a symptom in which a person feigns injury of illness in order to obtain hospital treatment' (CED) – in *The Lancet* in 1951. The next chapter will cast its net ever wider, in search of words that have dropped into, and out of, fashion.

chapter eleven

CHANGING
TIMES
CHANGING
TERMS

The first reference to
A MOBILE PHONE
– which was probably
the size of a phone box –
APPEARED IN 1945.

Changing Times, Changing Terms

This chapter traces the development of some words that have come to be associated with a particular era. Using a dictionary, it's easy to see when they came within the radar of the editors for the first time, but sometimes a different story emerges. Many fall into predictable patterns: during times of war, it's inevitable that certain words crop up. But words continue to surprise us: they're older – or younger – than they appear. Why do certain words keep developing, when others are dead and buried within a matter of months?

We love it when we get a new word: it's a new toy to play with. And linguistics experts get very excited when a word can be dated precisely. Take the word **dude**, which has been cited by the *OED* from in the *North Adams* (Massachusetts) *Transcript*[1] of 24 June 1883: 'The new coined word "dude" … has travelled over the country with a great deal of rapidity since but two months ago it grew into general use in New York.' When first introduced, it meant 'a name given in ridicule to a man affecting an exaggerated fastidiousness in dress, speech and deportment'. A bit of a **dandy**,[2] in other words, and most certainly not from the West Coast, although he might have enjoyed staying on a ranch for his holidays. The term 'dude ranch' (pre-1921) was developed specially to accommodate this sort of person. Since its coining, the word 'dude' has lost some of its fashion-consciousness. Popularized through black culture in the 1930s, it has become a general term of affection. Some would say that there is no greater

---

1 A local newspaper.
2 The *OED* has 'jack-a-dandy' from 1659: maybe this was a shortened form. Cited in a song around 1780, defined 'A man greatly concerned with smartness of dress.' (*CCD*)

compliment than being described as a **cool** 'dude', an adjective given a new currency by the jazz saxophonist Charlie Parker (1920–55) when he released the song 'Cool Blues' in 1947. Parker was one of the key figures in **bebop**, 'a type of jazz characterized by complex harmony and rhythms' (*Oxford Encylopedic Dictionary*). 'The bebop people have a language of their own,' wrote a dazzled *New Yorker* writer in 1948. 'Their expressions of approval include "cool"!'

Buzzwords impress themselves on our minds by encapsulating a topical interest or fashion in a memorable way, perhaps from the sound.[3] The current media obsession with celebrity – a very broad church, encompassing everyone from **superstars**[4] to **wannabes**[5] means that the word **celeb** is ubiquitous. Interestingly, though, it was first spotted in a Nebraska newspaper in 1913. Perhaps it was something to do with the burgeoning Hollywood film industry, which coined the term **It-girl**[6] a few years later ('it' being a euphemism for 'sex' or 'sexy'). But it transpired that Rudyard Kipling (1865–1936) had beaten them to it in 1904, when he wrote in *Traffics and Discoveries*: "Tisn't beauty, so to speak, nor good talk necessarily. It's just It. Some women'll stay in a man's memory if they once walk down a street.' It-girls have been with us in one form or another ever since, and like some of them, certain words don't show their age. Let's take a quick tour through the last 100 years or so to see which words may be older than we think and which ones had a relatively short use-by date (like certain other It-girls).

---

3 The *OED* defines a 1616 citation of the verb 'to buzz' as 'To spread as a rumour, with whispering or busy talk.' The word 'buzzword' was first used in Harvard Business School in 1946.
4 Superstars were invented by the Hollywood movie industry. The earliest *OED* citation is from 1925.
5 The first *OED*-cited wannabe is not what you might expect: it comes from a 1981 *Newsweek* article about people who want to be (i.e. 'wannabe') surfers. This was followed by 'wannabe gang members' (1985) and the pop-star 'Madonna-wannabes' (1986).
6 Clara Bow (1905–65), the American actress, sex symbol and archetypal Twenties flapper (see page 258), was the first It-girl. When she starred in the film *It* (1927), the *LA Times* and others dubbed her 'the "It" girl'.

The Twenties

During the 1920s, many of Britain's favourite words were transatlantic imports. This was no accident, since the axis of geopolitical power was turning that way too, but cinema and music were the biggest sources of new words. The **bee's knees**, like the **sparrow's kneecap**, used to mean something so tiny as to be almost invisible, but the 1920s changed all that. The 'bee's knees', like the **cat's whiskers** (or **cat's pyjamas**) came to mean 'an excellent person or thing' (*Oxford Encyclopedic Dictionary*). It also gave us the phrase **blind date** (1925) and to **carry a torch**, which *Vanity Fair* magazine defined that same year: 'When a fellow "carries the torch" it doesn't imply that he is "lit up" or drunk, but girl-less. His steady has quit him for another or he is lonesome for her.' Another of America's most famous writers from that period, Dorothy Parker (1893–1967), is credited with creating the phrase **scaredy-cat**[7] in 1933.

The first reference to **pop music** dates from 1921, though Bill Haley and the Comets didn't 'Rock around the Clock' until 1956. **Wizard**, in the sense of 'good', was first spotted in 1922, in *Babbitt*, the acclaimed novel by Sinclair Lewis about the moral hole in the middle of middle America, and the British writer J.B. Priestley (1894–1984) used it in 1943, when he wrote: 'The roofs are nicely camouflaged, and the stiff coloured netting … is a wizard show'. William Brown, the wonderfully naughty boy created by Richmal Crompton,[8] exclaimed in 1954, 'Gosh, that party of Ginger's last Christmas was wizard.' It was also a favourite word of Jennings and Derbyshire in the delightful school series by the late Anthony Buckeridge (1912–2004). The opposite was 'ozard'. How different,

---

7 'It's so nice to meet a man who isn't scaredy-cat about catching my beri-beri,' she wrote in *After Such Pleasures* (1933).
8 Real name Richmal Samuel Lanburn (1890–1969), a Classics teacher until he contracted polio in 1923. (*Chambers Dictionary of Quotations*)

you might think, from a much more recent expression of approval: **wicked**. A term coined on the streets of the Bronx, Harlem or South Central LA? Well, this quotation is certainly American: 'Tell 'em to play "Admiration"!' shouted Sloane … 'Phoebe and I are going to shake a wicked calf.' That line comes, in fact, from a stalwart of preppy – as opposed to homeboy – America: F. Scott Fitzgerald in *This Side of Paradise*, and it was written in 1920.

The musical show *Nifties* of 1923 by W. Collier and S. Bernard popularized the word **nifty** – 'Smart, stylish, attractive' according to the *OED*. It is a very welcome addition to the language, but it's a shame that its origin is unknown. The 1920s were a time of experimentation, and in 1928 the *Daily Telegraph* reported that a favourite example among high-school children was '**necking** in motor-cars in dark roads with the lights turned off'. The word 'necking', which means 'kissing', was in use until at least 1999 because the *OED* illustrates the word with a quotation ('Toyah is being necked by a hunk'[9]) from, of all places, the *Sunday Sport*.

But there are many other expressions from the 1920s, the decade of the **flappers**.[10] B. Mantle in *Best Plays of 1919–20* wrote that '"Jerry" Lamar is one of a band of pretty little salamanders known to Broadway as "gold-diggers", because they "dig" for the gold of their gentlemen friends and spend it being good to their mothers and their pet dogs.' That was the first metaphorical use of **gold-digger**, a term that probably gave some people the **heebie-jeebies**, though it's not known where these come from. The first written reference to 'heebie-jeebies' is from 1923 and is also, of course, American.

9 There is an earlier use from 1825, but only in the sense of 'embracing, caressing'. Tongues came later.
10 Flappers were 1920s good-time girls who kicked their legs up when they danced, causing the fringe on their skirt hems to flap.

The Thirties

A report in the *New York Times* on 25 February 1933 referred to **supermarkets**, which, it said, had sprung up in the previous two years and were already challenging 'both corporate chains and independent wholesale grocers'. In March it reported that one large supermarket in New Jersey had been taking $100,000 a week. In Britain, the *Spectator* of 25 September 1959 seemed to have got the point in a piece about supermarkets 'whose whole economy depends on people going in to buy a can of beans and coming out with a dazed expression and three pounds' worth of groceries'.

The rise of the supermarket is one of the most striking aspects of modern life on both sides of the Atlantic. In the UK, Marks and Spencer (founded 1926) has been experiencing a series of boardroom crises, though it can always take some comfort from the fact that its nickname **Marks and Sparks** earned its place in the *OED* in 1964 in the *Sunday Times*. It's an achievement that our other major food stores – from Waitrose and Sainsbury to Tesco and Asda – have been unable to match.

At the beginning of the twenty-first century we hear a lot about the growing habit of **dumbing down**,[11] but the expression has been around since 1933.[12] The word **racism** was also coined around that time.[13] On a lighter note, in 1935 American shoppers were the first to enjoy **Muzak**. Its inventor, shop-owner U.V. 'Bing' Muscio, told

---

11 'To simplify or reduce the intellectual content of (esp. published or broadcast material) in order to make it appealing or intelligible to a larger number of people.'
12 1933: H.T. Webster in *Forum*: 'I can cheer, too, for the Hollywood gag men in conference on a comedy which has been revealed as too subtle when they determine they must dumb it down.'
13 1936: L. Dennis *The Coming American Fascism* 'If ... it be assumed that one of our values should be a type of racism which excludes certain races from citizenship, then the plan of execution should provide for the annihilation, deportation, or sterilization of the excluded races.'

the *New York Times* in 1974, 'We needed a catchy name and the best-known trade name at that time was Kodak. So we just combined Kodak and music and got Muzak.'

The Forties

The 1940s gave us words reflecting changes that were social, technological and political. The first **mobile home** appeared in 1940, the **Wonderbra** in 1947, and the first reference to a **mobile phone** – which was probably the size of a phone box – appeared in 1945. In 1948, worried about television and politics of every stripe, George Orwell published his creepily powerful novel *1984*. From this we got a whole raft of expressions that seem ever more relevant: **Big Brother, doublethink, Room** 101. The expression 'Big Brother is watching you' came to denote complete authoritarian control. 'Room 101' was the room where dissidents were taken where they were confronted with that which they most feared. 'Doublethink' is an axiom of Orwell's totalitarian state, defined as 'The mental capacity to accept as equally valid two entirely contrary opinions or beliefs.' All these words have been appropriated in other contexts to describe suitably 'Orwellian' situations (such as those he might have devised) – from faceless bureaucracy to a police state.

The *OED* records almost three hundred new words entering the language per year during the Second World War. Many were what you might have expected from a state of war: the first **malfunction** happened in 1939, the first **jeep** appeared in 1941, as did **boffin**. **Arty** – short for 'artillery' – appeared in 1942, and the word **genocide** dates from 1944. The world's first **loud-hailer** went into service in 1941, and, not entirely unconnected, the world's first **marriage guidance counsellor** also dates from that year. In 1941 a **sprog** was army slang for a new recruit. By 1945, if the marriage guidance counsellor's advice had helped and the marriage had survived, 'sprog' meant youngster, child or baby.

A 1941 travel guide to Havana contains the first reference in print to **nightclubbing**, and, if you could wait just one more year, the *American Thesaurus of Slang* records the first **freebie** from 1942. You might have got in had you been wearing the first **zoot suit**, whose existence is recorded that same year in the song of the same name by Ray Gilbert and Bob O'Brien, 'I want a Zoot Suit with a reat pleat, with a drape shape.' **Smart casual** didn't appear until 1945, in the *New York Times*.

Telly, the shortened version of 'television', appears in print in 1942, three years before **bebop** (see page 256). 'Bebop', originally the name of a recording by jazz musician Dizzy Gillespie, was popular among **teenagers**, and 'teenagers' arrived on the pages of *Popular Science Monthly* in 1941, the same year that **existentialism** was translated into English by the philosopher Julius Kraft.

The Fifties

In the 1950s something irritating was described as **bugging** you, but if things were 'good', they were **cooking**. An enjoyable experience was a **blast**, as the editors of Harold Wentworth and Stuart Berg Flexner's 1960 *Dictionary of American Slang* noted: 'Maybe it's a little early in the day for their first blast,' meaning 'wild party' or 'good time'. They also noted that 'blast' had meant 'a strong gust of wind' ever since around the year 1000, and Chaucer in *Troilus and Criseyde* (1374) had written of a 'Reed that boweth dowen with every blaste'. It also came to mean 'a strong reprimand', but that was fully 953 years after its first use. When not having a 'blast', 1950s teenagers might have thought things were a **drag**. This is actually a fifteenth-century Old English word related to 'draw' that acquired a variety of meanings on its journey to the 1950s. These included a 'bonnet-denting car race', 'to dredge a river-bed', 'a major street or road' (as in 'the main drag'), 'women's clothes worn by men', 'a smelly thing that hounds will follow', 'a deep inhalation of a cigarette', 'a back-spin in cricket' and prison slang for a 'three-month sentence'.

In the 1950s, if you weren't **in the know** (first cited 1883), you were in **Nowheresville**, as a 1959 quotation from the *Washington Post* attests: 'Legally speaking, the Coffee and Confusion Club, the beat generation's contribution to Foggy Bottom,[14] was in Nowheresville yesterday.' It's not known for certain why this should have been the case, and the club no longer exists, but if it had waited another few years, it would probably have become fashionable again and been described – as Jack Kerouac put it in his beat novel *On the Road* (1957) – as **hip** (origin unknown).

For a while in the 1950s we fell in love with **U** and **non**-U words (U standing for upper class). The distinctions were invented by the British linguistics expert Alan Ross as a serious exercise, the idea being that people revealed their class and social aspirations through the vocabulary they used. Although his article appeared in an obscure journal, it came to the attention of the novelist Nancy Mitford (1904–73), who had great fun playing on England's uneasy class consciousness. Not surprisingly, it all went very badly for the middle classes, who fretted about whether they should be holding their 'napkins' or 'serviettes'.

---

14 One of Washington DC's oldest (nineteenth-century) areas, also the location of – and therefore a nickname for – the US Department of State.

U	Non-U
Bike	Cycle
Luncheon	Dinner
Vegetables	Greens
House	Home
Sick	Ill
Looking-glass	Mirror
Mad	Mental
Lavatory paper	Toilet paper
Rich	Wealthy

Along with social unease, the 1950s were the decade of the Cold War as characterized by **brinkmanship,** a word coined in 1956 by America's Secretary of State John Foster Dulles: the *New York Times* claimed that the US Democrat politician Adlai Stevenson 'derided [Dulles] for boasting of his brinkmanship – the art of bringing us to the edge of the nuclear abyss.' There is one earlier reference, in fact, from 1840, from the political writer John Stuart Mill: 'They had been brought to the brink of war.'

The Sixties

The Cold War continued on through the 1960s, bringing the world to within spitting distance of nuclear annihilation. Young people responded to the insanities of the adult world by living for the moment and lashing back at the perceived repression their parents' society. A growing sexual awareness, rock and roll music and the glamour of international fame led to a completely new and different sort of mania: **Beatlemania.** Combining biting wit with tuneful melodies, the Beatles' level of celebrity was unprecedented for a rock group. As well as becoming fashion icons, their thick Merseyside accents only added to their lustre, as did their distinctive vocabulary. The word **grotty** ('nasty or unattractive' – *CCD*) is credited to John Burke who wrote the novelization of the Beatles' 1964 film *A Hard Day's Night*, though the credit should go to Alun Owen, who wrote the screenplay. (The passage in the book reads: 'I wouldn't be seen dead in them. They're dead grotty.' Marshall stared. 'Grotty?' 'Yeah – grotesque.') The Beatles popularized many other sayings. The expression 'that's the gear' had been used to indicate approval since 1925 at least, but the Beatles made **gear** even more popular. The related expression **fab** – an abbreviation of 'fabulous' – is quoted in the supplement to Eric Partridge's *Dictionary of Slang* in 1961, but in the Beatles' mouths it achieved unprecedented prominence.

When the Beatles first sprang to fame, they were known affectionately as the 'Fab Four'. 'These lovable **"moptops"**', as the *New York Herald Tribune* referred to them – on account of their 'shaggy-dog' hairstyles – in February 1964, were cheeky but presentable. Meanwhile, other groups like the Rolling Stones, and the enigmatic Bob Dylan in America, were of more concern to the guardians of conventional mores. As the decade developed, and hairstyles grew longer, consciousnesses expanded under the influence of the prevailing social, musical and pharmaceutical trends. Trouser legs opened up into **flares**, and **hippy** clothes and **love-ins** came into vogue. **Psychedelia** was first named in a 1967 issue of the music magazine *Melody Maker*. **Pot**, the slang term for marijuana, is pre-war, and **pot-head** dates from 1959, as does the word **trip** – whether good or bad – for a hallucinogenic experience, but **acid**, the slang term for LSD, is cited from 1966. The aim of a drug experience was, of course, to get **high**, a term that had been in use to describe narcotic intoxication since the 1930s. On a 'bad trip', one might experience a **freak-out** (cited in the *Daily Telegraph*, August 1966). Or you might just wake up the next morning with a bad headache.

The Seventies

The 1970s started with **Watergate**[15] and ended with **punk**.[16] In political terms, they began with Nixon and Heath and ended with Reagan and Thatcher. In 1970 the proto-feminist Kate Millett wrote in *Sexual Politics* that 'A **sexual revolution** would require … an end of traditional sexual inhibitions and taboos.' Margaret Thatcher didn't promise that, but she was elected nonetheless after the **three-day week** put paid to the Labour government. Punk was great, **karaoke** was terrible, but punk is more or less dead and karaoke is still very much with us. **Trainers** came in, and so did **hypermarkets**,[17] the better to sell them.

The interest in drug culture led many people to explore eastern philosophies or religions like Buddhism and the Hare Krishna movement. The idea of using meditation to find oneself, and the search for peace (as in the slogan 'Make Love Not War') marked an ironic contrast with the violence and savagery of the war happening at the same time in Vietnam. Few people now use the expression **mind-fuck** to denote either 'an imaginary act of sexual intercourse' or 'a disturbing or revelatory experience' with anything like the frequency that its creators, novelist Erica Jong and rock writer Lester Bangs, used it in 1966 and 1971. But good luck to them if they do.

---

15 The name of a hotel in the Foggy Bottom district of Washington DC.
16 The word meant 'prostitute' in sixteenth-century England.
17 Hyper: the adjective was first cited in 1942. The *Guardian* described the first hypermarket in 1970 as 'a gigantic supermarket'.

The Eighties

Sometimes, it seems, we prefer to play safe. In a poll of favourite words by the *Sunday Times* in 1980, first place was won jointly by **melody** and **velvet**. Third place was shared between – hankies out now – **gossamer** and **crystal**, followed by **autumn, peace, tranquil, twilight, murmur, caress, mellifluous** and **whisper**. (Honestly, what were these people thinking?) Twenty-five years later, in September 2000, a BBC poll asked the same question. The winning word was **serendipity**;[18] **quidditch**[19] came in second, and – in a bracing victory for Anglo-Saxon straight talk – **bollocks** and **fuck** (see Chapter 9, pages 231 and 222) held joint ninth place. How times change.

In September 1981 the class struggle reared its head again, but this time U and non-U played no part in it. The *Guardian* reported: 'A couple of expressions have only come my way in the last month or so. One is **street wise** (though the *OED* has evidence of this from 1965) and the other **street cred**.' 'Street wise' means 'wise in the ways of modern urban life' (*Oxford Encyclopedic Dictionary*). To be 'street wise' meant that one knew how to look after oneself in an urban environment, originally American. 'Street credibility' was a post-punk version of non-U in which what counted was wearing the right clothes, seeing the right bands and having the right accent. In 1985 the *Sunday Times* claimed that 'Neil Kinnock, the Labour leader, lives in a "street cred" west London semi' (i.e. a road that was close enough to a run-down area to be electorally attractive, but not so close that one's house could be broken into every other night), though it didn't help him much in the election.

'C'mon, we're going out for an Indian,' says a character in a 1982

---

18 'The faculty of making fortunate discoveries by accident' (*CCD*), coined by Horace Walpole from the Persian fairytale 'The Three Princes of Serendip', in which the three heroes possess this gift.
19 After the game invented by Harry Potter creator J.K. Rowling.

episode of the Mersey soap *Brookside*, and the rest of the nation followed suit. We love **going for an Indian,** and **curry** (see Chapter 6, page 162) has been a favourite part of the British diet for some time, so much so that in 1998 the *Goodness Gracious Me* comedy series turned the tables and created its most famous sketch, called 'Going for an English'. The *OED* notes that in 1290, 'to curry' meant 'to rub down or dress a horse with a comb', and 'the currying or dressing of leather' is attested from 1430. In both these cases it derives from the thirteenth-century French word *corroi* ('preparation' in a later, Anglo-French formation). Since then it has meant 'tickle' (1598) and 'stroke' (with flattery) (*c.*1394). Is this where the phrase to **curry favour** comes from? No, that's simply a mishearing of 'to curry favel'. 'Favel' comes from the French *fauvel,* derived from *fauve,* meaning 'fallow-coloured'. Fauvel is the name of a horse in the allegorical French novel *Roman de Fauvel* (1310), which relates the exploits of a horse that is devious and manipulative and widely admired by the humans in the story, who pamper him in the hope of exploiting his talents to further their own aims. It's not clear if this is the first occurrence of a fallow horse as the symbol of dishonesty or not. In the 1980s you might have been a **yuppie** who liked currying favour over a **power lunch,** or you might have been a Sloane Ranger (in fact coined in 1975) canoodling with your **toy boy.** All were hallmarks of the decade where unfettered capitalism, stock market speculation, privatization and the Tory party resurgence came together. The *Independent* noted in December 1988 that '"Radical" … no longer has rebellious or left-wing connotations but means … wonderful or remarkable'.

The Nineties

In the 1990s we stopped pretending that computers weren't winning and just gave in: they had won, hands down. In came **netiquette** (though first attested in 1982), a new code of **online** manners, **emails** and emoticons, e-conferences, e-cards, e-shopping, e-banking and – it was only a matter of time – e-dating.

In the office we might have been **hot-desking**.[20] In our spare time we might have been tempted to **large it** (enjoy ourselves). This shows how an adjective can be changed into a verb – something that would have made William Shakespeare proud, as he was fond of doing that himself (see Chapter 4, page 122). Contemporary culture first 'larged it' in print in 1995, but we certainly weren't the first to do so. 'The wind larged with us again,' is from 1662, with a nautical sense.

The anxiety about the coming end of the millennium was nicely caught in this quote from the *Independent* in 1990: 'After the Eighties and the Nineties, what should we be calling the next decade? The Noughties?' Lots of people made the same joke, but, then, it was a good joke.

The Noughties

So far, the first decade of the twenty-first century hasn't been that naughty. We'll **sex things up**, refer occasionally to the **axis of evil**, and worry about the phenomenon of **happy slapping**,[21] but we won't ever mention chavs again: we've already done it too many times. Besides, we're probably too busy **texting** (see Chapter 12, page 284) our friends to see if they've found any good deals on eBay.

---

20 The work practice in a busy office with more people than desks: employees work at a number of desks, instead of keeping to one. Intention: to keep staff on their toes. Result: reduces staff to nervous hysteria. First *OED* reference 1994.
21 Commonly known as the act of striking a stranger – often in a public area – by one or more people while an accomplice records the incident on a camera phone.

When you study the English language you meet words from all over the world and from all periods of recorded history. The words in this chapter have all made their mark. Some may not wear their years too well, but they're still here, and still competing for our attention. And the great thing about language is that the field is still wide open. A word can enter at any time, and if it hangs in there for a few years, there's a good chance that it will be noticed. After that, it's in for good. But what if you're unhappy with a word and don't think it does justice to what it describes? Take **boyfriend** and **girlfriend**, for example. Do they describe the relationship between two people in a way that reflects the modern world? Perhaps you could do better. You might have a word in mind, either worked out on your own or with friends or – just possibly – with your boyfriend or girlfriend. This new word will, you think, sweep away both the other words. You are confident that we will all love your new word because it does exactly what we'd want the new word to do: imply sympathy, acquaintance, sex, intimacy and a system of shared values. But how do you bring it to the attention of the editors of the *OED*? The next chapter has some suggestions.

chapter twelve

ORIGIN UNKNOWN

YOU MAY NOT BE
TOO <u>INTERESTED</u>
in the first recorded
usage of the verb

"BARF" but it matters:
EVERY WORD MATTERS.

Origin Unknown

The *OED* contains many words marked 'etymology unknown', or 'origin obscure' or 'uncertain'. This is either very good news if you like a chase, or frustrating if you like your ends neatly tied. While we know what most of these words mean, it's much trickier to say how they came to enter the language. The uncertainty could be over which language they came from before entering English, or quite which language they came from – out of the dark – over a thousand years ago. Norse? Danish? Icelandic? It's not always clear.

Here are some examples for word detectives. The origin of **toodle-oo** (goodbye) is unclear. The *OED* has an illustrative quotation from a 1907 copy of *Punch* magazine: '"Toodle-oo, old sport." Mr. Punch turned round at the amazing words and gazed at his companion.' The next quotation, from 1908, is from T.E. Lawrence, but he says **tootle 'oo**. The *OED* says: 'Origin unknown: perhaps from toot'. That meant 'an act of tooting' in 1641, in other words, a blast on a horn. The *OED* compares 'toodle-oo' to the 'echoic' **pip-pip**, which is the sound made by a motorist on the horn of the car before leaving. Perhaps the two processes, imitating car sounds, are similar.

Now take **boffin**. 'Numerous conjectures have been made about the origin of the word but all lack foundation,' said the *OED* in its 1989 second edition. We know its definition, however: in 1941 it meant an 'elderly naval officer', but by 1945 it was a back-room boy, 'a person engaged in scientific or technical research'. Could it perhaps be related to the word **buff**? Among the *OED*'s seven entries for the noun 'buff' are a blow, a buffalo, a piece of armour, a fellow and foolish talk, but there is also a mention of the buff-coloured uniform worn by volunteer firemen in New York City, cited from the 1934 edition of *Webster's Dictionary*. And it adds, 'Hence generally an enthusiast or specialist', which it traces back to a 1903 copy of the *New York Sun*: 'The Buffs are men and boys whose love of fires, fire-fighting and firemen is a predominant characteristic.' So we have pinned down one meaning, but without further documentary sources, we can't get much closer to explaining the origins of 'boffin'.

Can someone explain the origin of the word **gimmick**? The *OED* says it's US slang, origin unknown. The first reference is to the 1926 *Wise-Crack Dictionary* by George H. Maines and Bruce Grant. 'Gimmick: device used for making a fair game crooked.' We are then directed towards a November 1936 copy of *Words* magazine. 'The word "gimac" means a "gadget",' says the writer. 'It is an anagram of the word "magic", and is used by magicians the same way as others use the word "thing-a-ma-bob".'[1] Can you do better?

Other twentieth-century words that mystify us include **hype** and **skiffle**. Like 'gimmick', these date from 1926, but we can't pin them down any more accurately than that. **Jive**[2] emerged in 1928, while **jalopy** (an American slang term for a battered old motor car) and **jitter** came along in 1929, but we don't know where from. Could it be, as the upstart *Online Etymological Dictionary* suggests, that many old American cars were sent to Jalapa in Mexico? To have the **jitters** or be **jittery** meant 'to be nervous', but why? Why should 'jittery' connote nervous energy? Could it be related to **chitter**, an ancient – Chaucer uses it – parallel form to **chatter**? No doubt 'jitter' inspired **jitterbug**, an energetic dance developed to accompany the Cab Calloway song of the same name from 1934.

---

1 Variant of *thingumabob* or *thingamabob*: 'A person or thing the name of which is unknown, temporarily forgotten, or deliberately overlooked.' (*CCD*)
2 Jive: 'A style of lively and jerky dance, popular esp. in the 1940s and 1950s.' (*CCD*) See also Chapter 7, page 187.

The derivation of the word **patsy** is also mysterious. It's an American slang term, meaning 'a person who is easily taken advantage of, especially by being deceived, cheated, or blamed for something; a dupe, a scapegoat'. To support this the *OED* cites a book by H.F. Reddall, called *Fact, Fancy and Fable* (1889), which quotes the following story: 'A party of minstrels in Boston, about twenty years ago, had a performance … When the pedagogue asked in a rage, "Who did that?", the boys would answer, "Patsy Bolivar!" … The phrase … spread beyond the limits of the minstrel performance, and when a scapegoat was alluded to, it was in the name of "Patsy Bolivar"… the one who is always blamed for everything.' Despite this detail, the *OED* can't say it's that for sure.

Can it be any more certain about the origin of the 1930 noun **woggle**? This is known to be a variant on the much older **toggle**, but where did it come from? The first 'woggle' was commented on in a 1930 issue of the *Daily News* as follows: 'Woggles have now become an established part of Scout uniform, and I have seen some very good examples made by Scouts.' You would think, would you not, that a man-made organization such as the Scouts would have been able to supply name and rank for all its terms. Evidently, someone was not fully prepared.

We don't know how **snazzy** came to mean 'excellent; attractive; classy, stylish, flashy' in 1932, though it may have come about through a felicitous coupling of **snappy** and **jazzy**. Nor are we absolutely clear on how **calypso** came to mean a 'West Indian ballad or song in African rhythm, usually improvised to comment on a topic of current interest' in 1934. Can this possibility be related to Calypso, the treacherous sea nymph in Homer's *Odyssey*? It seems hard to justify the connection at present. Perhaps we'll have more luck with **pizzazz** – 'zest, vim, vitality, liveliness' and 'flashiness, showiness'. The word was recorded in 1937, and in March of that year *Harper's Bazaar* magazine defined it thus: 'Pizazz, to quote the editor of the *Harvard Lampoon*, is an indefinable dynamic quality, the *je ne sais quoi* of function; as for instance, adding Scotch puts pizazz into a drink. Certain clothes have it, too… There's pizazz in this rust evening coat.' By May 1951, the word's original fizz had become a little coarsened. *Time* magazine was using it to describe new developments in aeroplane technology. 'Rentschler thinks the J-57 has more pizzazz than any other engine,' it wrote. 'Says he flatly: "It is more powerful than any jet engine ever flown."'

Aerospace research is an extremely expensive business that requires a great deal of **moolah** (money). This word was first spotted in 1939 in *Designs in Scarlet* by Courtney Ryley Cooper: 'What about it, baby, is it my fault I forgot my wallet?' says one character. 'I got plenty of mullah.'

Thrillers are, of course, known for their racy, perhaps even **raunchy**, storylines. This US slang term of unknown origin means – according to the CCD – 'lecherous or smutty', 'openly sexual; earthy', and 'slovenly, dirty'. But it also points us, for the purposes of comparison, to the adjective **ranchy**, which means 'dirty, disgusting, indecent', offering the following two quotations as evidence. The first is dated 1903: 'Then they brought the monkey in,' wrote A.M. Binstead in *Pitcher in Paradise*, 'the sad-faced, bare-based, flea-ranchy old monk.' The second is from Lord Kinross's *Innocents at Home* (1959): 'The bridegroom, an Englishman, declared his intention of having the English as opposed to the American marriage service. This included … the worshipping of her with his body. There was an embarrassed pause at this; and then one of the bridesmaids remarked, "A bit ranchy, that."' The earliest spelling of 'raunchy' is dated from 1939, but these days it's more common.

Should we care about these word mysteries, or should we just give up and rejoice in their mysteriousness? A scientist who has identified a new species of plant or animal must classify the find, and consequently has an unpleasant task: the plant has to be torn from the ground, or the animal, no matter how rare, has to be caught and killed. Only then can the process of classification take place. But linguists face a different challenge. Language is not living in the same sense as plants and animals. Few linguists would relish that uncluttered feeling of certain words, the sense of their rootlessness. These words are born out of linguistic wedlock: we cannot leave them alone to their unhitched status. The classifying part of our brain wants to tie them down. These words are like beautiful, mysterious strangers at a party whom others view from afar, wondering where they have come from. But party guests come and go. Words are different: they're here to stay.

Starting from scratch

The current research team on the *OED* has announced its intention to revise the whole dictionary for the first time since it was published. The third edition of the *OED* needs your help to extend its knowledge and solve some of the most intractable puzzles. Your evidence could revise ideas about pronunciation or etymology, serve to extend the chronological range of examples in existing entries, fill in gaps, or help refine existing definitions. It might even be used to draft entirely new entries.

Each *OED Online* newsletter contains an appeal. At the time of writing it asks for help with **antedating**, which involves finding an earlier citation than the one quoted at present. Let's take an example: **to piss on from a great height** (to humiliate utterly). The

earliest current reference for this is from 1992: can you antedate it?
Other examples from the letter P for which help is needed include:

> **pony** *n.* an act of defecation; faeces; nonsense [antedate 1958]
> **pony** *adj.* worthless, useless [antedate 1964]
> **poo(h)** *n.* faeces [antedate 1981]
> **poo(h)** *v.* to defecate [antedate 1975]
> **popular beat combo**[3] *n.* [antedate 1990]
> **pork scratchings** *n.* [antedate 1982]
> **post-maritally** *adv.* [antedate 1952]

In addition, the editors also want to know if you can **postdate**,
i.e. find a later reference, for **portrayment** *n.* portrayal (1891) and
postless *adj.* without a postal service (1934). It sometimes happens
that there is a large gap between two citations, as with **postlike** *adj.*
resembling a wooden post (1617 and 1976). Can you help **interdate**
this? The flood of responses to previous requests has allowed the
editors to antedate **password** (to 1799 from *c.*1817), **patio** (to 1764
from 1828), **pastry-cook** (to 1656 from 1712), **passionately** (to *c.*1487
from 1590) and **parrotwise** (to 1795 from 1856). These achievements
are significant, helping to improve the accuracy of the great *OED*.
However, the project is constantly evolving and the search never ends.

The search for evidence could take you along paths that snake
ever deeper into the past, or simply lead you into dead ends, but
the hunt will never be boring. In the July 1999 newsletter a
Washington DC researcher describes how her researches in the
Library of Congress could take her from the Newspapers and
Current Periodicals Reading Room to the Copyright Office, the
Performing Arts Reading Room, the Motion Pictures and Recorded
Sound Division, the Manuscripts Division and the Law Library.

---

3 Informally defined as the description of a pop group from the early days of
rock and roll.

A search for examples of **garbanzo** (chickpea), for instance, led her to a 1770 letter from the American president Benjamin Franklin (1706–90) to the American botanist John Bartram (1699–1777). Franklin wrote:

> I send ... some Chinese Garavances, with Father Navaretta's account of the universal use of a cheese made of them, in China ... Some runnings of salt (I suppose runnet) is put into water when the meal is in it, to turn it to curds. I think we have Garavances with us; but I know not whether they are same with these, which actually came from China, and are what the Tau-fu is made of.

The researcher conjectures that **garavances** is a variant of 'garbanzos', but she was particularly pleased to come across this reference to Chinese *tau-fu* (**tofu**) since it antedates the earliest example currently in the *OED* by more than 100 years. 'The editors have not yet considered it for publication, and further research may be necessary,' she adds, but she is optimistic of the outcome.

Widening the net

To a linguist, no matter how many times you pick up a word and shake it, if it is marked 'unknown' in the dictionary, it remains a puzzle. Linguists and lexicographers want to get to know how words work. A word that comes into the language without revealing how it arrived is a mystery. Sometimes words send us on false chases, and yet we have to pursue those leads, if only to eliminate them. Some examples are given below. For each one, as we peer back through history, the outline of the word becomes increasingly vague. Eventually, like a ship surrounded by fog, it disappears and we have to make do with pure conjecture.

By ante-dating words the *OED* researchers are cleaving their way through the fog and, in a way, ceaselessly working to undercut their earlier efforts. Sometimes it seems that they will never rest until every single word is sucked back into one vast **ur-text**[4] (original source *c.* AD 1150), perhaps into a giant word representing a linguistic Big Bang, from which every word in the English language originally spread.

Ante-dating also sheds light on society. For example, the second edition of the *OED* defines the noun **oldie** as 'an old or elderly person; an adult; an "old hand". Frequently in ironical contexts.' The accompanying quotation, dated 1874, is from the writer Laura Troubridge (1858–1929): 'I am now in my seventeenth year – isn't it sad? I shall soon be an "oldy".' That seems reasonable, and we would supposedly accept as fair that the writer was describing her ambivalent feelings towards growing old. Maybe we even feel that the writer invented, or came close to inventing, the term, or somehow picked it out of the air. Looking at other pages in the dictionary, we note the first reference to **old age pension** from 1879, the first recorded use of **old boy** (1868) at Haileybury School, and the use of **old-fangled** by the poet Robert Browning in *The Pied Piper of Hamelin* (1842). We sense that we are slipping back in time, but are content that the process has to stop, or start, somewhere. The March 2004 *OED Online* newsletter reveals that 'oldie' has been sighted further back towards the horizon – as early as 1799, in fact: 'Oldy, you don't understand this. Young people must love, and, of course, whine,' (from *Reconciliation* by C. Ludger, translated by A. von Kotzebue). Suddenly the word, which had been standing on the shoulders of other nineteenth-century words, has upended the pyramid, brought it crashing down, and re-enters the structure at a much lower point, carrying more weight on its own shoulders.

---

4 Ur-: prefix, first citation 1889. Denoting 'primitive, original, earliest'.

We should be pleased: this is how dictionaries work. People were being gently mocking about 'oldies' eighty-five years earlier than we had at first thought.

But the *OED* has been drawing on sources from an ever-widening circle. In its 1972 Supplement it made use, for the first time, of a script from a broadcast programme. Written for the comedian Tony Hancock by Ray Galton and Alan Simpson, *Four Hancock Scripts for Television* contained gems that kept the British laughing throughout the 1950s and 1960s, and also shed light on vernacular speech of the time. One of the words Hancock muttered (in 1961) was **bonkers**, as in 'By half-past three he'll be raving bonkers'. The lexicographer Eric Partridge had defined it in his *Dictionary of Forces' Slang* (1948) as 'light in the head; slightly drunk'. By the 1960s, it meant something more like 'crazy', and it was in this sense that Hancock used it and popularized it. The *OED* also notes the use in the scripts of expressions such as **Charlie** (fool) and **cor[5] blimey**. However, according to the September 2003 *OED Online* newsletter, the scripts also provided a successful ante-dating of **stone me** (from 1967 to 1961), which went into the fourth volume of the *OED* Supplement in 1986.

The use of such scripts is extremely useful to lexicographers, since the expressions they contain gained a wide audience and were therefore bound to influence – or reflect – speech patterns. When Ben Elton and Richard Curtis wrote the TV comedy *Blackadder the Third* in 1987, it was a particularly riotous programme that positively relished its use of anachronistic language. Take **mud-wrestling**, for example, which first burst on to the linguistic scene in a 1981 issue of the *Washington Post*: 'One night a week [we found] women who mud-wrestle for appreciative female audiences.' In 1987 Sir Edmund Blackadder yanked it back in time when he said, 'I'd mud-wrestle

---

5 Cor – a vulgar corruption of 'God', is first attested from 1931.

my own mother for a ton of cash, an amusing clock and a sack of French porn.'

It's worth noting that **porn** is a low-register abbreviation of a slightly higher register word, **pornography**. (See Chapter 1, page 35 for an explanation of 'register'.) In his book *A History of English Words*, the linguist Geoffrey Hughes lists several words in which the more formal version of the word comes first, such as the Middle English **physiognomy**, then the short one registers its own breakthrough, appearing as the more *déclassé* **phiz** (1688). In the same way, **fanatic** (1553) shortens to **fan** (1889), **obstreperous** (1600) to **stroppy** (1951) and **perquisites** (1565) to **perks** (1869).

Elton and Curtis also made great play of the phrase **big girl's blouse**, which was in conversational use at the time. ('Oh Mr Byron, don't be such a big girl's blouse!') The *OED* notes that there was an opinion circulating in internet circles at the time that it had been a catchphrase in the stage act of the comedienne Hylda Baker during the 1940s and 1950s, but without any written or recorded evidence of her in performance, this was hard to substantiate. However, when Hylda Baker went on to appear in a TV comedy series called *Nearest and Dearest* (1968–1972) she imported many of the phrases that had made her one of the biggest box-office draws in Britain. The *OED* contacted an archivist at Granada Television, who was able to provide a camera script of the show, and this furnished the evidence required. The line, from series two, episode one, is as follows:

> **Eli:** Go round talking like that, you'll be hearing from our solicitor.
> **Nellie:** He is our solicitor, you big girl's blouse.

This is a good joke, implying that Eli is 'a person regarded as feeble, cowardly or emotionally over-sensitive; an ineffectual or effeminate man'. But again, it shows how the phrase mulches down in time, how it goes from the smack-in-the-face quality of novelty to something more cosy, almost affectionate. The phrase also occurs in *The Balloons in the Black Bag* (1978) by the late William Donaldson: 'The big girl's blouse was sat seated on the bench, eyes closed, a look of foolish rapture on his face.'

Ever since they were first admitted by the *OED*, television and radio scripts have been an invaluable source of admissible evidence. A camera script from a 1973 episode of *Whatever Happened to the Likely Lads?* by Dick Clement and Ian La Frenais provides an ante-dated use of the phrase the **big E** (big elbow, i.e. brush-off). The film script for the 1956 Ealing comedy thriller *The Long Arm of the Law* contains an early recorded slang use of the word **magic** (as in 'fantastic'). Doubtless this reliance on scripts to trace developments in the language will continue, aided by the spread of electronic databases.

Television also captured the cheeky new meaning that **lunchbox** acquired during the 1990s: 'British slang: a man's genitals, especially when conspicuous in tight clothing'. 'Lunchbox' came into prominence, so to speak, in 1998 when the *Daily Mirror* (amongst others) noticed that the Lycra shorts worn by the British sprinter Linford Christie left little to the imagination and coined the euphemism, though it seemed a rather inept comparison, since a box is flat and rectangular. But that wasn't the first reference. We can backdate the word to an 11 May 1972 (Issue 108) cover photo of a nude David Cassidy on *Rolling Stone* magazine and to the punning caption 'Naked lunchbox', a reference to William Burroughs' 1959 novel *The Naked Lunch*.

Ante-dating is a very exact science, and written evidence is the ultimate proof. It could be that Stone Age man and woman woke up each morning and mouthed exactly the same expression to each other for hundreds of years, but until someone wrote it down in a form that survives to this day, in linguistic terms it never happened.

Old, new and in-between

It remains to be seen how the dictionary deals with the phenomenon of **text messaging** or **chat rooms**, in which new words are thrown up with the same sort of frenzy that the McDonald's corporation opens up franchises worldwide (currently two a day and counting). 'Instant messaging', whether via computer or by mobile phone, may not be very elegant, but its truncated spellings are an aid to rapid communication. Schools are having to drill their pupils extra-hard to prevent this usage spilling over into essays and examination papers as micro-words like GR8 (great) and L8 (late) are now more familiar to most teenagers than their conventionally spelt versions. Two generations ago, people used telegrams to communicate with each other, and modified the rules of grammar, punctuation and spelling accordingly. A similar process is taking place today. When you're **texting**, you can't let long words slow you down, hence the profusion of acronyms like AFAIK (as far as I know), BRB (be right back), BTW (by the way), GR8 (great), IMHO (in my humble opinion), TLK2UL8R (talk to you later) and ROTFLMAO (rolling on the floor laughing my arse off).

At present, though, it doesn't matter whether the word's first use is in a folio[6] edition of Shakespeare, on a page of the *Topper* comic, or in a notice above a public lavatory. What counts is that it was committed to writing. It is we, the non-lexicographical specialists,

6 'Shakespeare's earliest published plays are referred to as folios or quartos according to the folding of the printed sheets and therefore the size of the book: folios being large, tall volumes and the quartos being smaller and squarer.' From the *Oxford Companion to English Literature*, ed. M. Drabble (1985)

who can only watch, admire and sometimes add judgements, such as in the case of who *barfed* first. You may not be too interested in the first recorded usage of the verb 'barf', but it matters: every word matters.

In lexicography, every ball is permanently in the air, and no word can ever be declared closed. At present, therefore, the world's first 'barf' is recorded in Wentworth and Flexner's *Dictionary of American Slang*. Would it not have been preferable, though, to have found a non-dictionary reference? The very fact that Wentworth and Flexner had netted it implies that someone, somewhere had used it, written it down and printed it before then. Someone must, in other words, have had a 'barf' earlier than 1960.

You can help

The greatest dictionary of the English language, which was originally published in full in 1928, needs an upgrade, and the public is once again being offered the chance to enter this massive project and have a say. The *OED* is currently trying to find the earliest verifiable usage of every single word in English – currently around 600,000, but still counting – and of every separate meaning of every word.

In June 2005 the BBC launched its own search called Wordhunt in association with the TV series *Balderdash & Piffle*, which spawned this book. The fifty words in the list below represent some of the most intriguing and baffling mysteries in the English language. The year given next to them corresponds to the earliest dated evidence that the dictionary currently has. Can you improve on it? Perhaps you had a **balti** before 1984, or a **mullet** earlier than 1994. If you did, you might know how they got their names. The *OED* can't always establish with certainty how a particular word came to be. If you can help, and your theory is convincing or your evidence compelling, you could be helping to rewrite the dictionary.

BBC Wordhunt appeal

back to square one* (1960)
balti* *n.* (1984)
Beeb *n.* (1967)
bitch-slap *v.* (1987)
boffin* *n.* (1941)
bog-standard *adj.* (1983)
bomber jacket *n.* (1973)
bonk (sexual intercourse) *v.* (1975)
bouncy castle *n.* (1986)
chattering classes pl. *n.* (1985)
codswallop* *n.* (1960)
Crimble *n.* (1963)
cyberspace *n.* (1982)
cyborg *n.* (1960)
ditsy* (scatterbrained) *adj.* (1978)
dosh* *n.* (1953)
full monty* (1985)
gas mark *n.* (1963)
gay (homosexual sense) *adj.* (1935)
handbags at dawn (1987)
her indoors *n.* (1979)
jaffa* (cricketing term) *n.* (YEAR UNKNOWN)
Mackem (native of the city of Sunderland) *n.* (1991)
minger *n.* (1995)
minted *adj.* (1995)
moony, moonie *n.* (1990)

muller* (in sport – to comprehensively outplay) *v.* (1993)
mullet* (hairstyle) *n.* (1994)
mushy peas *n.* (1975)
naff* *adj.* (1966)
nerd* *n.* (1950)
nip and tuck *n.* (1980)
nit nurse *n.* (1985)
nutmeg* (in football – to play the ball through your opponent's legs) *v.* (1979)
Old Bill (police) *n.* (1958)
on the pull (1988)
pass the parcel (children's partygame) *n.* (1967)
pear-shaped *adj.* (1983)
phwoar (1980)
pick and mix *adj.* (1959)
ploughman's lunch *n.* (1970)
pop one's clogs *v.* (1977)
porky *n.* (1985)
posh* *adj.* (1915)
ska* *n.* (1964)
smart casual *adj.* (1945)
snazzy* *adj.* (1932)
something for the weekend *n.* (1990)
throw one's toys out of the pram (or cot) *v.* (1989)
tikka masala *n.* (1975)

* = origin unknown or origin uncertain

So far, at the time of writing, about half the words on the list opposite have been ante-dated thanks to an impressive response from the public. But there is no end to the trail, so help is still needed, and all are welcome to join in. To get started, simply log on to the website www.oed.com/bbcwordhunt, click on your chosen word and you will see part of the *OED* entry for that word, including the researchers' best guess as to its origins.

Whether your information is academic or general, whether you come across an earlier citing of the word in a book, magazine, film script or fanzine, or in unpublished papers, a letter or a postmarked postcard, the main thing is that your evidence must be dated. Please email it to: wordhunt@bbc.co.uk or post it to: BBC Wordhunt, 132 Grafton Road, London NW5 4BA. If the research team agree with you, it could appear in the revised *OED*.

Endword

Although this section might be described as an afterthought, it is actually the most important of all because it looks into the future. Scientists may continue to dispute whether we live in an expanding physical universe, but there is no doubt that as far as words are concerned, the boundaries just keep stretching, and we are in the forefront of that growth.

New words – and new uses for old words – are being invented all the time. From the moment we wake up we are all experimenting with language. We hear words all the time, we use words to suit our own purposes, and many of them are novel in some way. They are there for us to use, abuse and subvert. Many of our favourites exist in a small, enclosed world: our favourite word for the telly, or our pet name for the car. How would it feel if that word became a celebrity in its own right, taking its place in the grandest vocabulary shop window of them all – the *OED*?

We are part of this incredible process because we all use language with just as much facility as any scholar or writer. We are all at the outer limits of our own linguistic borders, which is why we have a fantastic opportunity to put that knowledge to good use. We don't always concentrate on what is being said: sometimes we're working, or half-asleep, or 'on the train'. But we are witnesses to a constant process of linguistic innovation. This book, and the TV series that prompted it, is based on the belief that we should share that process more widely.

The *OED* normally waits five years to see if a word will 'bed down' into the language because it does not want to be overwhelmed by noisy, one-hit wonders. The waiting period gives the media a chance to absorb the novelty acts without getting over-excited, and to sort out the flourishing from the perished. Of course, long-dead vogue words such as **tatterdemalion**[1] and **ruffles**[2] do appear in the *OED*, having once been just as live an issue as **chavs** and **ASBOs** are now. But these days, given the sheer size of the internet, the *OED* has its work cut out in weighing up the hundreds of new words being coined each week. A period of consolidation is necessary, therefore, and this is where you can do your bit.

Traditionally, the *OED* has relied on its Reading Programme to solicit information from readers around the world about which words are coming into the language. With the expansion of the *OED Online*, there is an unprecedented range of ways in which readers can become involved. You are invited to tell the *OED* researchers about the words you hear or use. Perhaps, for example, you and your circle of friends have a particular word for 'happy', or you always refer to a certain drink by a particular name. If you feel that that word is rather good and does its job well, why not submit it for wider circulation? For details on how to submit to the *OED*, contact Oxford University Press or visit their website (see Useful Addresses & Websites, page 294).

We don't know how many of the words we use first arose out of a smog of Celtic, Anglo-Saxon or Norman French vowel-and-consonant clusters back in the mists of time. The word that became 'dog' took shape in a different part of post-Stone Age man's mouth from the word that became 'house', and it was a very long haul that led to it being taken up and used by everyone. But what we can do these days is to begin that chain reaction (see Chapter 8, page 216)

---

1 *c*.1611: 'A person in tattered clothing; a ragged or beggarly fellow; a ragamuffin.'
2 Victorian slang for handcuffs. W.H. Ainsworth *Jack Sheppard* (1839): '"I'll accommodate you with a pair of ruffles." And he proceeded to handcuff his captive.'

ourselves. The doors to the *OED* are open as never before, and if you know how the system works, you can squeeze in and leave your mark.

Say you have a particular nickname by which you refer to your partner. In times past it's likely that no one outside your own domestic set-up would have been privy to that word, but now, via a wider social structure that includes newspapers, chat rooms, gyms, football matches, radio broadcasts and television shows, that word could be passed on and adopted by whole sections of the country. It might be a long process, and easier to achieve if you have a high profile, but it does happen.

Back in the 1980s the comedian Jasper Carrott, a native of Birmingham, hated the anodyne term **spot** for a skin blemish, which he had heard since arriving in London. So he brazenly announced his intention to move the word zit from Brummy dialect into greater prominence. It was obviously a live issue for him – he was much younger at the time and acne was clearly very much on his mind, as well as all over his face – but it worked, and 'zit' entered the language. But you don't have to be a comedian, still less a chat-show host, sports person, pop singer or film star to take advantage of the same process. All that's needed is to get a word used, push it into circulation, and you could find that it suddenly catches a wave and off it goes into popular usage.

There's no point in telling the *OED* researchers when the word is still being popularized. But words can emerge from a private language. They can get on to the street and into people's houses, clubs or places of work. That's the challenge.

What do you think is the biggest new word on your street at the moment? Let us know and you could be making your mark on English in a more permanent way than you ever thought possible.

Acknowledgements

My thanks go to the staff of the British Library, the London Library (especially Christopher Phipps), and Mount Pleasant writers' retreat, where sections of this book were written. I'm grateful to Julian Alexander at LAW, to Archie Baron, Neil Cameron, Kate Carter, Helena Braun and Rob Silva of Takeaway Media; to lexicographer Jane McCauley, who read through the text so scrupulously and to Peter Gilliver, who painstakingly checked the *OED* chapter. Thanks, too, for their good-humoured thoroughness, to Cameron Fitch and Stuart Cooper at BBC Books. Any errors, though it pains me to admit it, are mine.

Thanks also to Matthew Batstone and Tony Cryer for past kindnesses, to Walter Becker, Donald Fagen and Paul Weller for the music, and particularly to Tim Jackson. I am also indebted, on a more elemental level, to Esther, Fergus and Edie.

Finally, my thanks to two great – if occasionally terrifying – Classics school teachers: Eric Marston and the late H.J.K. (John) Usher. Apologies to anyone I've overlooked.

Further Reading

Introduction – The Power of Words
Frederick Bodmer, *The Loom of Language* (Allen & Unwin, London, 1944)
Susie Dent, *Larpers and Shroomers* (Oxford University Press, 2004)
Michael Quinion, *POSH* (Penguin, London, 2004)
Lynne Truss, *Eats, Shoots and Leaves* (Profile, London, 2003)

Chapter 1 – Our Mongrel Tongue
Melvyn Bragg, *The Adventure of English* (Hodder & Stoughton, London, 2003)
Geoffrey Chaucer, *The Canterbury Tales* (1386) (Penguin, London, 2003)
David Crystal, *The Cambridge Encyclopedia of Language* (Cambridge University Press, 1987)
Richard A. Firmage, *The Alphabet Abecedarium* (Bloomsbury, London, 2000)
Geoffrey Hughes, *A History of English Words* (Blackwell, Oxford, 2000)
David Sacks, *The Alphabet* (Hutchinson, London, 2003)

Chapter 2 – Dr Johnson's Big Idea
James Boswell, *The Life of Samuel Johnson* (H. Baldwin, London, 1791)
Samuel Johnson, *Dictionary of the English Language* (Papermac, London, 1982)
Samuel Johnson, *Dictionary of the English Language*, ed. Jack Lynch (Walker & Company, New York, 2003)
Samuel Johnson's Dictionary: Selections from the 1755 Work That Defined the English Language, ed. Jack Lynch (Atlantic, London, 2004)
Henry Hitchings, *Dr Johnson's Dictionary: The Extraordinary Life of the Book that Defined the World* (John Murray, London, 2005)

Chapter 3 – From 0800 Number to Zyxt
The Concise Oxford English Dictionary, eds. H.W. and F.G. Fowler (Oxford University Press, 1911, 2004)
Jonathon Green, *Chasing the Sun: Dictionary Makers and the Dictionaries They Made* (Jonathan Cape, London, 1996)
Lynda Mugglestone, *Lost for Words: The Hidden History of the Oxford English Dictionary* (Yale University Press, New Haven, 2005)
K.M. Elisabeth Murray, *Caught in the Web of Words: James A.H. Murray and the Oxford English Dictionary* (Yale University Press, New Haven, 1977)

A New English Dictionary on Historical Principles, eds. Frederick Furnivall, James Murray (Oxford University Press, 1884–1928)

The Oxford English Dictionary, eds. Frederick Furnivall, James Murray, Henry Bradley, William Craigie, C.T. Onions, Robert Burchfield (Oxford University Press, 1928, 1933, 1989)

OED Online (www.oed.com) (launched 2000)

The Oxford English Reference Dictionary, eds. Judy Pearsall and Bill Trumble (Oxford University Press, 1995, 2002)

The Oxford School Dictionary of Word Origins, ed. John Ayto with Jessica Feinstein (Oxford University Press, 2002)

The Pocket Oxford Dictionary, first edition eds. F.G. and H.W. Fowler, 1924; 10th edition ed. Catherine Soanes, with Sara Hawker and Julia Elliott (Oxford University Press, 2005)

The Shorter Oxford English Dictionary, eds. William Little, H.W. Fowler and Jesse Coulson (Oxford University Press, 1933, 2002)

The Visual English Dictionary, eds. Jean-Claude Corbeil and Ariane Archambault (Oxford University Press, 2002)

Simon Winchester, *The Meaning of Everything: The Story of the Oxford English Dictionary* (Oxford University Press, 2003)

Chapter 4 – Desert Island Texts

The Holy Bible, pref. the King James version (Nelson Bibles, Nashville, 2003)

Frank Kermode, *Shakespeare's Language* (Allen Lane, London, 2000)

Alister E. McGrath, *In the Beginning: The Story of the King James Bible and How It Changed a Nation, a Language, and a Culture* (Doubleday, New York, 2001)

William Shakespeare: *The Complete Works* (Oxford University Press, 2005)

George Steiner, After Babel (Oxford University Press, 1975)

Chapter 5 – Local Lingo

The New Shorter OED (Oxford University Press, 1993)

Iona and Peter Opie, *The Lore and Language of Schoolchildren* (Clarendon Press, Oxford, 1959)

Harold Orton, The Linguistic Atlas of England (Croom Helm, London, 1978)

John Walker, *Critical Pronouncing Dictionary and Expositor of the English Language* (G.G. and J. Robinson and T. Cadell, London, 1791)

Joseph Wright, *English Dialect Dictionary* (Henry Frowde, Oxford, 1898)

Chapter 6 – Global Lingo

Collins Concise Dictionary & Thesaurus (HarperCollins, London, 2003)

David Crystal, *English as a Global Language*, (Cambridge University Press, 1998)

Ivor Lewis, *Sahibs, Nabobs and Boxwallahs* (Oxford University Press, 1991)

Paroo Nihalani, R.K. Tongue and Priya Hosali, *Indian and British English: A Handbook of Usage and Pronunciation* (Oxford University Press, 1979)

F. Richards, *Old-Soldier Sahib* (Faber & Faber, London, 1936)

The Times English Dictionary (HarperCollins, London, 2000)

Sir Henry Yule and A.C. Burnell, *Anglo-Indian Dictionary aka Hobson-Jobson* (J. Murray, London, 1886)

Chapter 7 – That's Entertainment

Chambers English Dictionary (Chambers Harrap, Edinburgh, 2003)

Wilfred Granville, *Dictionary of Theatrical Terms* (A. Deutsch, London, 1952)

Francis Grose, *Classical Dictionary of the Vulgar Tongue* (S. Hooper, London, 1785)

Steven Johnson, *Everything Bad is Good for You: How Popular Culture is Making us Smarter* (Allen Lane, London, 2005)

Nigel Rees, *A Word in Your Shell-Like: 6,000 Curious & Everyday Phrases Explained* (HarperCollins, London, 2004)

Chapter 8 – The Appliance of Science

Edmund Blunden, *Undertones of War* (R. Cobden-Sanderson, London, 1928)

Paul Fussell, *The Great War and Modern Memory* (Oxford University Press, 1975)

Ewart Alan Mackintosh, *War, the Liberator* (J. Lane, London, 1918)

Steven Pinker, *The Language Instinct: The New Science of Language and Mind* (Penguin Science, Penguin Books, London, 1995)

Chapter 9 – Mind Your Language

Paul Baker, *Polari, the Lost Language of Gay Men* (Routledge Studies in Linguistics) (Taylor & Francis, London, 2002)

The F-Word, ed. Jesse Sheidlower (Faber & Faber, London, 1999)

Jonathon Green and Kipper Williams, *The Big Book of Filth* (Cassell, London, 2000)

Geoffrey Hughes, *Swearing: A Social History of Foul Language, Oaths and Profanity in English* (Penguin Books, London, 1998)

The Language, Ethnicity and Race Reader, eds. Roxy Harris and Ben Rampton, (Routledge, London, 2003)

Eric Partridge, *The Dictionary of Slang* (Greenwood Press, New York, 1951)

Noel Perrin, *Dr Bowdler's Legacy: A History of Expurgated Books in England and America* (Athenum, New York, 1969)

Percy Walker, *The Message in the Bottle: How Queer Man Is - How Queer Language Is - and What One Has to Do with the Other* (Farrar, Strauss and Giroux, New York, 1975, 2000)

Chapter 10 – To Er ... is Human

Fifty Years Among the New Words: A Dictionary of Neologisms, 1941–1991, ed. John Algeo (Cambridge University Press, 1991)

Leo H. Grindon, *Figurative Language: Its Origin and Constitution* (James Spiers, London, 1879)

Patrick Scrivenor, *Egg on Your Interface: A Dictionary of Modern Nonsense* (Buchan & Enright, London, 1989)

Robert D. Sutherland, *Language and Lewis Carroll* (Mouton, The Hague, 1970)

Chapter 11 – Changing Times, Changing Terms

The Cassell Dictionary of Slang, ed. Jonathon Green (Cassell, London, 2000)

R.W. Holder, *A Dictionary of Euphemisms: How Not to Say What You Mean* (Oxford Paperback Reference, 2003)

The Oxford Encylopedic English Dictionary, eds. Joyce M. Hawkins and Robert Allen (Oxford University Press, 1991)

Harold Wentworth and Stuart Berg Flexner, *Dictionary of American Slang* (T. Crowell, New York, 1960)

Chapter 12 – Origin Unknown

George H. Maines and Bruce Grant, *Wise–Crack Dictionary* (1926)

Online Etymological Dictionary (www.etymonline.com)

Eric Partridge, *Dictionary of Forces' Slang* (Seckler & Warburg, 1948)

H.F. Reddall, *Fact, Fancy and Fable* (1889)

Noah Webster, *An American Dictionary of the English Language*, 1st edition 1828, 3rd edition (Merriam-Webster, Springfield MA, USA, 1961), also available online at www.merriam-webster.com

Useful General References

David Crystal, *The Stories of English* (Allen Lane, London, 2004)

Susie Dent, *The Language Report* (Oxford University Press, 2005)
An editor and translator, Susie Dent appears regularly on TV's *Countdown* quiz as the resident dictionary expert. Her annual *Language Report* covers the year's latest crop of new words. The 2005 edition is called *Fanboys and Overdogs*.

Albert Jack, *Red Herrings and White Elephants: The Origins of the Phrases We Use Every Day* (Metro Publishing, London, 2004).
Also available at www.albertjack.com
Contains explanations of phrases such as 'above board', 'Bob's your uncle' and 'scratch my back and I'll scratch yours'.

Paul McFedries, *Word Spy: The Word Lover's Guide to Modern Culture* (Broadway Books, New York, 2004).
Also available at www.wordspy.com
This book is an entertaining introduction to the explosion of new words, from 'affluenza' to 'zoo rage'.

David Wilton, *Word Myths: Debunking Linguistic Urban Legends* (Oxford University Press USA, 2004)

Useful Addresses & Websites

BBC Wordhunt
132 Grafton Road
London NW5 4BA
Email: wordhunt@bbc.co.uk
Website: www.bbc.co.uk/wordhunt

Dr Johnson's House
17 Gough Square
London EC4A 3DE
Tel: 020 7353 3745
Email: curator@drjohnsonshouse.org
Website: www.drjh.dircon.co.uk

The Johnson Society
The Birthplace Museum
Breadmarket Street, Lichfield
Staffordshire WS13 6LG
Email: edmanmail-johnsoc@yahoo.co.uk
Website: www.lichfieldrambler.co.uk

The Oxford English Dictionary
Oxford University Press
Great Clarendon Street
Oxford OX2 6DP
Tel: 01865 353660
Email: oed3@oup.com

**http://encarta.msn.com/encnet/
features/dictionary/dictionaryhome.aspx**
MSN Encarta: Online dictionary with over
100,000 entries, definitions, and pronunciations

http://portal.unesco.org
Initiative B@bel uses Information and
Communication Technologies (ICTs) to
support linguistic and cultural diversity, and to
protect and preserve languages in danger of
disappearance.

www.collins.co.uk/wordexchange
The HarperCollins site includes an online
dictionary and a weekly bulletin by Jeremy
Butterfield, editor-in-chief of Collins
dictionaries.

www.dictionary.oed.com
The website of *The Oxford English Dictionary*.
Comprehensive information on the *OED*,
and home to *OED* Online. Its archive
includes previous newsletters back to January
1995, much valuable material from the vaults
and an information resource.

www.en.wikipedia.org
The biggest independently edited
encyclopaedia on the net.

www.ethnologue.com
Ethnologue – Languages of the World: an
encyclopedic reference work cataloguing all
the world's 6912 known living languages.

www.ogmios.org
Foundation for Endangered Languages – aims
to raise awareness and support the use of
endangered languages.

www.phrases.org.uk
Offers word meanings, origins, a thesaurus
and a discussion group.

www.urbandictionary.com
An online slang dictionary, with entries and
definitions supplied and updated by readers.

www.wordorigins.org
The website of David Wilton, author of *Word
Myths*, discusses commonly misunderstood
words and phrases and includes a weekly
newsletter, A Way with Words.

www.worldwidewords.org
Michael Quinion, author of *POSH and Other
Language Myths* (see Introduction, page 32) is
the nation's foremost word-sleuth.

www.wordwizard.com
Word site that includes quotations, insults
and neologisms.

Index